371.1209794
C153se
No. 121, 125

59.95
Educ

CSET 121-125

Chemistry
Teacher Certification Exam

D0746560

By: Sharon Wynne, M.S
Southern Connecticut State University

"And, while there's no reason yet to panic, I think it's only prudent that we make preparations to panic."

XAMonline, INC.
Boston

Copyright © 2007 XAMonline, Inc.
All rights reserved. No part of the material protected by this copyright notice may be reproduced or utilized in any form or by any means, electronic or mechanical, including photocopying, recording or by any information storage and retrievable system, without written permission from the copyright holder.

To obtain permission(s) to use the material from this work for any purpose including workshops or seminars, please submit a written request to:

XAMonline, Inc.
21 Orient Ave.
Melrose, MA 02176
Toll Free 1-800-301-4647
Email: info@xamonline.com
Web www.xamonline.com
Fax: 1-781-662-9268

Library of Congress Cataloging-in-Publication Data

Wynne, Sharon A.
    Chemistry 121-125: Teacher Certification / Sharon A. Wynne. -2nd ed.
    ISBN 978-1-58197-395-2
    1. Chemistry 121-125.   2. Study Guides.   3. CSET
    4. Teachers' Certification & Licensure.   5. Careers

Disclaimer:
The opinions expressed in this publication are the sole works of XAMonline and were created independently from the National Education Association, Educational Testing Service, or any State Department of Education, National Evaluation Systems or other testing affiliates.

Between the time of publication and printing, state specific standards as well as testing formats and website information may change that is not included in part or in whole within this product. Sample test questions are developed by XAMonline and reflect similar content as on real tests; however, they are not former tests. XAMonline assembles content that aligns with state standards but makes no claims nor guarantees teacher candidates a passing score. Numerical scores are determined by testing companies such as NES or ETS and then are compared with individual state standards. A passing score varies from state to state.

Printed in the United States of America

CSET: Chemistry 121-125
ISBN: 978-1-58197-395-2

About the CSET Subject Examinations in Chemistry

Nothing in life is to be feared, it is only to be understood. Now is the time to understand more, so that we may fear less.

—Marie Curie

Purpose: The exams are designed to test the knowledge and competencies of prospective chemistry teachers. Test questions were developed using textbooks, California curriculum syllabi, teacher education curricula, and teacher credentialing standards. The questions were developed in consultation with and approved by committees of educators, teacher educators, and other content and assessment specialists. The exam question bank is undergoing constant revision.

Credential Version and CSET Tests Required: California offers two Single Subject Teaching Credentials in chemistry. State licensure requirements may change, so consult your educational institution's teaching preparation counselor or the California Commission on Teacher Credentialing to verify which tests you should take.

A credential in *Chemistry* authorizes instruction in chemistry, general science, and integrated science. The *Chemistry* credential requires the successful passage of three exams. Content domains in **boldface** are chemistry-specific and covered by this guide.

CSET examinations required for credential in *Chemistry*

Exam title (CSET number)	Part I Content Domains	Multiple choice questions		Constructed-response items	
		Number of questions	Proportion of score	Number of questions	Proportion of score
Science Subtest I: General Science (118)	Astronomy	7		none	
	Geodynamics	15		1	
	Earth Resources	7		none	
	Waves	8	80%	none	20%
	Forces/Motion	15		1	
	Electricity/Magnetism	6		none	
		total: 58		total: 2	
Science Subtest II: General Science (119)	Ecology	8		none	
	Genetics/Evolution	14		none	
	Molecular Biology/Biochemistry	7		1	
	Cell and Organismal Biology	7	80%	1	20%
	Heat Transfer/Thermodynamics	7		none	
	Structure and Properties of Matter	15		none	
		total: 58		total: 2	
Science Subtest III: Chemistry (121)	Atomic and Molecular Structure Chemical Reactions Kinetic Molecular Theory Solution Chemistry Chemical Thermodynamics Organic Chemistry/Biochemistry Nuclear Processes	total: 50	70%	total: 3	30%

A credential in *Chemistry (specialized)* authorizes instruction in chemistry only. This credential requires the passage of two examinations. Subtest IV (#125) tests the same content domains as the chemistry-specific portion of subtest II (#119).

CSET examinations required for credential in *Chemistry (specialized)*

Exam title (CSET number)	Part I Content Domains	Multiple choice questions		Constructed-response items	
		Number of questions	Proportion of score	Number of questions	Proportion of score
Science Subtest III: Chemistry (121)	**Atomic and Molecular Structure Chemical Reactions Kinetic Molecular Theory Solution Chemistry Chemical Thermodynamics Organic Chemistry/Biochemistry Nuclear Processes**	total: 50	70%	total: 3	30%
Science Subtest IV: Chemistry (specialized) (125)	**Heat Transfer/Thermodynamics Structure and Properties of Matter**	total: 40	80%	total: 1	20%

Every CSET science exam also tests material for the following content domains:

CSET Science Part II content domains

Investigation and Experimentation
Nature of Science
Science and Society

Time allowance: You may register for one, two, or three subtests in one session, and you will have five hours to complete all subtests for which you have registered. Unless you have a compelling need for rapid certification, there is no reason to register for three subtests during one sitting. If your preparation time will be limited or you are concerned about time pressure, register for one subtest at a time.

Calculators: Scientific calculators (model Texas Instruments TI-30Xa, TI-30 Xs, or TI-30X IIs) will be provided for examinees. Directions for the use of the calculator will not be provided. You will not be allowed to use your own calculator.

Additional information: The CSET is developed by *National Evaluation Systems, Inc.* (NES) of Amherst, MA, and their website (www.cset.nesinc.com), provides additional information, including registration, preparation and testing procedures, and study materials. The California Commission on Teacher Credentialing (CCTC) is charged with the evaluation and issuance of teaching credentials for public school teachers in California. Their website (www.ctc.ca.gov) provides up-to-date teacher credential information for the state.

Massachusetts Tests for Educator Licensure®

Test Date: March 4, 2006

See reverse side for an explanation of how to read your score report.

MARC SHELIKOFF has met the qualifying score on the following test(s) as of March 4, 2006:
    12 Chemistry

MARC SHELIKOFF

Your scores have been reported to the Massachusetts Department of Education.

---

12 Chemistry

Your Score: 94   **Minimum Qualifying Score: 70**   **Status: Met the Qualifying Score**

Number of Questions	Subarea Name	Graphic Display
1 to 10	The Nature of Chemical Inquiry..	
11 to 20	Matter and Atomic Structure..	
11 to 20	Energy/Chemical Bonds/Molecular Struct...........................	
11 to 20	Chemical Reactions..	
1 to 10	Quantitative Relationships..	
11 to 20	Chemistry, Society, and the Environment...........................	
2	Open-Response Items..	

BIOGRAPHICAL INFORMATION FOR MARC SHELIKOFF:

In high school, Mr. Shelikoff received first place for short story in the Scholastic Magazine Writing Competition and was a National Merit Scholarship finalist.

As an undergraduate at Penn State, he was awarded the Omega Chi Epsilon Award for outstanding chemical engineer and was fiction editor of *Kalliope*, the Penn State Literary Magazine.

He received a National Science Foundation fellowship for his graduate studies. At M.I.T., he has authored research papers in the field of protein glycosylation and presented his work at several conferences.

Mr. Shelikoff has tutored many high school students in math and science since 1999. He recently received his teacher's certification in Chemistry from Massachusetts by passing the MTEL.

Table of Contents

Part II Content Domains: Subject Matter Skills and Abilities Applicable to the Content Domains in Science (all CSET science exams)

[Notice: For those of you using the state of California topical guide, please note that they omit letters f and g. XAMonline has taken that fact into account and properly sequenced the letters.]

Study and Testing Tips

What to study in order to prepare for the subject assessments is the focus of this study guide but equally important is *how* you study. You can increase your chances of truly mastering the information by taking some simple, but effective steps.

Study Tips:

1. **Some foods aid the learning process.** Foods such as milk, nuts, seeds, rice, and oats help your study efforts by releasing natural memory enhancers called CCKs (*cholecystokinin*) composed of *tryptophan*, *choline*, and *phenylalanine*. All of these chemicals enhance the neurotransmitters associated with memory. Before studying, try a light, protein-rich meal of eggs, turkey, and fish. All of these foods release the memory enhancing chemicals. The better the connections, the more you comprehend.

Likewise, before you take a test, stick to a light snack of energy boosting and relaxing foods. A glass of milk, a piece of fruit, or some peanuts all release various memory-boosting chemicals and help you to relax and focus on the subject at hand.

2. **Learn to take great notes.** A by-product of our modern culture is that we have grown accustomed to getting our information in short doses (i.e. TV news sound bites or USA Today style newspaper articles.)

Consequently, we've subconsciously trained ourselves to assimilate information better in neat little packages. If your notes are scrawled all over the paper, It fragments the flow of the information. Strive for clarity. Newspapers use a standard format to achieve clarity. Your notes can be much clearer through use of proper formatting. A very effective format is called the *"Cornell Method."*

> Take a sheet of loose-leaf lined notebook paper and draw a line all the way down the paper about 1-2" from the left-hand edge.

> Draw another line across the width of the paper about 1-2" up from the bottom. Repeat this process on the reverse side of the page.

Look at the highly effective result. You have ample room for notes, a left hand margin for special emphasis items or inserting supplementary data from the textbook, a large area at the bottom for a brief summary, and a little rectangular space for just about anything you want.

3. <u>Get the concept then the details.</u> Too often we focus on the details and don't gather an understanding of the concept. However, if you simply memorize only dates, places, or names, you may well miss the whole point of the subject.

A key way to understand things is to put them in your own words. If you are working from a textbook, automatically summarize each paragraph in your mind. If you are outlining text, don't simply copy the author's words.

Rephrase them in your own words. You remember your own thoughts and words much better than someone else's, and subconsciously tend to associate the important details to the core concepts.

4. <u>Ask Why?</u> Pull apart written material paragraph by paragraph and don't forget the captions under the illustrations.

Example: If the heading is "Stream Erosion", flip it around to read "Why do streams erode?" Then answer the questions.

If you train your mind to think in a series of questions and answers, not only will you learn more, but it also helps to lessen the test anxiety because you are used to answering questions.

5. <u>Read for reinforcement and future needs</u>. Even if you only have 10 minutes, put your notes or a book in your hand. Your mind is similar to a computer; you have to input data in order to have it processed. *By reading, you are creating the neural connections for future retrieval.* The more times you read something, the more you reinforce the learning of ideas.

Even if you don't fully understand something on the first pass, *your mind stores much of the material for later recall.*

6. <u>Relax to learn so go into exile.</u> Our bodies respond to an inner clock called biorhythms. Burning the midnight oil works well for some people, but not everyone.

If possible, set aside a particular place to study that is free of distractions. Shut off the television, cell phone, pager and exile your friends and family during your study period.

If you really are bothered by silence, try background music. Light classical music at a low volume has been shown to aid in concentration over other types. Music that evokes pleasant emotions without lyrics are highly suggested. Try just about anything by Mozart. It relaxes you.

7. <u>Use arrows not highlighters</u>. At best, it's difficult to read a page full of yellow, pink, blue, and green streaks. Try staring at a neon sign for a while and you'll soon see that the horde of colors obscure the message.

A quick note, a brief dash of color, an underline, and an arrow pointing to a particular passage is much clearer than a horde of highlighted words.

8. <u>Budget your study time</u>. Although you shouldn't ignore any of the material, *allocate your available study time in the same ratio that topics may appear on the test.*

Testing Tips:

1. <u>Get smart, play dumb</u>. Don't read anything into the question. Don't make an assumption that the test writer is looking for something else than what is asked. Stick to the question as written and don't read extra things into it.

2. <u>Read the question and all the choices *twice* before answering the question</u>.
You may miss something by not carefully reading, and then re-reading both the question and the answers.

If you really don't have a clue as to the right answer, leave it blank on the first time through. Go on to the other questions, as they may provide a clue as to how to answer the skipped questions.

If later on, you still can't answer the skipped ones . . . *Guess.* The only penalty for guessing is that you *might* get it wrong. Only one thing is certain; if you don't put anything down, you will get it wrong!

3. <u>Turn the question into a statement</u>. Look at the way the questions are worded. The syntax of the question usually provides a clue. Does it seem more familiar as a statement rather than as a question? Does it sound strange?

By turning a question into a statement, you may be able to spot if an answer sounds right, and it may also trigger memories of material you have read.

4. <u>Look for hidden clues</u>. It's actually very difficult to compose multiple-foil (choice) questions without giving away part of the answer in the options presented.

In most multiple-choice questions you can often readily eliminate one or two of the potential answers. This leaves you with only two real possibilities and automatically your odds go to Fifty-Fifty for very little work.

5. <u>Trust your instincts</u>. For every fact that you have read, you subconsciously retain something of that knowledge. On questions that you aren't really certain about, go with your basic instincts. **Your first impression on how to answer a question is usually correct.**

6. <u>Mark your answers directly on the test booklet</u>. Don't bother trying to fill in the optical scan sheet on the first pass through the test.

Just be very careful not to miss-mark your answers when you eventually transcribe them to the scan sheet.

7. <u>Watch the clock</u>! You have a set amount of time to answer the questions. Don't get bogged down trying to answer a single question at the expense of 10 questions you can more readily answer.

Periodic Table of the Elements

Group	1 IA	2 IIA	3 IIIB	4 IVB	5 VB	6 VIB	7 VIIB	8 VIIIB	9 VIIIB	10 VIIIB	11 IB	12 IIB	13 IIIA	14 IVA	15 VA	16 VIA	17 VIIA	18 VIIIA
Period 1	hydrogen 1 H 1.0079																	helium 2 He 4.0026
2	lithium 3 Li 6.941	beryllium 4 Be 9.0122											boron 5 B 10.811	carbon 6 C 12.011	nitrogen 7 N 14.007	oxygen 8 O 15.999	fluorine 9 F 18.998	neon 10 Ne 20.180
3	sodium 11 Na 22.990	magnesium 12 Mg 24.305											aluminum 13 Al 26.982	silicon 14 Si 28.086	phosphorus 15 P 30.974	sulfur 16 S 32.065	chlorine 17 Cl 35.453	argon 18 Ar 39.948
4	potassium 19 K 39.098	calcium 20 Ca 40.078	scandium 21 Sc 44.956	titanium 22 Ti 47.867	vanadium 23 V 50.942	chromium 24 Cr 51.996	manganese 25 Mn 54.938	iron 26 Fe 55.845	cobalt 27 Co 58.933	nickel 28 Ni 58.693	copper 29 Cu 63.546	zinc 30 Zn 65.409	gallium 31 Ga 69.723	germanium 32 Ge 72.64	arsenic 33 As 74.922	selenium 34 Se 78.96	bromine 35 Br 79.904	krypton 36 Kr 83.798
5	rubidium 37 Rb 85.468	strontium 38 Sr 87.62	yttrium 39 Y 88.906	zirconium 40 Zr 91.224	niobium 41 Nb 92.906	molybdenum 42 Mo 95.94	technetium 43 Tc [98]	ruthenium 44 Ru 101.07	rhodium 45 Rh 102.91	palladium 46 Pd 106.42	silver 47 Ag 107.87	cadmium 48 Cd 112.41	indium 49 In 114.82	tin 50 Sn 118.71	antimony 51 Sb 121.76	tellurium 52 Te 127.60	iodine 53 I 126.90	xenon 54 Xe 131.29
6	cesium 55 Cs 132.91	barium 56 Ba 137.33	57-71 *	hafnium 72 Hf 178.49	tantalum 73 Ta 180.95	tungsten 74 W 183.84	rhenium 75 Re 186.21	osmium 76 Os 190.23	iridium 77 Ir 192.22	platinum 78 Pt 195.08	gold 79 Au 196.97	mercury 80 Hg 200.59	thallium 81 Tl 204.38	lead 82 Pb 207.2	bismuth 83 Bi 208.98	polonium 84 Po [209]	astatine 85 At [210]	radon 86 Rn [222]
7	francium 87 Fr [223]	radium 88 Ra [226]	89-103 **	rutherfordium 104 Rf [261]	dubnium 105 Db [262]	seaborgium 106 Sg [266]	bohrium 107 Bh [264]	hassium 108 Hs [277]	meitnerium 109 Mt [268]	darmstadtium 110 Ds [271]	roentgenium 111 Rg [272]							

*Lanthanoids

lanthanum 57 La 138.91	cerium 58 Ce 140.12	praseodymium 59 Pr 140.91	neodymium 60 Nd 144.24	promethium 61 Pm [145]	samarium 62 Sm 150.36	europium 63 Eu 151.96	gadolinium 64 Gd 157.25	terbium 65 Tb 158.93	dysprosium 66 Dy 162.50	holmium 67 Ho 164.93	erbium 68 Er 167.26	thulium 69 Tm 168.93	ytterbium 70 Yb 173.04	lutetium 71 Lu 174.97

**Actinoids

actinium 89 Ac [227]	thorium 90 Th 232.04	protactinium 91 Pa 231.04	uranium 92 U 238.03	neptunium 93 Np [237]	plutonium 94 Pu [244]	americium 95 Am [243]	curium 96 Cm [247]	berkelium 97 Bk [247]	californium 98 Cf [251]	einsteinium 99 Es [252]	fermium 100 Fm [257]	mendelevium 101 Md [258]	nobelium 102 No [259]	lawrencium 103 Lr [262]

Atomic mass values from IUPAC review (2001): http://www.iupac.org/reports/periodic_table/

Domains for Chemistry Subtest III (121)

This book follows the California numbering system for labeling all chemistry Subject Matter Requirement (SMR) Domains. Domains 1 through 7 in this section are refered to as Chemistry Domains. Domains 11 and 12 in the following section are refered to as General Chemistry Domains enumerated within the broader scope of general science.

Domain 1: Atomic and Molecular Structure, Competency 1.1: Periodic Table and Periodicity

What the ocean was to the child, the Periodic Table is to the chemist.
—K. Barry Sharpless (Nobel prize in Chemistry, 2001)

Skill 1.1a-Differentiate periodic groups and families of elements and their properties

The construction and organization of the periodic table are described in **Skill 12.1k**.

Groups 1, 2, 17, and 18 are often identified with the group names shown on the table to the right. Groups 3 through 12 are called the **transition metals**. The lanthanoid series is contained in period 6, and the actinoid series is in period 7. The two series together are called the **inner transition metals**. The locations of the transition and inner transition metals in the periodic table are discussed further in **Skill 1.1b**. Elements in the periodic table are also divided into broad categories of metals, nonmetals, and semimetals as discussed in **Skill 12.1l**.

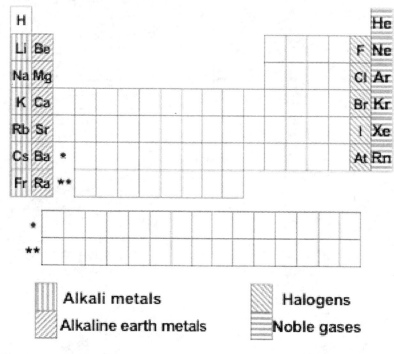

Several elements are found as **diatomic molecules**: **(H_2, N_2, O_2, and the halogens: F_2, Cl_2, Br_2, and I_2)**. Mnemonic devices to remember the diatomic elements are: "$Br_2I_2N_2Cl_2H_2O_2F_2$" (pronounced "Brinklehof") and "**H**ave **N**o **F**ear **O**f **I**ce **C**old **B**eer." These molecules are attracted to one another using **weak London dispersion forces** (see **Skill 1.3d**).

Note that **hydrogen** is <u>not</u> an alkali metal. Hydrogen is a colorless gas and is the most abundant element in the universe, but H_2 is very rare in the atmosphere because it is light enough to escape gravity and reach outer space. Hydrogen atoms form more compounds than any other element.

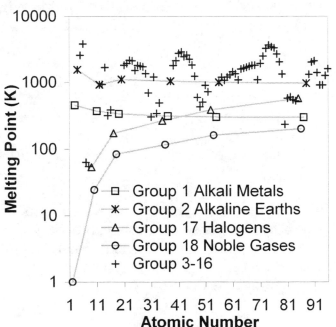

Alkali metals are shiny, soft, metallic solids. They have **low melting points and low densities** compared with other metals because they have a weaker metallic bond (see the square data points in the figures to the left and below). Measures of intermolecular attractions including their **melting points decrease further down the periodic table due to weaker metallic bonds** as the size of atoms increases. See **Skill 1.3d** for a discussion of metallic bonding. Most salts with an alkali metal cation are always soluble (see **Skill 4.1a**).

Alkaline earth metals (group 2 elements) are grey, metallic solids. They are harder, denser, and have a higher melting point than the alkali metals (see asterisk data points in the figures), but values for these properties are still low compared to most of the transition metals. Measures of metallic bond strength like melting points for alkaline earths do not follow a simple trend down the periodic table.

When cut by a knife, the exposed surface of an **alkali metal or alkaline earth metal** quickly turns into an oxide. These elements **do not occur in nature as free metals**. Instead, they

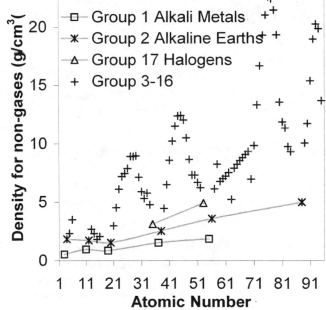

react with many other elements to form white or grey water-soluble salts. With some exceptions, the oxides of group 1 elements have the formula M_2O, their hydrides are MH, and their halides are MX (for example, NaCl). The oxides of group 2 elements have the formula MO, their hydrides are MH_2, and their halides are MX_2.

Copper, silver, and gold (group 11) are known as the **noble metals** or **coinage metals** because they are very unreactive.

Halogens (group 17 elements) have an irritating odor. Unlike the metallic bonds between alkali metals, weak **London forces between halogen molecules increase in strength further down the periodic table**, increasing their melting points as shown by the triangular data points in the figures on the previous page. Weak London forces (see **Skill 1.3d**) make Br_2 a liquid and I_2 a solid at 25 °C. The lighter halogens are gases. Halogens form a wide variety of oxides and also combine with other halogens. They combine with hydrogen to form HX gases, and these compounds are also commonly used as acids (hydrofluoric, hydrochloric, etc.) in aqueous solution. Halogens form salts with metals by gaining electrons to become X^- ions. Halogen compounds are called halides. Astatine is an exception to many of these properties because it is an artificial metalloid.

Noble gases (group 18 elements) have no color or odor and exist as **individual gas atoms** that experience London forces. These attractions also increase with period number as shown by the circular data points in the figures on the previous page. Noble gases are **nearly chemically inert**. The heavier noble gases form a number of compounds with oxygen and fluorine such as KrF_2 and XeO_4

Skill 1.1b-Relate valence electrons and the electron shell structures to an element's position in the periodic table

The position of an element in the periodic table may be related to its electron configuration, and this configuration in turn results from the quantum theory describing the filling of a shell of electrons. In this skill, we will take this theory as our starting point. However, it should be remembered that it is the correlation with properties—not with electron arrangements—that have placed the periodic table at the beginning of most chemistry texts.

Quantum numbers
The quantum-mechanical solutions from the Schrödinger Equation (see **Skill 1.2a**) utilize three quantum numbers (n, l, and m_l) to describe an orbital and a fourth (m_s) to describe an electron in an orbital. This model is useful for understanding the frequencies of radiation emitted and absorbed by atoms and chemical properties of atoms.

The **principal quantum number n** may have positive integer values (1, 2, 3, …). n is a measure of the **distance** of an orbital from the nucleus, and orbitals with the same value of n are said to be in the same **shell**. This is analogous to the Bohr model of the atom (see **Skill 1.2a**). Each shell may contain up to $2n^2$ electrons.

The **azimuthal quantum number** l may have integer values from 0 to n-1. l describes the angular momentum of an orbital. This determines the orbital's **shape**. Orbitals with the same value of n and l are in the same **subshell**, and each subshell may contain up to $4l + 2$ electrons. Subshells are usually referred to by the principle quantum number followed by a letter corresponding to l as shown in the following table:

Azimuthal quantum number l	0	1	2	3	4
Subshell designation	s	p	d	f	g

The **magnetic quantum number** m_l or m may have integer values from $-l$ to l. m_l is a measure of how an individual orbital responds to an external magnetic field, and it often describes an orbital's **orientation**. A subscript—either the value of m_l or a function of the x-, y-, and z-axes—is used to designate a specific orbital. See **Skill 1.2a** for images of electron density regions for a few orbitals of hydrogen. $n=3$, $l=2$, and $m_l=0$ for the $3d_0$ orbital. Each orbital may hold up to two electrons.

The **spin quantum number** m_s or s has one of two possible values: $-1/2$ or $+1/2$. m_s differentiates between the two possible electrons occupying an orbital. Electrons moving through a magnet behave as if they were tiny magnets themselves spinning on their axis in either a clockwise or counterclockwise direction. These two spins may be described as $m_s = -1/2$ and $+1/2$ or as down and up.

The **Pauli exclusion principle** states that **no two electrons in an atom may have the same set of four quantum numbers**.

The following table summarizes the relationship among n, l, and m_l through $n=3$:

n	l	Subshell	m_l	Orbitals in subshell	Maximum number of electrons in subshell
1	0	1s	0	1	2
2	0	2s	0	1	2
	1	2p	−1, 0, 1	3	6
3	0	3s	0	1	2
	1	3p	−1, 0, 1	3	6
	2	3d	−2, −1, 0, 1, 2	5	10

Subshell energy levels
In single-electron atoms (H, He$^+$, and Li^{2+}) above the ground state, subshells within a shell are all at the same energy level, and an orbital's energy level is only determined by n. However, in all other atoms, multiple electrons repel each other. Electrons in orbitals closer to the nucleus create a screening or **shielding effect** on electrons further away from the nucleus, preventing them from receiving the full attractive force of the nucleus. **In multi-electron atoms, both n and l determine the energy level of an orbital.** In the absence of a magnetic field, **orbitals in the same subshell with different m_l all have the same energy** and are said to be **degenerate orbitals**.

The following list orders subshells by increasing energy level:
$1s < 2s < 2p < 3s < 3p < 4s < 3d < 4p < 5s < 4d < 5p < 6s < 4f < 5d < 6p < 7s < 5f < \ldots$

This list may be constructed by arranging the subshells according to n and l and drawing diagonal arrows as shown below:

$1s$

$2s$ $2p$

$3s$ $3p$ $3d$

$4s$ $4p$ $4d$ $4f$

$5s$ $5p$ $5d$ $5f$ $5g$

$6s$ $6p$ $6d$ $6f$ $6g$

$7s$ $7p$ $7d$ $7f$ $7g$

$8s$ $8p$ $8d$ $8f$ $8g$

Drawing electron shell structures
Electron shell structures (also called electron arrangements) in an atom may be represented using three methods: an **electron configuration**, an **orbital diagram**, or an **energy level diagram**.

All three methods require knowledge of the subshells occupied by electrons in a certain atom. The **Aufbau principle** or **building-up rule** states that **electrons at ground state fill orbitals starting at the lowest available energy levels**.

An **electron configuration** is a **list of subshells** with superscripts representing the **number of electrons** in each subshell. For example, an atom of boron has 5 electrons. According to the Aufbau principle, two will fill the $1s$ subshell, two will fill the higher energy $2s$ subshell, and one will occupy the $2p$ subshell which has an even higher energy. The electron configuration of boron is $1s^2 2s^2 2p^1$. Similarly, the electron configuration of a vanadium atom with 23 electrons is:
$$1s^2 2s^2 2p^6 3s^2 3p^6 4s^2 3d^3.$$

Configurations are also written with their principle quantum numbers together:
$$1s^2 2s^2 2p^6 3s^2 3p^6 3d^3 4s^2.$$

Electron configurations are often written to emphasize the outermost electrons. This is done by writing the symbol in brackets for the element with a full p subshell from the previous shell and adding the **outer electron configuration** onto that configuration. The element with the last full p subshell will always be a noble gas from the right-most column of the periodic table (see **Skill 1.1a** and **Skill 12.1l**). For the vanadium example, the element with the last full p subshell has the configuration $1s^2 2s^2 2p^6 3s^2 3p^6$. This is $_{18}$Ar. The configuration of vanadium may then be written as $[Ar]4s^2 3d^3$ where $4s^2 3d^3$ is the outer electron configuration.

Electron shell structures may also be written by noting the number of electrons in each shell. For vanadium, this would be:

2, 8, 11, 2.

Orbital diagrams assign electrons to individual orbitals so the energy state of individual electrons may be found. This requires knowledge of how electrons occupy orbitals within a subshell. **Hund's rule** states that **before any two electrons occupy the same orbital, other orbitals in that subshell must first contain one electron each with parallel spins**. Electrons with up and down spins are shown by half-arrows, and these are placed in lines of orbitals (represented as boxes or dashes) according to Hund's rule, the Aufbau principle, and the Pauli exclusion principle. Below is the orbital diagram for vanadium:

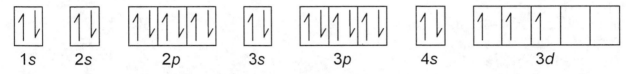

An **energy level diagram** is an orbital diagram that shows subshells with higher energy levels higher up on the page. The energy level diagram of vanadium is:

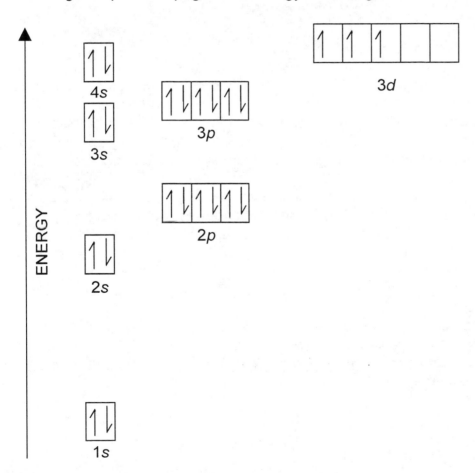

Valence shell electrons and the periodic table

Electrons in the **outermost shell** are called **valence shell electrons**. For example, the electron configuration of Se is $[Ar]4s^2 3d^{10} 4p^4$, and its valence shell electron configuration is $4s^2 4p^4$.

The **periodic table** may be related to the electron shell structure of any element. The table may be divided up into **blocks corresponding to the subshell** designation of the most recent orbital to be filled by the building-up rule.

Elements in the s- and p-blocks are known as **main-group elements**. The d-block elements are called **transition metals.** The f-block elements are called **inner transition metals**.

The maximum number of electrons in each subshell (2, 6, 10, or 14) determines the number of elements in each block, and the order of energy

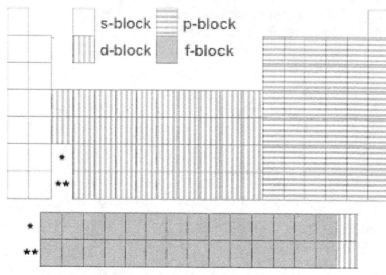

levels for subshells create the pattern of blocks. These blocks also usually correspond to the value of *l* for the **outermost electron** of the atom. This has important consequences for the physical and chemical properties of the elements as shown in **Skill 1.1c**. The outermost shell or valence shell principle quantum number (for example, 4 for Se) is also the period number for the element in the table.

Atoms in the d- and f-blocks often have unexpected electron shell structures that cannot be explained using simple rules. Some heavy atoms have unknown electron configurations because the number of different frequencies of radiation emitted and absorbed by these atoms is very large.

http://www.cowtownproductions.com/cowtown/genchem/08_07T1.htm contains a brief tutorial on energy level diagrams.
http://www.colorado.edu/physics/2000/applets/a2.html contains (among other things) energy level diagrams and animations of electron shells and nuclei.
http://intro.chem.okstate.edu/WorkshopFolder/Electronconfnew.html animates the building up of energy level diagrams.

Skill 1.1c-Predict periodic trends including electronegativity, ionization energy, and the relative sizes of ions and atoms

Electronegativity

Electronegativity measures the ability of an atom to attract electrons in a chemical bond. The most metallic elements (see **Skill 12.1I**) at the lower left of the periodic table have the lowest electronegativity. The most nonmetallic have the highest electronegativity. The impact of electronegativity on chemical bonding is discussed in **Skill 1.3a**.

Physics of electrons and stability of electron configurations

For an isolated atom, the **most stable system of valence electrons is a filled set of orbitals** (see **Skill 1.1b** and **Skill 12.1I**). For the main group elements, this corresponds to group 18 (ns^2np^6 and $1s^2$ for helium), and, to a lesser extent, group 2 (ns^2). The next most stable state is a set of degenerate half-filled orbitals. These occur in group 15 (ns^2np^3). The least stable valence electron configuration is a single electron with no other electrons in similar orbitals. This occurs in group 1 (ns^1) and to a lesser extent in group 13 (ns^2np^1)).

An atom's first **ionization energy** is the energy required to remove one electron by the reaction $M(g) \rightarrow M^+(g) + e^-$. Periodicity is in the opposite direction from the trend for atomic radius. The most metallic atoms have electrons further from the nucleus, and these are easier to remove.

An atom's **electron affinity** is the energy released when one electron is added by the reaction $M(g) + e^- \rightarrow M^-(g)$.

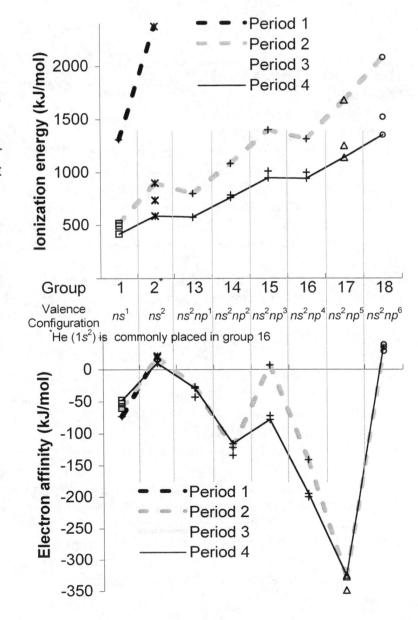

A large negative number for the exothermic reaction indicates a high electron affinity. Halogens have the highest electron affinities.

Trends in **ionization energy and electron affinity** within a period reflect the **stability of valence electron configurations**. A stable system requires more energy to change and releases less when changed. Note the peaks in stability for groups 2, 13, and 16 to the right.

The **size of an atom** is not an exact distance due to of the probabilistic nature of electron density (see Skill 1.2a), but we may compare radii among different atoms using some standard. As seen to the right, the sizes of neutral atoms increase

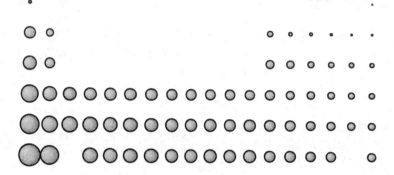

with period number and decrease with group number. As period number increases, the outermost electrons are shielded from the positive charge of the nucleus by more electrons in shells further in, so they are held less tightly. As group number increases, electrons are added to the same shell, so they experience little additional shielding, but the increased number of protons holds them in more closely. This trend is similar to the trend for metallic character. The smallest atom is helium.

The **size of an ion** is also not an exact distance due to the probabilistic nature of electron density, but different ion sizes may be compared. The size of different ions with the same number of electrons decreases as the number of protons increases because more protons provide a greater attractive force (e.g., the size of O^{2-} > F^- > Ne > Na^+ > Mg^{2+} > Al^{3+} for ions with 10 electrons). Cations are smaller than the same parent atom (Na^+ < Na) because of decreased repulsion among electrons and anions are larger than the same parent atom (Cl^- > Cl) because of increased electron repulsion. Ions of the same charge show periodic trends identical to the trends for neutral atoms. Sizes increase with period number (F^- < Cl^- < Br^- < I^-) and decrease with group number (Na^+ > Mg^+ > Al^+).

Periodic trends in **melting point** and **density** were charted in **Skill 1.1a**. **Intermolecular forces contribute to density** by bringing nuclei closer to each other, so the periodicity in density is similar to trends for melting point. However, group-to-group differences are superimposed on a general trend for **density** to **increase with period number** because heavier nuclei make the material denser. See **Skill 1.3d** for other properties altered by intermolecular forces.

Metal oxides form basic solutions in water because the ionic bonds break apart and the O^{2-} ion reacts to form hydroxide ions:

$$\text{metal oxide} \rightarrow \text{metal cation}(aq) + O^{2-}(aq) \quad \text{and} \quad O^{2-}(aq) + H_2O(l) \rightarrow 2\ OH^-(aq)$$

Ionic oxides containing a large cation with a low charge (Rb_2O, for example) are most soluble and form the strongest bases.

Covalent oxides form acidic solutions in water by reacting with water. For example:

$$SO_3(l) + H_2O(l) \rightarrow H_2SO_4(aq) \rightarrow H^+(aq) + HSO_4^-(aq)$$

$$Cl_2O_7(l) + H_2O(l) \rightarrow 2HClO_4(aq) \rightarrow 2H^+(aq) + 2ClO_4^-(aq)$$

Covalent oxides at high oxidation states and high electronegativities form the strongest acids. Acids and bases are discussed in **Competency 4.2**. For this skill, note that the periodic trends for acid and base strength of the oxide of an element follows the same pattern we've seen before.

Summary

A summary of periodic trends is shown to the right. The properties tend to decrease or increase as shown depending on a given element's proximity to fluorine in the table.

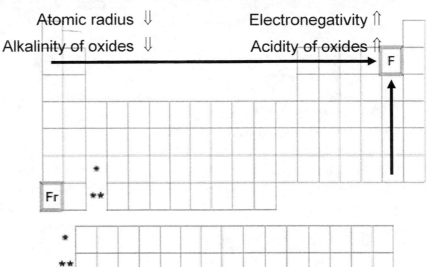

Metallic character ⇓   Ionization energy ⇑

Ionic character of halides ⇓ Covalent character of halides ⇑

Atomic radius ⇓   Electronegativity ⇑

Alkalinity of oxides ⇓   Acidity of oxides ⇑

http://jcrystal.com/steffenweber/JAVA/jpt/jpt.html contains an applet of the periodic table and trends.

http://www.webelements.com is an on-line reference for information on the elements.

http://www.uky.edu/Projects/Chemcomics/ has comic book pages for each element.

Competency 1.2: Atomic Structure

Skill 1.2a-Analyze the evolution of the atomic model

Dalton

The existence of fundamental units of matter called atoms of different types called elements was proposed by ancient philosophers without any evidence to support the belief. Modern atomic theory is credited to the work of **John Dalton** published in 1803-1807. Observations made by him and others about the composition, properties, and reactions of many compounds led him to develop the following postulates:

1) Each element is composed of small particles called atoms.
2) All atoms of a given element are identical in mass and other properties.
3) Atoms of different elements have different masses and differ in other properties.
4) Atoms of an element are not created, destroyed, or changed into a different type of atom by chemical reactions.
5) Compounds form when atoms of more than one element combine.
6) In a given compound, the relative number and kind of atoms are constant.

Dalton's table of atomic symbols and masses

Dalton determined and published the known relative masses of a number of different atoms. He also formulated the law of partial pressures (see **Skill 3.1f**). Dalton's work focused on the ability of atoms to arrange themselves into molecules and to rearrange themselves via chemical reactions, but he did not investigate the composition of atoms themselves. **Dalton's model of the atom** was a tiny, indivisible, indestructible **particle** of a certain mass, size, and chemical behavior, but Dalton did not deny the possibility that atoms might have a substructure.

Thomson

Joseph John Thomson, often known as **J. J. Thomson**, was the first to examine this substructure. In the mid-1800s, scientists had studied a form of radiation called "cathode rays" or "electrons" that originated from the negative electrode (cathode) when electrical current was forced through an evacuated tube. Thomson determined in 1897 that **electrons have mass**, and because many different cathode materials release electrons, Thomson proposed that the **electron is a subatomic particle**. **Thomson's model of the atom** was a uniformly positive particle with electrons contained in the interior.

This has been called the "plum-pudding" model of the atom where the pudding represents the uniform sphere of positive electricity and the bits of plum represent electrons. For more on Thomson, see http://www.aip.org/history/electron/jjhome.htm.

Planck

Max Planck determined in 1900 that **energy is transferred by radiation in exact multiples of a discrete unit of energy called a quantum**. Quanta of energy are extremely small, and may be found from the frequency of the radiation, v, using the equation:

$$\Delta E = hv,\ 2hv,\ 3hv,\ \dots$$

where h is Planck's constant and hv is a quantum of energy.

Rutherford

Ernest Rutherford studied atomic structure in 1910-1911 by firing a beam of alpha particles (see **Skill 7.1b**) at thin layers of gold leaf. According to Thomson's model, the path of an alpha particle should be deflected only slightly if it struck an atom, but Rutherford observed some alpha particles bouncing almost backwards, suggesting that **nearly all the mass of an atom is contained in a small positively charged nucleus**. **Rutherford's model of the atom** was an analogy to the sun and the planets. A small positively charged nucleus is surrounded by circling electrons and mostly by empty space. Rutherford's experiment is explained in greater detail in this flash animation: http://www.mhhe.com/physsci/chemistry/essentialchemistry/flash/ruther14.swf.

De Broglie

Depending on the experiment, radiation appears to have wave-like or particle-like traits. In 1923-1924, Louis de Broglie applied this **wave/particle duality to all matter with momentum**. The discrete distances from the nucleus described by Bohr corresponded to permissible distances where standing waves could exist. **De Broglie's model of the atom** described electrons as **matter waves in standing wave orbits** around the nucleus. The first three standing waves corresponding to the first three discrete distances are shown in the figure. An applet of de Broglie's model may be found here: http://artsci-ccwin.concordia.ca/facstaff/a-c/bird/c241/D1-part2.html.

Bohr

Niels Bohr incorporated Planck's quantum concept into Rutherford's model of the atom in 1913 to explain the **discrete frequencies of radiation emitted and absorbed by atoms with one electron** (H, He^+, and Li^{2+}). This electron is attracted to the positive nucleus and is closest to the nucleus at the **ground state** of the atom. When the electron absorbs energy, it moves into an orbit further from the nucleus and the atom is said to be in an electronically **excited state**. If sufficient energy is absorbed, the electron separates from the nucleus entirely, and the atom is ionized:

$$H \rightarrow H^+ + e^-$$

The energy required for ionization from the ground state is called the atom's **ionization energy**. The discrete frequencies of radiation emitted and absorbed by the atom correspond (using Planck's constant) to discrete energies and in turn to discrete distances from the nucleus. **Bohr's model of the atom** was a small positively charged nucleus surrounded mostly by empty space and by electrons orbiting at certain discrete distances ("shells") corresponding to discrete energy levels. Animations utilizing the Bohr model may be found at the following two URLs: http://artsci-ccwin.concordia.ca/facstaff/a-c/bird/c241/D1.html and http://www.mhhe.com/physsci/chemistry/essentialchemistry/flash/linesp16.swf.

Heisenberg

The realization that both matter and radiation interact as waves led Werner Heisenberg to the conclusion in 1927 that the act of observation and measurement requires the interaction of one wave with another, resulting in an **inherent uncertainty** in the location and momentum of particles. This inability to measure phenomena at the subatomic level is known as the **Heisenberg uncertainty principle**. A discussion of the principle and Heisenberg's other contributions to quantum theory is located here: http://www.aip.org/history/heisenberg/.

Schrödinger
When Erwin Schrödinger studied the atom in 1925, he replaced the idea of precise orbits with regions in space called **orbitals** where electrons were likely to be found. **The Schrödinger equation** describes the **probability** that an electron will be in a given region of space, a quantity known as **electron density** or ψ^2. The diagrams below are surfaces of constant ψ^2 found by solving the Schrödinger equation for the hydrogen atom $1s$, $2p_z$ and $3d_0$ orbitals (see **Skill 1.1b**). Additional representations of solutions may be found here: http://library.wolfram.com/webMathematica/Physics/Hydrogen.jsp. **Schrödinger's model of the atom** is a mathematical formulation of quantum mechanics that describes the electron density of orbitals. It is the atomic model that has been in use from shortly after it was introduced up to the present.

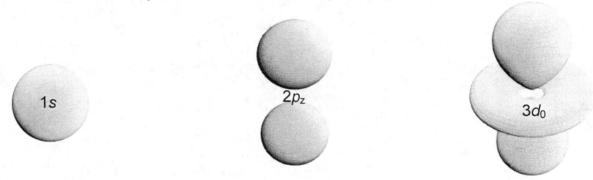

Skill 1.2b-Relate atomic spectroscopy and the photoelectric effect to the quantum structure of the atom

The quantum structure of the atom describes electrons in discrete energy levels surrounding the nucleus (see **Skill 1.2a**). When an electron moves from a high energy orbital to a lower energy orbital, a quantum of electromagnetic radiation is emitted, and for an electron to move from a low energy to a higher energy level, a quantum of radiation must be absorbed. The particle that carries this electromagnetic force is called a **photon** . The quantum structure of the atom predicts that only photons corresponding to certain wavelengths of light will be emitted or absorbed by atoms. These distinct wavelengths are measured by **atomic spectroscopy**.

In **atomic absorption spectroscopy**, a continuous spectrum (light consisting of all wavelengths) is passed through the element. The frequencies of absorbed photons are then determined as the electrons increase in energy. An **absorption spectrum** in the visible region usually appears as a rainbow of color stretching from red to violet interrupted by a few black lines corresponding to distinct wavelengths of absorption.

In **atomic emission spectroscopy**, the electrons of an element are excited by heating or by an electric discharge. The frequencies of emitted photons are then determined as the electrons release energy.

An **emission spectrum** in the visible region typically consists of lines of light at certain colors corresponding to distinct wavelengths of emission. The bands of emitted or absorbed light at these wavelengths are called **spectral lines**. **Each element has a unique line spectrum**. Light from a star (including the sun) may be analyzed to determine what elements are present.

A simple optical spectroscope separates visible light into distinct wavelengths by passing the light through a prism or diffraction grating. When electrons in hydrogen gas are excited inside a discharge tube, the emission spectroscope shown below detects photons at four visible wavelengths.

Visible spectral lines for hydrogen	Wavelength λ
Purple	411 nm
Blue	434 nm
Green	486 nm
Orange-red	656 nm

Quantum #	Radius
$n \rightarrow \infty$	$r_\infty \rightarrow \infty$
$\vdots$	$\vdots$
$n = 5$	$r_5 = 25a_0$
$n = 4$	$r_4 = 16a_0$
$n = 3$	$r_3 = 9a_0$
$n = 2$	$r_2 = 4a_0$
$n = 1$ $\oplus$ (H nucleus)	$r_1 = a_0$

An electron may exist at distinct radial distances (r_n) from the nucleus. These distances are proportional to the square of the **principal quantum number**, n. For a hydrogen atom (shown at left), the proportionality constant is called the **Bohr radius** ($a_0 = 5.29 \times 10^{-11}$ m). This value is the mean distance of an electron from the nucleus at the ground state of $n = 1$. The distances of other electron shells are found by the formula:

$$r_n = a_0 n^2 .$$

As $n \rightarrow \infty$, the electron is no longer part of the hydrogen atom. Ionization occurs and the atom become an H^+ ion.

Photon wavelength (λ) in meters and frequency (ν) in reciprocal seconds are inversely proportional to each other. The proportionality constant between them is the **speed of light** ($c = 3.00 \times 10^8$ m/s):

$$\lambda = \frac{c}{\nu} \quad \text{and} \quad \nu = \frac{c}{\lambda} .$$

A quantum of energy (ΔE) emitted from or absorbed by an electron transition is directly proportional to the frequency of radiation. The proportionality constant between them is **Planck's constant** ($h = 6.63 \times 10^{-34}$ J·s):

$$\Delta E = h\nu \quad \text{and} \quad \Delta E = \frac{hc}{\lambda}.$$

Visible wavelengths stretch from about 400 to 700 nm, and occupy only a small portion of the **electromagnetic spectrum** (shown at right) describing all possible types of electromagnetic radiation.

Wavelength λ (m)	Radiation class	Frequency ν (s^{-1})	Energy ΔE (J)
$10^{-12} = 1$ pm	Gamma rays	3×10^{20}	2×10^{-13}
$10^{-11} = 10$ pm	Gamma rays	3×10^{19}	2×10^{-14}
$10^{-10} = 100$ pm		3×10^{18}	2×10^{-15}
$10^{-9} = 1$ nm	X-rays	3×10^{17}	2×10^{-16}
$10^{-8} = 10$ nm		3×10^{16}	2×10^{-17}
$10^{-7} = 100$ nm	Ultraviolet	3×10^{15}	2×10^{-18}
$10^{-6} = 1$ µm	Visible	3×10^{14}	2×10^{-19}
$10^{-5} = 10$ µm	Infrared	3×10^{13}	2×10^{-20}
$10^{-4} = 100$ µm		3×10^{12}	2×10^{-21}
$10^{-3} = 1$ mm		3×10^{11}	2×10^{-22}
$10^{-2} = 1$ cm	Microwaves	3×10^{10}	2×10^{-23}
$10^{-1} = 1$ dm	Radio	3×10^{9}	2×10^{-24}
1 m	Broadcasts	3×10^{8}	2×10^{-25}

The energy of an electron (E_n) is inversely proportional to its radius from the nucleus. For a hydrogen atom (shown below left), only the principle quantum number determines the energy of an electron by the **Rydberg constant** ($R_H = 2.18 \times 10^{-18}$ J):

Quantum #	Energy
$n \to \infty$	$E_\infty \to 0$
$n = 3$	$E_3 = -\dfrac{R_H}{9}$
$n = 2$	$E_2 = -\dfrac{R_H}{4}$
$n = 1$	$E_1 = -R_H$

$$E_n = -\frac{R_H}{n^2}.$$

The Rydberg constant is used to determine the energy of a photon emitted or absorbed by an electron transition from one shell to another in the H atom:

$$\Delta E = R_H \left(\frac{1}{n_{initial}^2} - \frac{1}{n_{final}^2} \right).$$

When a photon is absorbed, n_{final} is greater than $n_{initial}$, resulting in positive values corresponding to an endothermic process. Ionization occurs when sufficient energy is added for the atom to lose its electron from the ground state. This corresponds to an electron transition from $n_{initial} = 1$ to $n_{final} \to \infty$. The Rydberg constant is the energy required to ionize one atom of hydrogen. Photon emission causes negative values corresponding to an exothermic process because $n_{initial}$ is greater than n_{final}.

Planck's constant and the speed of light are often used to express the Rydberg constant in units of s^{-1} or length. The formulas below determine the photon frequency or wavelength corresponding to a given electron transition:

$$v_{photon} = \left(\frac{R_H}{h}\right) \left| \frac{1}{n^2_{initial}} - \frac{1}{n^2_{final}} \right| \quad \text{and} \quad \lambda_{photon} = \frac{1}{\left(\frac{R_H}{hc}\right) \left| \frac{1}{n^2_{initial}} - \frac{1}{n^2_{final}} \right|}.$$

These formulas **relate observed lines in the hydrogen spectrum to individual transitions** from one quantum state to another.

Every line in the hydrogen spectrum corresponds to a transition between electron energy levels. The four spectral lines from hydrogen emission spectroscopy in the visible range were discussed on the first page of this skill. These lines correspond to electron transitions from n = 3, 4, 5, and 6 to n =2 as shown in the table below.

Radiation type	Wavelength λ (nm)	Frequency v (s^{-1})	Energy change ΔE (J)	Electron transition $n_{initial} \rightarrow n_{final}$	
Ultraviolet	≤397	≥7.55×10^{14}	≤−5.00×10^{-19}	$\infty \rightarrow 1$, ... $2 \rightarrow 1$ $\infty \rightarrow 2$, ... $7 \rightarrow 2$	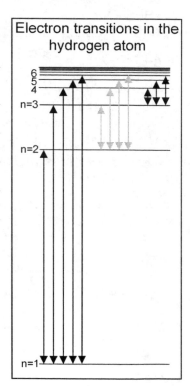
Purple	411	7.31×10^{14}	−4.84×10^{-19}	$6 \rightarrow 2$	
Blue	434	6.90×10^{14}	−4.58×10^{-19}	$5 \rightarrow 2$	
Green	486	6.17×10^{14}	−4.09×10^{-19}	$4 \rightarrow 2$	
Orange-red	656	4.57×10^{14}	−3.03×10^{-19}	$3 \rightarrow 2$	
Infrared and beyond	≥821	≤3.65×10^{14}	≥−2.42×10^{-19}	$\infty \rightarrow 3$, ... $4 \rightarrow 3$ $\infty \rightarrow 4$, ... $5 \rightarrow 4$ ⋮	

Electron transitions in the hydrogen atom

Most lines in the hydrogen spectrum are not at visible wavelengths. Larger energy transitions produce ultraviolet radiation and smaller energy transitions produce infrared or longer wavelengths of radiation. Transitions between the first three and the first six energy levels of the hydrogen atom are shown in the diagram to the right. The energy transitions producing the four visible spectral lines are colored grey.

The **photoelectric effect** occurs when **light shining on a clean metal surface causes the surface to emit electrons** towards a region of the metal kept in the dark. The energy of an absorbed photon is transferred to an electron as shown to the right. If this energy is greater than the binding energy holding the electron close to nearby nuclei then the electron will move. A high energy (high frequency, low wavelength) photon will not only dislodge an electron from the

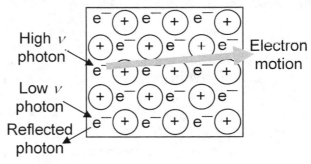

"electron sea" of a metal (**See Skill 1.3d**), but it will also impart kinetic energy to the electron, making it move rapidly. These electrons in motion will produce an electric current if a circuit is present. **Solar cells** use this effect to produce electricity from sunlight. For every metal there is a minimum frequency required for the photoelectric effect to occur.

A **large number of low-energy photons will not cause the photoelectric effect** because each photon does not impart sufficient energy to overcome binding energy. Instead of setting the electron in motion, the electron simply emits another photon. Non-quantum **classical theories predicted that an electron could slowly build up energy** from low-energy photon absorptions and eventually accumulate enough energy to free itself from nearby nuclei, but this is not observed. The quantum structure of the atom predicts that the energy from a photon absorption event will not be stored by the electron in an intermediate energy state. **Quantum events are "all or nothing,"** and this is what is observed by photoelectric effect experiments.

Skill 1.2c-Illustrate the position and describe the properties of quarks, protons, neutrons, and electrons within atoms

Protons have a positive charge, **neutrons** have no charge, and **electrons** have a negative charge. Atoms have no net charge and thus have an equal number of protons and electrons. **Anions** are negative ions and contain more electrons than protons. **Cations** are positive ions and contain more protons than electrons. Protons and neutrons are contained in a small volume at the center of the atom called the **nucleus**. Electrons move in the remaining space of the atom and have very little mass—about 1/1800 of the mass of a proton or neutron. Electrons are prevented from flying away from the nucleus by the attraction that exists between opposite electrical charges. This force is known as **electrostatic** or **coulombic** attraction.

Protons and neutrons each contain three **quarks**. A neutron consists of one *up* quark and two down quarks. A proton consists of two up quarks and one *down* quark. Other quarks are named *strange*, *charm*, *bottom*, and *top*., but these four are not part of atoms. Quarks are a fundamental constituent of matter according to current standard model of particle physics, but individual quarks are not seen. Instead they are always confined within other subatomic particles. There is no need to consider quarks when describing chemical interactions. **Only electrons are involved in chemical reactions**. The position and sizes of these particles in a helium atom is indicated in the diagram at right. A diagram like this one could never be drawn to scale. If a proton were drawn 1 cm in diameter, the atom's diameter would require a page about 1 km long and a quark's diameter would be less than 1 μm.

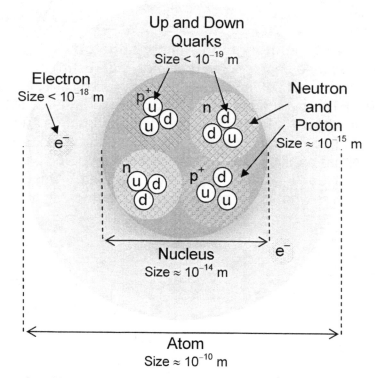

Up and Down Quarks
Size < 10^{-19} m

Electron
Size < 10^{-18} m

Neutron and Proton
Size ≈ 10^{-15} m

Nucleus
Size ≈ 10^{-14} m

Atom
Size ≈ 10^{-10} m

Competency 1.3: Molecular Structure and Chemical Bonds

Skill 1.3a-Compare types of molecular bonds including ionic, covalent, and hydrogen bonds

An **ionic bond** occurs **between a metal and a nonmetal.** In an ionic bond, the metal "gives" an electron to the nonmetal. A **covalent bond is favored between nonmetals.** In a covalent bond both atoms attract electrons and share electrons between them. A **metallic bond is favored between metals.** In a metallic bond, atoms lose electrons to a matrix of free electrons surrounding them. Many bonds have some characteristics of more than one of the above basic bond types. Electronegativity and the location of metallic and nonmetallic elements on the periodic table are described in **Skill 1.1c and 12.1l.**

Ionic bonds

An **ionic bond** describes the electrostatic forces that exist between **particles of opposite charge.** Elements that form an ionic bond with each other have a large difference in their electronegativity. Anions and cations pack together into a crystal **lattice** as shown to the right for NaCl. Ionic compounds are also known as **salts.**

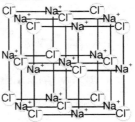

All common salts are solids at room temperature. **Salts are brittle, have a high melting point**, and do not conduct electricity because their ions are not free to move in the crystal lattice. Salts do conduct electricity in molten form. The formation of a salt from a metal and a nonmetal is a highly exothermic reaction.

Salts in solid form are generally stable compounds, but in molten form or in solution, their component ions often react to form a more stable salt. The reactivities of these ions vary with the electronegativity of the respective element as described in **Skill 12.1m.**

Some salts decompose to form more stable salts, as in the decomposition of molten potassium chlorate to form potassium chloride and oxygen:

$$2KClO_3(l) \rightarrow 2KCl(s) + 3O_2(g).$$

Single and multiple covalent bonds

Nonmetals typically react with other nonmetals to form **covalent bonds**. A covalent bond is formed between two atoms by **sharing a pair of electrons**. The simplest covalent bond is between the two single electrons of hydrogen atoms. Covalent bonds may be represented by an electron pair (a pair of dots) or a line as shown below. The shared pair of electrons provides each H atom with two electrons in its valence shell (the $1s$ orbital), so both have the stable electron configuration of helium.

$$H\cdot \ + \ \cdot H \longrightarrow \begin{array}{c} H{:}H \\ H{-\!\!-}H \end{array}$$

Chlorine molecules have 7 electrons in their valence shell and share a pair of electrons so both have the stable electron configuration of argon.

$$:\ddot{\underset{..}{Cl}}\cdot \ + \ \cdot \ddot{\underset{..}{Cl}}: \ \longrightarrow \ \begin{array}{c} :\ddot{\underset{..}{Cl}}{:}\ddot{\underset{..}{Cl}}: \\ :\ddot{\underset{..}{Cl}}{-\!\!-}\ddot{\underset{..}{Cl}}: \end{array}$$

In the previous two examples, a single pair of electrons was shared, and the resulting bond is referred to as a **single bond**. When two electron pairs are shared, two lines are drawn, representing a **double bond**, and three shared pairs of electrons represents a **triple bond** as shown below for CO_2 and N_2. The remaining electrons are in **unshared pairs**.

$$\ddot{O}{:}{:}C{:}{:}\ddot{O} \qquad :N{:}{:}{:}N:$$

$$\ddot{O}{=\!\!=}C{=\!\!=}\ddot{O} \qquad :N{\equiv}N:$$

Covalent bonds in a network solid

A covalent network solid may be considered **one large molecule connected by covalent bonds**. These materials are **very hard, strong, and have a high melting point**. Diamond, C_n or C_∞, and quartz, $(SiO_2)_n$ or $(SiO_2)_\infty$, are two examples.

Electronegativity and polar/nonpolar covalent bonds

Electron pairs shared between **two atoms of the same element are shared equally**. At the other extreme, **for ionic bonding there is no electron sharing** because the electron is transferred completely from one atom to the other. Most bonds fall somewhere between these two extremes, and the electrons are **shared unequally**. This will increase the probability that the shared electrons will be located on one of the two atoms, giving that atom a **partial negative charge**, and the other atom a **partial positive charge** as shown below for gaseous HCl. Such bonds are referred to as **polar bonds**. A particle with a positive and a negative region is called a **dipole**. A lower-case delta (δ) is used to indicate partial charge or an arrow is draw from the partial positive to the partial negative atom.

$$\overset{\delta+ \quad \delta-}{H\!-\!Cl} \qquad \overset{\longrightarrow}{H\!-\!Cl}$$

Electronegativity is a measure of **the ability of an atom to attract electrons** in a chemical bond. Metallic elements have low electronegativities and nonmetallic elements have high electronegativities (see **Skill 1.1c**).

H
2.2

Li	Be		B	C	N	O	F
1.0	1.6		1.8	2.5	3.0	3.4	4.0
Na	Mg		Al	Si	P	S	Cl
0.9	1.3		1.6	1.9	2.2	2.6	3.2

Linus Pauling developed the concept of electronegativity and its relationship to different types of bonds in the 1930s.

A **large electronegativity difference** (greater than 1.7) results in an **ionic bond**. Any bond composed of two different atoms will be slightly polar, but for a **small electronegativity difference** (less than 0.4), the distribution of charge in the bond is so nearly equal that the result is called a **nonpolar covalent bond**. An **intermediate electronegativity difference** (from 0.4 to 1.7) results in a **polar covalent bond**. HCl is polar covalent because Cl has a very high electronegativity (it is near F in the periodic table) and H is a nonmetal (and so it will form a covalent bond with Cl), but H is near the dividing line between metals and nonmetals, so there is still a significant electronegativity difference between H and Cl. Using the numbers in the table above, the electronegativity for Cl is 3.2 and it is 2.2 for H. The difference of 3.2 – 2.2 = 1.0 places this bond in the middle of the range for polar covalent bonds.

Bond type is actually a continuum as shown in the following chart for common bonds. Note that the **C-H bond** is considered **nonpolar**.

Type of bonding	Electronegativity difference	Bond
		Fr^+—F^-
Very ionic		Na^+—F^-
	3.0	
⋮	⋮	⋮
Ionic		Na^+—Cl^-
	2.0	Na^+—Br^-
Mostly ionic		Na^+—I^-
Mostly polar covalent	1.5	$C^{\delta+}$—$F^{\delta-}$
		$H^{\delta+}$—$O^{\delta-}$
Polar covalent	1.0	$H^{\delta+}$—$Cl^{\delta-}$
		$C^{\delta+}$=$O^{\delta-}$
		$H^{\delta+}$—$N^{\delta-}$
		$C^{\delta+}$—$Cl^{\delta-}$
	0.5	$C^{\delta+}$≡$N^{\delta-}$
Mostly nonpolar covalent		C—H
Fully nonpolar covalent	0	H_2, N_2, O_2, F_2, Cl_2, Br_2, I_2, C—C, S—S

Increasing ionic character ⇑

Metallic bonds
The physical properties of metals are attributed to the **electron sea model of metallic bonds** shown on the right. Metals **conduct heat and electricity** because electrons are not associated with the bonding between two specific atoms and they are able to flow through the material. They are called **delocalized** electrons. Metals are **lustrous** because electrons at their surface reflect light at many different wavelengths.

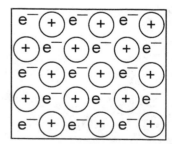

Metals are **malleable** and **ductile** because the electrons are able to rearrange their positions to maintain the integrity of the solid when the metallic lattice is deformed, acting like glue between the cations. The strengths of different metallic bonds can be related to the relative amounts and positions of electrons in this glue.

Alkali metals contain only one valence electron ("less glue"), and that electron is a considerable distance away from the nucleus ("weaker glue") because it is shielded from nuclear attraction by the noble gas configuration of the remaining electrons. The result is a weak metallic bond and a low melting point. Heavier alkali metals contain a valence electron even further from the nucleus, resulting in a very weak metallic bond and a lowering of the melting point. With two valence electrons and smaller atoms, alkaline earth metals have stronger metallic bonds than the alkali metals. This explains some of the periodic trends described in **Skill 2.1**.

The metal with the weakest metallic bonds is mercury. Hg is a liquid at room temperature because Hg atoms hold on tightly to a stable valence configuration of full s, f, and d subshells. Fewer electrons are shared to create bonds than in other metals.

The reactivity of metals increases with lower electronegativity in reactions with nonmetals to form ionic bonds. See the reactivity series in **Skill 2.2**.

Hydrogen bonds
Except in larger molecules, hydrogen bonds are usually an intermolecular force, not a bonding mechanism within a single molecule. Intermolecular forces are also sometimes described as "secondary molecular bonds". Hydrogen bonds will be described in **Skill 1.3d**.

Skill 1.3b-Draw Lewis dot structures for compounds and ions

Noble gases have stable electron configurations because the subshells corresponding to their valence electrons are completely filled. Atoms often gain, lose, or share electrons in order to achieve the **same number of electrons as the noble gas nearest to them in the periodic table**. Helium has a $1s^2$ valence electron configuration, and every other noble gas has an ns^2np^6 valence electron configuration for a total of **eight valence electrons**. The observation that **many reaction products have eight valence electrons** is known as the **octet rule**.

Lewis dot structures are a method for keeping track of each atom's valence electrons in a molecule. Drawing Lewis structures is a three-step process:

1) Add the number of valence shell electrons for each atom. See **Skill 1.1b** for using the periodic table to do this. If the compound is an anion, add the charge of the ion to the total electron count because anions have "extra" electrons. If the compound is a cation, subtract the charge of the ion.
2) Write the symbols for each atom showing how the atoms connect to each other.
3) Draw a single bond (one pair of electron dots or a line) between each pair of connected atoms. Place the remaining electrons around the atoms as unshared pairs. If every atom has an octet of electrons except H atoms with two electrons, the Lewis structure is complete. Shared electrons count towards both atoms. If there are too few electron pairs to do this, draw multiple bonds (two or three pairs of electron dots between the atoms) until an octet is around each atom (except H atoms with two). If there are two many electron pairs to complete the octets with single bonds then the octet rule Is broken for this compound.

Example: Draw the Lewis structure of HCN.
Solution:
1) From their locations in the main group of the periodic table, we know that each atom contributes the following number of electrons: H—1, C—4, N—5. Because it is a neutral compound, the molecule will have a total of 10 valence electrons.
2) The atoms are connected with C at the center and will be drawn as: H C N. Having H as the central atom is impossible because H has one valence electron and will always only have a single bond to one other atom. If N were the central atom then the formula would probably be written as HNC.
3) Connecting the atoms with 10 electrons in single bonds gives the structure to the right. H has two electrons to fill its valence subshells, but C and N only have six each. A triple bond between these atoms fulfills the octet rule for C and N and is the correct Lewis structure.

$$\text{H} : \text{C} ::: \text{N} :$$

Skill 1.3c-Predict molecular geometries using Lewis dot structures and hybridized atomic orbitals, e.g., valence shell electron pair repulsion model (VSEPR)

Resonance
O_2 contains a total of 12 valence electrons and the following Lewis structure:

Ozone, O_3, has a total of 18 valence electrons, and two Lewis structures are possible for this molecule

Equivalent Lewis structures are called **resonance forms**. A double-headed arrow is used to indicate resonance. The actual molecule does not have a double bond on one bond and a single bond on the other. The **molecular structure is in an average state between the resonance forms**.

Hybridized atomic orbitals
Electron shell structures (see **Skill 1.1b**) are built up by considering different energy levels for different subshells to explain spectroscopic data about individual atoms (see **Skill 1.2b**). However, when Lewis dot structures are drawn (**Skill 1.3b**) or molecular geometries are determined (later in this skill), all valence electrons are treated identically to explain the bonding between atoms regardless of whether the electrons once belonged to the s or the p subshell of their atom. Reconciling these views of the individual and the bonded atom requires a theory known as hybridization.

Hybridization describes the pre-bonding **promotion of one or more electrons** from a lower energy subshell to a higher energy subshell followed by a **combination** of the orbitals into degenerate **hybrid orbitals**.

Example: A boron atom has the valence electron configuration $2s^2 2p^1$ as shown to the right. Before bonding to three other atoms, the capability to form three equivalent bonds is achieved by hybridization. First a $2s$ electron is promoted to an empty p orbital. Next the occupied orbitals combine into three hybrid $2sp^2$ orbitals. Now three electrons in degenerate orbitals are available to create covalent bonds with three atoms.

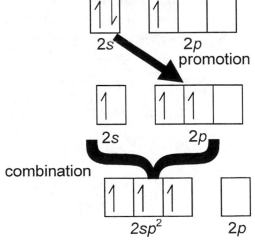

Hybridization occurs for atoms with a valence electron configuration of ns^2, ns^2np^1, or ns^2p^2. For period 2, this corresponds with Be, B, C, and N in the NH_3^+ ion.

An atom joined to its neighbor by **multiple covalent bonds** is prepared for bonding by hybridization with incomplete combination. Electrons that remain in p orbitals can contribute additional bonds between the same two atoms.

Example: An isolated carbon atom has the valence electron configuration $2s^2 2p^2$. Hybridization to four $2sp^3$ orbitals occurs before bonding to four atoms. Three hybrid sp^2 orbitals form if there is a double bond so the C atom is bonded to three atoms and one electron remains in the p orbital. Two hybrid sp orbitals occur if there is a triple bond or two double bonds. In this case, C is bonded to two atoms with two electrons remaining in p orbitals.

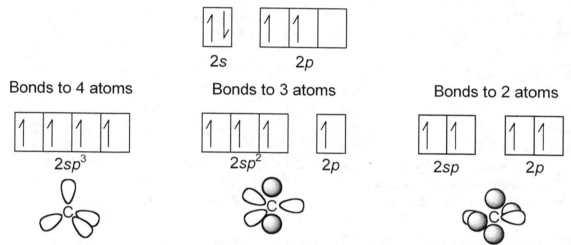

Note: p orbitals are shaded in the diagrams. These models are meant to illustrate the **locations** and **angles** of hybrid and p orbitals relative to the central atom. A mathematical solution would also show that each type of hybrid orbital (sp^3, sp^2, and sp) has a slightly different shape from the other two. See **Skill 1.2a** for an image of electron density in a p orbital.

See http://www.mhhe.com/physsci/chemistry/essentialchemistry/flash/hybrv18.swf for a flash animation tutorial of hybridization.

Molecular Orbital Theory
The electron configurations of isolated atoms are found in atomic orbitals; the configurations of atoms about to bond are represented by atomic and hybridized atomic orbitals; and **the electron configurations of molecules are represented by molecular orbitals**. Molecular orbital theory is an advanced topic, but it may be simplified to representing the **bonds between atoms as overlapping electron density shapes from atomic orbitals**. There are two typical locations for molecular orbitals.

The **bonding sigma orbital** (σ) surrounds a **line drawn between the two atoms** in a bond. At least one electron pair in every bond is in a bonding σ orbital. Sigma bonds get their name from s orbitals because the spherical electron density shapes of two s orbitals overlap to form a σ orbital. A drawing of this overlap and the resulting molecular orbital is shown to the right for H_2. Hybrid or p atomic orbitals also form a σ orbital when they overlap such that the axis between the bonded atoms runs through the center of the combined electron density.

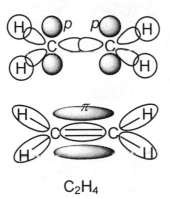

C_2H_4

The **bonding pi orbital** (π) follows regions **separate from a line drawn between the two atoms** in a bond. Two overlapping p orbitals will form π bonds to contain the additional shared electrons in molecules with double or triple bonds. π bonds prevent atoms from rotating about the central axis between them. The atomic orbitals that form the compound C_2H_4 are shown above to the left. Each H atom contains one electron in an s orbital and each C atom contains 4 valence electrons in three hybrid sp^2 orbitals and one p orbital. The compound itself contains the molecular orbitals shown below to the left. There are five σ bonds (white ovals) and one π bond (the shaded shapes). For additional examples of π bonds in carbon compounds, see **Skill 6.1a.**

Molecular orbital theory also predicts **antibonding orbitals** that **prevent bonding** because they are at a higher energy level than the electrons on individual atoms. Antibonding electrons play a role in explaining why molecules like H_2 form while molecules like He_2 do not, but they are not required to predict molecular structures. For more on this aspect of molecular orbital theory, see http://www.chem.ufl.edu/~chm2040/Notes/Chapter_12/theory.html.

Electron Pairs

Molecular geometry is predicted using the valence-shell electron-pair repulsion or **VSEPR** model. VSEPR uses the fact that **electron pairs around the central atom of a molecule repel each other**. Imagine you are one of two pairs of electrons in bonds around a central atom (like a bonds in BeH_2 in the table below). You want to be as far away from the other electron pair as possible, so you will be on one side of the atom and the other pair will be on the other side. There is a straight line (or a 180° angle) between you to the other electron pair on the other side of the nucleus. In general, electron pairs lie at the **largest possible angles** from each other.

Electron pairs	Geometrical arrangement		Predicted bond angles	Example
2		Linear	180°	
3		Trigonal planar	120°	
4		Tetrahedral	109.5°	
5		Trigonal bipyramidal	120° and 90°	
6		Octahedral	90°	

X represents a generic central atom. Lone pair electrons on F are not shown in the example molecules.

Unshared Electron Pairs

The **shape of a molecule is given by the location of its atoms**. These are connected to central atoms by shared electrons, but unshared electrons also have an important impact on molecular shape. Unshared electrons may determine the angles between atoms. Molecular shapes in the following table take into account total and unshared electron pairs.

Electron pairs	Molecular shape				
	All shared pairs	1 unshared pair	2 unshared pairs	3 unshared pairs	4 unshared pairs
2	A—X—A Linear				
3	Trigonal planar	Bent			
4	Tetrahedral	Trigonal pyramidal	Bent		
5	Trigonal bipyramidal	Seesaw or sawhorse	T-shaped	Linear	
6	Octohedral	Square pyramidal	Square planar	T-shaped	Linear

X represents a generic central atom bonded to atoms labeled A.

Altered Bond Angles

Unpaired electrons also have a less dramatic impact on molecular shape. Imagine you are an unshared electron pair around a molecule's central atom. The shared electron pairs are each attracted partially to the central atom and partially to the other atom in the bond, but you are different. You are attracted to the central atom, but there's nothing on your other side, so you are free to expand in that direction. That expansion means that you take up more room than the other electron pairs, and they are all squeezed a little closer together because of you. Multiple bonds have a similar effect because more space is required for more electrons. In general, **unshared electron pairs and multiple bonds decrease the angles between the remaining bonds**. A few examples are shown in the following tables.

Compound	CH_4	NH_3	H_2O
Unshared electrons	0	1	2
Shape	Tetrahedral	Trigonal pyramidal	Bent

Compound	BF_3	C_2H_4 (ethylene)
Multiple bonds	0	1
Shape	Trigonal planar	Trigonal planar

Summary

In order to use VSEPR to predict molecular geometry, perform the following steps:

1) Write out Lewis dot structures using **Skill 1.3b**.
2) Use the Lewis structure to determine the number of unshared electron pairs and bonds around each central atom counting multiple bonds as one (for now).
3) The second table of this skill gives the arrangement of total and unshared electron pairs to account for electron repulsions around each central atom.
4) For multiple bonds or unshared electron pairs, decrease the angles slightly between the remaining bonds around the central atom.
5) Combine results from the previous two steps to determine the molecular shape.

http://www.shef.ac.uk/chemistry/vsepr/ is a good site for explaining and visualizing molecular geometries using VSEPR.
http://cowtownproductions.com/cowtown/genchem/09_16T.htm provides more practice.

Skill 1.3d-Relate intermolecular electrostatic forces, including Van der Waals, polar and induced polar, and ionic, to their expected states of matter and their characteristic physical properties

Polar and nonpolar molecules
A **polar molecule** has positive and negative regions as shown below for HCl.

$$\delta+ \quad \delta- \qquad \longrightarrow$$
$$H\!-\!Cl \qquad H\!-\!Cl$$

Bond polarity (see **Skill 1.3a**) is **necessary but not sufficient for molecular polarity**. A molecule containing polar bonds will still be nonpolar if the most negative and most positive location occurs at the same point. In other words, **in a polar molecule, bond polarities must not cancel**.

To determine if a molecule is polar perform the following steps.

1) Draw the molecular structure (see **Skill 1.3c**).
2) Assign a polarity to each bond with an arrow (remember C-H is nonpolar). If none of the bonds are polar, the molecule is nonpolar.
3) Determine if the polarities cancel each other in space. If they do, the molecule is nonpolar. Otherwise the molecule is polar.

Examples: Which of the following are polar molecules: CO_2, CH_2Cl_2, CCl_4.

Solution: 1)

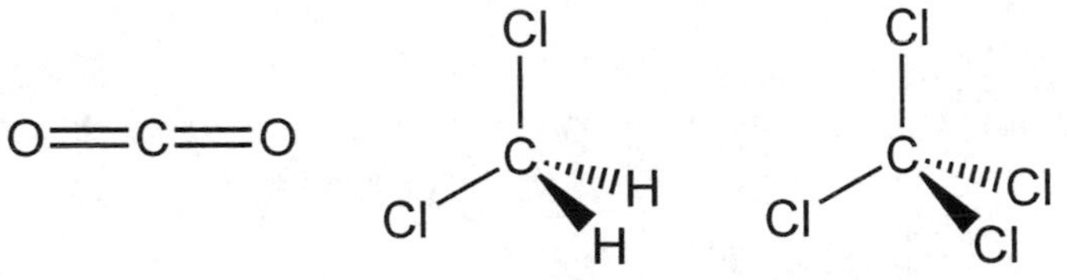

$$O\!=\!C\!=\!O$$

CO_2 CH_2Cl_2 CCl_4

2)

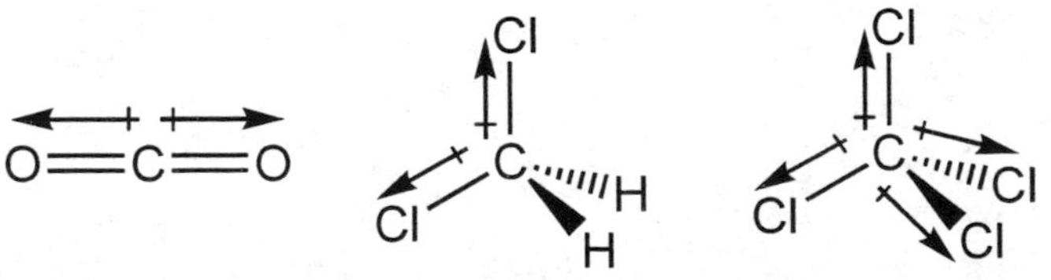

3)   charges cancel   net dipole   charges cancel

nonpolar   polar   nonpolar

The polarity of molecules is critical for determining a good solvent for a given solute (see **Skill 4.1c**). Additional practice on the topic of polar bonds and molecules is available at http://cowtownproductions.com/cowtown/genchem/09_17M.htm.

The following intermolecular forces between molecules are usually weaker than covalent, ionic, and metallic bonds. They are listed from the strongest force to the weakest.

Ion-dipole interactions
Salts tend to dissolve in several polar solvents. An ion with a full charge in a polar solvent will **orient nearby solvent molecules** so that their opposite partial charges are pointing towards the ion. In aqueous solution, certain salts react to form solid **precipitates** if a combination of their ions is insoluble. See **Skill 4.1c** for more about salts in solution including an example of an ion-dipole interaction for a Na^+ ion in water.

Hydrogen bonds
Hydrogen bonds are particularly **strong dipole-dipole interactions** that form between the H-atom of one molecule and an **F, O, or N** atom of an adjacent molecule. The partial positive charge on the hydrogen atom is attracted to the partial negative charge on the electron pair of the other atom. The hydrogen bond between two water molecules is shown as the dashed line below:

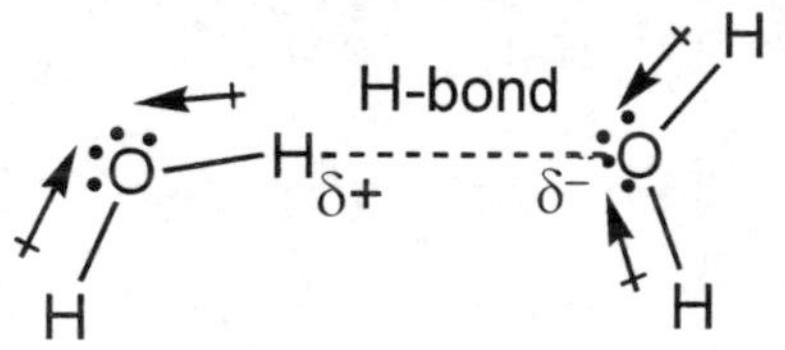

Dipole-dipole interactions
The intermolecular forces between polar molecules are known as dipole-dipole interactions. The partial positive charge of one molecule is attracted to the partial negative charge of its neighbor.

Ion-induced dipole

When a nonpolar molecule (or a noble gas atom) encounters an ion, its **electron density is temporarily distorted** resulting in an **induced dipole** that will be attracted to the ion. Intermolecular attractions due to induced dipoles in a nonpolar molecule are known as **London forces or Van der Waals interactions**. These are very weak intermolecular forces.

For example, carbon tetrachloride, CCl_4, has polar bonds but is a nonpolar molecule due to the symmetry of those bonds. An aluminum cation will draw the unbonded electrons of the chlorine atom towards it, distorting the molecule (this distortion has been exaggerated in the figure) and creating an attractive force as shown by the dashed line below.

Dipole-induced dipole

The partial charge of **a permanent dipole may also induce a dipole in a nonpolar molecule** resulting in an attraction similar to—but weaker than—that created by an ion.

London dispersion force: induced dipole-induced dipole

The above two examples required a permanent charge to induce a dipole in a nonpolar molecule. A nonpolar molecule may also induce a temporary dipole on its identical neighbor in a pure substance. These forces occur because at any given moment, electrons are located within a certain region of the molecule, and **the instantaneous location of electrons will induce a temporary dipole** on neighboring molecules. For example, an isolated helium atom consists of a nucleus with a 2+ charge and two electrons in a spherical electron density cloud. An attraction of He atoms due to London dispersion forces (shown below by the dashed line) occurs because when the electrons happen to be distributed unevenly on one atom, a dipole is induced on its neighbor. This dipole is due to intermolecular repulsion of electrons and the attraction of electrons to neighboring nuclei.

The strength of London dispersion forces **increases for larger molecules** because a larger electron cloud is more easily polarized. The strength of London dispersion forces also **increases for molecules with a larger surface area** because there is greater opportunity for electrons to influence neighboring molecules if there is more potential contact between the molecules.

Paraffin in candles is an example of a solid held together by weak London forces between large molecules. These materials are soft.

Impact on physical properties
The impact of intermolecular forces on substances is best understood by imagining ourselves shrinking down to the size of molecules and picturing what happens when we stick more strongly to molecules nearby. It will take more energy (higher temperatures) to pull us away from our neighbors.

If two substances are being compared, the material with the **greater intermolecular attractive forces** (i.e. the stronger intermolecular bond) will have the following properties relative to the other substance:

For solids:
Higher melting point
Higher enthalpy of fusion
Greater hardness
Lower vapor pressure

For liquids:
Higher boiling point
Higher critical temperature
Higher critical pressure
Higher enthalpy of vaporization
Higher viscosity
Higher surface tension
Lower vapor pressure

For gases:
Intermolecular attractive forces are neglected for ideal gases.

For example, covalent networks, salts, and metals are nearly always solids at room temperature because the strength of these bonds results in a high melting point. H_2O and NH_3 are liquids at room temperature because they contain hydrogen bonds. These bonds are of intermediate strength, so the melting point of these compounds is lower than room temperature and their boiling point is higher than room temperature. H_2S contains weaker dipole-dipole interactions than H_2O because the sulfer atoms do not form hydrogen bonds. Therefore, H_2S is a gas at room temperature due to its low boiling point. Finally, small non-polar molecules such as CO_2 (44.01 u), N_2.or atoms such as He will be gases at room temperature due to very weak London forces, but larger non-polar molecules such as octane (114.22 u) or CCl_4 (153.82 u) may be liquids, and very large non-polar molecules such as paraffins will be soft solids.

Domain 2: Chemical Reactions, Competency 2.1: Conservation of Matter and Stoichiometry

Skill 2.1a-Calculate molar mass, mass, number of particles, and volume, at standard temperature and pressure (STP) for elements and compounds

A single atom or molecule weighs very little in grams and cannot be measured using a balance the lab. It's useful to have a system that permits a large number of chemical particles to be described as one unit, analogous to a dozen as 12 of something or one gross as 144. A useful number of atoms, molecules, or formula units is **that number whose mass in grams is numerically equal to the atomic mass, molecular mass, or formula mass** of the substance. This quantity is called the **mole**, abbreviated mol. Because the ^{12}C isotope is assigned an exact value of 12 atomic mass units, there are exactly 12 g of ^{12}C in one mole of ^{12}C. The atomic mass unit is also called a Dalton, and either "u" (for "unified atomic mass unit") or "Da" may be used as an abbreviation. Older texts use "amu." To find the molar mass of a substance, use the periodic table before skill 1.1 to determine the molecular weight of each atom in the substance and multiply by the number of each atom present. For example:

$$Al_2(SO_4)_3 \text{ molecular weight} = 2\left(26.982 \text{ u for Al}\right) + 3\left(32.065 \text{ u for S}\right) + 12\left(15.999 \text{ u for O}\right)$$

$$= 342.147 \text{ u.}$$

Therefore 1 mol $Al_2(SO_4)_3 = 342.147$ g $Al_2(SO_4)_3$.

It's been found experimentally that this number of atoms, ions, molecules, or anything else in one mole is 6.022045×10^{23}. For most purposes, three significant digits are sufficient, and 6.02×10^{23} will be used. This value was named in honor of Amedeo Avogadro after his death and it is referred to as **Avogadro's number**. The following table illustrates why the mole and Avogadro's number are useful. These concepts permit us to think about interactions among individual molecules and atoms while measuring many grams of a substance.

Name	Formula	Formula weight (u)	Mass of 1 mol of formula units (g)	Number and kind of particles in 1 mol
Atomic hydrogen	H	1.0079	1.0079	6.02×10^{23} H atoms
Molecular hydrogen	H_2	2.0158	2.0158	6.02×10^{23} H_2 molecules $2(6.02 \times 10^{23})$ H atoms
Silver	Ag	107.87	107.87	6.02×10^{23} Ag atoms
Silver ions	Ag^+	107.87	107.87	6.02×10^{23} Ag^+ ions
Barium chloride	$BaCl_2$	208.24	208.24	6.02×10^{23} $BaCl_2$ units 6.02×10^{23} Ba^{2+} ions $2(6.02 \times 10^{23})$ Cl^- ions

Many problems are given at "**standard temperature and pressure**" or "**STP**." Standard conditions are *exactly* **1 atm** (101.325 kPa) and **0 °C (273.15 K)**. At STP, one mole of an ideal gas has a volume of 22.4 L. This value is known as the **standard molar volume of any gas at STP**, and it is calculated in **Skill 3.1c**.

The volume of liquids and solids may be determined from their density. See **Skill 12.1g**. The **percent composition** of a substance is the **percentage by mass of each element**. See **Skill 4.1b**.

Skill 2.1b-Calculate the masses of reactants and products, and percent yield using balanced chemical equations, including problems with a limiting reagent

Balanced chemical equations
A properly written chemical equation must contain properly written formulas and must be **balanced**. Chemical equations are written to describe a certain number of moles of reactants becoming a certain number of moles of reaction products. The number of moles of each compound is indicated by its **stoichiometric coefficient**.

Example: In the reaction

$$2H_2(g) + O_2(g) \rightarrow 2H_2O(l),$$

hydrogen has a stoichiometric coefficient of two, oxygen has a coefficient of one, and water has a coefficient of two because 2 moles of hydrogen react with 1 mole of oxygen to form two moles of water.

In a balanced equation, the stoichiometric coefficients are chosen such that the equation contains an **equal number of each type of atom on each side**. In our example, there are four H atoms and two O atoms on both sides.

Antoine **Lavoisier** is called **the father of modern chemistry** because he carefully weighed material before and after chemical reactions to determine that **chemical reactions do not alter total mass**. This principle is called **conservation of matter**. It does not apply to nuclear reactions (see **Skill 7.1a**). The mass of individual atoms does not change, so placing an equal number of each type of atom on both sides of a chemical equation insures conservation of matter will be represented.

Reactions among ions in aqueous solution may often be represented in three ways. When solutions of hydrochloric acid and sodium hydroxide are mixed, a reaction occurs and heat is produced. The **molecular equation** for this reaction is:

$$HCl(aq) + NaOH(aq) \rightarrow H_2O(l) + NaCl(aq).$$

It is called a molecular equation because the **complete chemical formulas** of reactants and products are shown. But in reality, both HCl and NaOH are strong electrolytes and exist in solution as ions (see **Competency 4.1**). This is represented by a **complete ionic equation** that shows all the dissolved ions:

$$H^+(aq) + Cl^-(aq) + Na^+(aq) + OH^-(aq) \rightarrow H_2O(l) + Na^+(aq) + Cl^-(aq).$$

Because $Na^+(aq)$ and $Cl^-(aq)$ appear as both reactants and products, they play no role in the reaction. Ions that appear in identical chemical forms on both sides of an ionic equation are called **spectator ions** because they aren't part of the action. When spectator ions are removed from a complete ionic equation, the result is a **net ionic equation** that shows the actual changes that occur to the chemicals when these two solutions are mixed together:

$$H^+(aq) + OH^-(aq) \rightarrow H_2O(l)$$

An additional requirement for **redox** reactions (see **Skill 2.1d**) is that the equation contains an **equal charge on each side**. Redox reactions may be divided into half-reactions which either gain or lose electrons.

Balancing equations (other than redox reactions) is a four-step process.

1) Connect reactants to products, by an arrow creating an **unbalanced equation**.
2) Determine the **number of each type of atom on each side** of the equation to find if the equation is balanced.
3) Assume that **the molecule with the most atoms** has a stoichiometric coefficient of one, and determine the other stoichiometric coefficients required to create the **same number of atoms on each side** of the equation.
4) Multiply all the stoichiometric coefficients by a whole number if necessary to eliminate fractional coefficients.

Example: Balance the chemical equation describing the combustion (see **Skill 2.1c**) of methanol (CH_4O) in oxygen to produce only CO_2 and water.

Solution:
1) The unbalanced equation is: $CH_4O + O_2 \rightarrow CO_2 + H_2O.$

2) On the left there are 1C, 4H, and 3O. On the right, there are 1C, 2H, and 3O. It seems close to being balanced, but there's work to do.

3) Assuming that CH_4O has a stoichiometric coefficient of one means that the left side has 1C and 4H that also must be present on the right. Therefore the stoichiometric coefficient of CO_2 will be 1 to balance C and the stoichiometric coefficient of H_2O will be 2 to balance H. Now we have:

$$CH_4O + ?O_2 \rightarrow CO_2 + 2H_2O.$$

and only oxygen remains unbalanced. There are 4O on the right and one of these is accounted for by methanol leaving 3O to be accounted for by O_2. This gives a stoichiometric coefficient of 3/2 and a balanced equation:

$$CH_4O + \frac{3}{2}O_2 \rightarrow CO_2 + 2H_2O.$$

4) Whole-number coefficients are achieved by multiplying by two:

$$2CH_4O + 3O_2 \rightarrow 2CO_2 + 4H_2O.$$

Mass-mass stoichiometry problems

In a mass-mass stoichiometry problem, the mass of one compound that participates in a reaction is given and the mass of a different compound is required. Solving these problems is a three-step process:

1) Grams of the given compound are converted to moles (**Skill 2.1a**).
2) Moles of the given compound are related to moles of the second compound by relating their stoichiometric coefficients.
3) Moles of the second compound are converted to grams (**Skill 2.1a**).

These steps are often combined in one series of multiplications, which may be described as **"grams to moles to moles to grams."**

Example: What mass of oxygen is required to consume 95.0 g of ethane in this reaction: $2C_2H_6 + 7O_2 \rightarrow 4CO_2 + 6H_2O$?

$$\begin{array}{ccccc} & \text{step 1} & \text{step 2} & \text{step 3} & \\ \text{Solution:} & & & & \\ 95.0 \text{ g } C_2H_6 \times & \dfrac{1 \text{ mol } C_2H_6}{30.1 \text{ g } C_2H_6} & \times \dfrac{7 \text{ mol } O_2}{2 \text{ mol } C_2H_6} & \times \dfrac{32.0 \text{ g } O_2}{1 \text{ mol } O_2} & = 359 \text{ g } O_2 \end{array}$$

Limiting reagent problems

The **limiting reagent** of a reaction is the **reactant that runs out first**. This reactant **determines the amount of product formed**, and any **other reactants remain unconverted** to product and are called **excess reagents**.

Example: Consider the reaction $3H_2 + N_2 \rightarrow 2NH_3$ and suppose that 3 mol H_2 and 3 mol N_2 are available for this reaction. What is the limiting reagent?

Solution: The equation tells us that 3 mol H_2 will react with one mol N_2 to produce 2 mol NH_3. This means that 2 mol N_2 will remain and H_2 is the limiting reagent because it runs out first.

The limiting reagent may be determined by **dividing the number of moles of each reactant by its stoichiometric coefficient.** This determines the moles of reaction if each reactant were limiting. The **lowest result** will indicate the actual limiting reagent. Remember to use moles and not grams for these calculations.

Example: 50.0 g Al and 400. g Br_2 react according the the following equation:

$$2Al + 3Br_2 \rightarrow 2AlBr_3$$

until the limiting reagent is completely consumed. Find the limiting reagent, the mass of $AlBr_3$ expected to form, and the excess reagent expected to remain after the limiting reagent is consumed.

Solution: First convert both reactants to moles:

$$50.0 \text{ g Al} \times \frac{1 \text{ mol Al}}{26.982 \text{ g Al}} = 1.853 \text{ mol Al} \quad \text{and} \quad 400. \text{ g Br}_2 \times \frac{1 \text{ mol Br}_2}{159.808 \text{ g Br}_2} = 2.503 \text{ mol Br}_2.$$

The final digits in the intermediate results above are italicized because they are insignificant. Dividing by stoichiometric coefficients gives:

$$1.853 \text{ mol Al} \times \frac{\text{mol reaction}}{2 \text{ mol Al}} = 0.9265 \text{ mol reaction if Al is limiting}$$

$$2.503 \text{ mol Br}_2 \times \frac{\text{mol reaction}}{3 \text{ mol Br}_2} = 0.8343 \text{ mol reaction if Br}_2 \text{ is limiting.}$$

Br_2 is the lower value and is limiting reagent.
The reaction is expected to produce:

$$2.503 \text{ mol Br}_2 \times \frac{2 \text{ mol AlBr}_3}{3 \text{ mol Br}_2} \times \frac{266.694 \text{ g AlBr}_3}{\text{mol AlBr}_3} = 445 \text{ g AlBr}_3.$$

The reaction is expected to consume:

$$2.503 \text{ mol Br}_2 \times \frac{2 \text{ mol Al}}{3 \text{ mol Br}_2} \times \frac{26.982 \text{ g Al}}{\text{mol Al}} = 45.0 \text{ g Al.}$$

50.0 g Al − 45.0 g Al = 5.0 g Al are expected to remain.

Percent Yield

The **yield of a reaction is the amount of product** obtained. This value is nearly always less than what would be predicted from a stoichiometric balance because side-reactions may produce different products, the reverse reaction may occur, and some material may be lost during the procedure. The yield from a stoichiometric balance on the limiting reagent is called the theoretical yield. **Percent yield is the actual yield divided by the theoretical yield:**

$$\text{Percent yield} = \frac{\text{Actual yield}}{\text{Theoretical yield}} \times 100\%.$$

Example: 387 g $AlBr_3$ are produced by the reaction described in the previous example. What is the percent yield?

Solution: $\dfrac{387 \text{ g AlBr}_3}{445 \text{ g AlBr}_3} \times 100\% = 87.0\% \text{ yield.}$

Skill 2.1c-Distinguish reaction types, including single replacement, double replacement, synthesis, decomposition, and combustion

General reaction types are listed in the following table. Some reaction types have multiple names.

Reaction type	General equation	Example
Combination Synthesis	$A + B \rightarrow C$	$2H_2 + O_2 \rightarrow 2H_2O$
Decomposition	$A \rightarrow B + C$	$2KClO_3 \rightarrow 2KCl + 3O_2$
Single substitution Single displacement Single replacement	$A + BC \rightarrow AB + B$	$Mg + 2HCl \rightarrow MgCl_2 + H_2$
Double substitution Double displacement Double replacement Ion exchange Metathesis	$AC + BD \rightarrow AD + BC$	$HCl + NaOH \rightarrow NaCl + H_2O$
Isomerization	$A \rightarrow A'$	

Many **specific reaction types** also exist. The most common specific reaction types are summarized in the following table:

Reaction type	General equation	Example
Precipitation (**Skill 4.1a**)	Molecular: $AC(aq) + BD(aq) \rightarrow AD(s \text{ or } g) + BC(aq)$	Molecular: $NiCl_2(aq) + Na_2S(aq) \rightarrow NiS(s) + 2NaCl(aq)$
	Net ionic: $A^+(aq) + D^-(aq) \rightarrow AD(s \text{ or } g)$	Net ionic: $Ni^{2+}(aq) + S^{2-}(aq) \rightarrow NiS(s)$
Acid-base neutralization (**Skill 4.2a**)	Arrhenius: $H^+ + OH^- \rightarrow H_2O$	Arrhenius: $HNO_3 + NaOH \rightarrow NaNO_3 + H_2O$ $H^+ + OH^- \rightarrow H_2O$ (net ionic)
	Brønsted-Lowry: $HA + B \rightarrow HB + A$	Brønsted-Lowry: $HNO_3 + KCN \rightarrow HCN + KNO_3$ $H^+ + CN^- \rightarrow HCN$ (net ionic)
	Lewis: $A + :B \rightarrow A:B$	Lewis:
Redox (**Skill 2.1d**)	Full reaction: $A + B \rightarrow C + D$	$Ni + CuSO_4 \rightarrow NiSO_4 + Cu$ $Ni + Cu^{2+} \rightarrow Ni^{2+} + Cu$ (net ionic)
	Half reactions: $A \rightarrow C + e^-$ and $e^- + B \rightarrow D$	$Ni \rightarrow Ni^{2+} + 2e^-$ $2e^- + Cu^{2+} \rightarrow Cu$
Combustion (**Skill 11.1e**)	organic molecule $+ O_2 \rightarrow CO_2 + H_2O + $ heat	$2C_2H_6 + 7O_2 \rightarrow 4CO_2 + 6H_2O$

Whether precipitation occurs among a group of ions—and which compound will form the precipitate—may be determined by the solubility rules in **Skill 4.1a**.

If protons are available (**Skill 4.2a**) for combination or substitution then it's likely they are being transferred from an acid to a base. An unshared electron pair on one of the reactants may form a bond in a Lewis acid-base reaction.

The possibility that oxidation numbers (**Skill 2.1d**) may change among the reactants indicates an electron transfer and a redox reaction. Combustion reactants consist of an organic molecule and oxygen.

Skill 2.1d-Utilize the rules of oxidation states to balance oxidation-reduction reactions

Oxidation states

The **oxidation state of an ion is its charge**. The oxidation state of an atom sharing its electrons is **the charge it would have if the bonding were ionic**. The periodicy of oxidation states is discussed in **Skill 12.1n**. Oxidation states are also called oxidation numbers. There are four rules for determining oxidation number:

1) The oxidation number of an element (i.e., a Cl atom in Cl_2) is zero because the electrons in the bond are shared equally.

2) In a compound, the more electronegative atoms (see **Skill 1.1c**) are assigned negative oxidation numbers and the less electronegative atoms are assigned positive oxidation numbers equal to the number of shared electron-pair bonds. For example, hydrogen may only have an oxidation number of −1 when bonded to a less electronegative element or +1 when bonded to a more electronegative element. Oxygen almost always has an oxidation number of −2. Fluorine always has an oxidation number of −1 (except in F_2).

3) The oxidation numbers in a compound must add up to zero, and the sum of oxidation numbers in a polyatomic ion must equal the overall charge of the ion.

Example: What is the oxidation state of nitrogen in the nitrate ion, NO_3^-? Oxygen has the oxidation number of −2 (rule 2), and the sum of the oxidation numbers must be −1 (rule 3). The oxidation number for N may be found by solving for x in the equation $x + 3 \times (-2) = -1$. The oxidation number of N in NO_3^- is +5.

Identifying oxidation-reduction reactions and their components

Reduction is the **gain of an electron** by a molecule, atom, or ion, thus decreasing its oxidation number. **Oxidation** is the **loss of an electron**, thus increasing the oxidation number of the molecule, atom, or ion. These two processes always occur together in **oxidation-reduction reactions, also called redox reactions**. Electrons lost by one substance are gained by the other.

The easiest redox processes to identify are those involving monatomic ions with altered charges. For example, the reaction

$$Zn(s) + Cu^{2+}(aq) \rightarrow Zn^{2+}(aq) + Cu(s)$$

is a redox process because electrons are transferred from Zn to Cu.

However, many redox reactions involve the transfer of electrons from one molecular compound to another. In these cases, **oxidation numbers must be determined**. For example, the reaction

$$H_2 + F_2 \rightarrow 2HF$$

is a redox process because the oxidation numbers of atoms are altered. The oxidation numbers of elements are always zero, and oxidation numbers in a compound are never zero.

Fluorine is the more electronegative element, so in HF it has an oxidation number of -1 and hydrogen has an oxidation number of $+1$. This is a redox process where electrons are transferred from H_2 to F_2 to create HF.

In the reaction

$$HCl + NaOH \rightarrow NaCl + H_2O,$$

the H-atoms on both sides of the reaction have an oxidation number of $+1$, the atom of Cl has an oxidation number of -1, the Na-atom has an oxidation number of $+1$, and the atom of O has an oxidation number of -2. **This is not a redox process because oxidation numbers remain unchanged** by the reaction.

An **oxidizing agent** (also called an oxidant or oxidizer) has the ability to oxidize other substances by removing electrons from them. The **oxidizing agent is reduced** in the process. A **reducing agent** (also called a reductive agent, reductant or reducer) is a substance that has the ability to reduce other substances by transferring electrons to them. The **reducing agent is oxidized** in the process.

Redox reactions may always be written as **two half-reactions**, a **reduction half-reaction** with **electrons as a reactant** and an **oxidation half-reaction** with **electrons as a product**.

For example, the redox reactions considered previously:

$$Zn(s) + Cu^{2+}(aq) \rightarrow Zn^{2+}(aq) + Cu(s) \quad \text{and} \quad H_2 + F_2 \rightarrow 2HF$$

may be written in terms of the half-reactions:

$$2e^- + Cu^{2+}(aq) \rightarrow Cu(s) \qquad 2e^- + F_2 \rightarrow 2F^-$$
$$\text{and}$$
$$Zn(s) \rightarrow Zn^{2+}(aq) + 2e^-. \qquad H_2 \rightarrow 2H^+ + 2e^-.$$

An additional (non-redox) reaction, $2F^- + 2H^+ \rightarrow 2HF$, achieves the final products for the second reaction.

57 videos of redox experiments are presented here:
http://chemmovies.unl.edu/chemistry/redoxlp/redox000.html.

Charge balance

Balancing redox reactions requires an additional step because there must be a **charge balance**. For example, the equation:

$$Sn^{2+} + Fe^{3+} \rightarrow Sn^{4+} + Fe^{2+}$$

contains one Sn and one Fe atom on each side but it is not balanced because the sum of charges on the left side of the equation is $+5$ and the sum on the right side is $+6$. A charge balance is obtained by considering each half-reaction separately before multiplying by an appropriate factor so that the number of electrons gained by one half-reaction is the same as the number lost in the other. The two half-reactions may then be combined again into one reaction.

For the example presented above, one electron is gained in the reduction half-reaction ($Fe^{3+} + e^- \rightarrow Fe^{2+}$), but two are lost in the oxidation half-reaction ($Sn^{2+} \rightarrow Sn^{4+} + 2e^-$). A charge balance is obtained by multiplying the reduction half-reaction by two to obtain the half-reactions:

$$2Fe^{3+} + 2e^- \rightarrow 2Fe^{2+}$$

$$Sn^{2+} \rightarrow Sn^{4+} + 2e^-.$$

The equation:

$$Sn^{2+} + 2Fe^{3+} \rightarrow Sn^{4+} + 2Fe^{2+}$$

is properly balanced because both sides contain the same sum of charges (+8).

Oxidation states as a tool for balancing equations

Oxidation states are often useful to balance equations more rapidly than the method described in **Skill 2.1b** alone. For example, consider the unbalanced reaction between copper and nitric acid:

$$Cu(s) + HNO_3(aq) \rightarrow Cu(NO_3)_2(aq) + NO(g) + H_2O(g).$$

Let's first try balancing this equation using the method in **Skill 2.1b**. There is one Cu on both sides, but none of the other atoms are balanced. If we assume that $Cu(NO_3)_2$ has a stoichiometric coefficient of one, then Cu(s) will also have a coefficient of one, but the other coefficients are difficult to balance right away. We could use algebra, and assign variable names to the other coefficients:

$$Cu(s) + xHNO_3(aq) \rightarrow Cu(NO_3)_2(aq) + yNO(g) + zH_2O(g)$$

Then we could solve these three equations:

From the balance on H: $x = 2z$

From the balance on N: $x = 2 + y$

From the balance on O: $3x = 6 + y + z$

With a lot more work to solve three equations and three unknowns, we could determine that $x = 8/3$, $y = 2/3$, and $z = 4/3$, and we'd almost be finished.

Next let's try using oxidation states to help us balance the equation.

Cu is oxidized from an oxidation state of 0 to +2, an increase of 2. The N that will form NO is reduced from an oxidation state of +5 to +2, a decrease of 3. Therefore, three Cu atoms must be oxidized from Cu(s) (for a net change of +6) for every two N atoms that are reduced to NO(g) (for a net change of –6). We may write:

$$3Cu(s) + ?HNO_3(aq) \rightarrow ?Cu(NO_3)_2(aq) + 2NO(g) + ?H_2O(g).$$

A balance on Cu gives a stoichiometric coefficient of 3 for $Cu(NO_3)_2$. This means there are 8 N on the right. A balance on N gives a coefficient of 8 for HNO_3. This means there are 8 H on the left side. A balance on H gives a coefficient of 4 for H_2O. This yields the following equation:

$$3Cu(s) + 8HNO_3(aq) \rightarrow 3Cu(NO_3)_2(aq) + 2NO(g) + 4H_2O(g)$$

Before declaring that the equation is balanced, we also must confirm that the O atoms and the charges balance. There are 24 O on each side and there is a charge balance because all species are neutral.

Competency 2.2: Reaction rates and Chemical Equilibrium

Skill 2.2a-Predict the effect of temperature, pressure, and concentration on chemical equilibrium (LeChatelier's principle) and the reaction rate
Introduction to dynamic equilibrium
A dynamic equilibrium consists of two **opposing reversible processes** that both occur at the **same rate**. *Balance* is a synonym for equilibrium. A system at equilibrium is stable; it does not change with time. Equilibria are drawn with a double arrow.

When a process at equilibrium is observed, it often doesn't seem like anything is happening, but **at a microscopic scale, two events are taking place that balance each other**. An example is given to the right. Arrows in this diagram represent the movement of molecules. When water is placed in a closed container, the water evaporates until the air in the container is saturated. After this occurs, the water level no longer changes, so an observer at the macroscopic scale would say that evaporation has stopped, but the reality on a microscopic scale is that both evaporation and condensation are taking place at the same rate. All equilibria between different phases of matter (see **Skill 5.1b**) have this dynamic character on a microscopic scale.

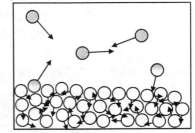

Liquid ⬚ evaporation/condensation Vapor

Chemical reactions often do not "go to completion." Instead, products are generated from reactants up to a certain point when the reaction no longer seems to occur, leaving some reactant unaltered. At this point, the system is in a state of **chemical equilibrium** because **the rate of the forward reaction is equal to the rate of the reverse reaction**. An example is shown to the right. Arrows in this diagram represent the chemical reactions of individual molecules. An observer at the macroscopic scale might say that no reaction is taking place at equilibrium, but at a microscopic scale, both the forward and reverse reactions are occurring at the same rate.

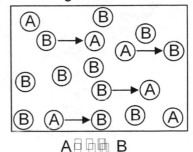

A ⬚ B

Homogeneous equilibrium refers to a chemical equilibrium among reactants and products that are all in the same phase of matter. **Heterogeneous equilibrium** takes place between two or more chemicals in different phases.

A reaction at equilibrium contains a constant ratio of chemical species. The nature of these ratios is determined by an **equilibrium constant** (see **Skill 2.2d**).

If equilibrium is disturbed by changing concentration, pressure, or temperature, the state of balance is upset for a period of time before the equilibrium shifts to achieve a new state of balance.

Le Chatelier's principle states that equilibrium will shift to partially offset the impact of an altered condition.

Le Chatelier: Change in reactant and product concentrations

If a chemical reaction is at equilibrium, Le Chatelier's principle predicts that **adding a substance**—either a reactant or a product—will shift the reaction so **a new equilibrium is established by consuming some of the added substance**. Removing a substance will cause the reaction to move in the direction that forms more of that substance.

Example: The reaction $CO + 2H_2 \rightleftharpoons CH_3OH$ is used to synthesize methanol. Equilibrium is established, and then additional CO is added to the reaction vessel. Predict the impact on each reaction component after CO is added.

Solution: Le Chatelier's principle states that the reaction will shift to partially offset the impact of the added CO. Therefore, CO concentration will decrease, and the reaction will "shift to the right." H_2 concentration will also decrease and CH_3OH concentration will increase.

Le Chatelier: Change in pressure for gases at equilibrium

If a chemical reaction is at equilibrium in the gas phase, Le Chatelier's principle predicts that **an increase in pressure** will shift the reaction so **a new equilibrium is established by decreasing the number of gas moles present**. A decrease in the number of moles partially offsets this rise in pressure. Decreasing pressure will cause the reaction to move in the direction that forms more moles of gas. These changes in pressure might result from altering the volume of the reaction vessel at constant temperature.

Example: The reaction $N_2 + 3H_2 \rightleftharpoons 2NH_3$ is used to synthesize ammonia. Equilibrium is established. Next the reaction vessel is expanded at constant temperature. Predict the impact on each reaction component after this expansion occurs.

Solution: The expansion will result in a decrease in pressure (see Boyle's Law in **Skill 3.1a**). Le Chatelier's principle states that the reaction will shift to partially offset this decrease by increasing the number of moles present. There are 4 moles on the left side of the equation and 2 moles on the right, so the reaction will shift to the left. N_2 and H_2 concentration will increase. NH_3 concentration will decrease.

Le Chatelier: Change in temperature

Le Chatelier's principle predicts that **when heat is added** at constant pressure to a system at equilibrium, **the reaction will shift in the direction that absorbs heat** until a new equilibrium is established. For an endothermic process, the reaction will shift to the right towards product formation.

For an exothermic process, the reaction will shift to the left towards reactant formation. If you understand the application of Le Chatelier's principle to concentration changes then writing "heat" on the appropriate side of the equation will help you understand its application to changes in temperature. The impact of temperature on solubility reactions will be discussed in **Skill 4.1d**.

Example: $N_2 + 3H_2 \rightleftharpoons 2NH_3$ is an exothermic reaction. First equilibrium is established and then the temperature is decreased. Predict the impact of the lower temperature on each reaction component.

Solution: Since the reaction is exothermic, we may write it as: $N_2 + 3H_2 \rightleftharpoons 2NH_3 + Heat$. For the purpose of finding the impact of temperature on equilibrium processes, we may consider heat as if it were a reaction component. Le Chatelier's principle states that after a temperature decrease, the reaction will shift to partially offset the impact of a loss of heat. Therefore more heat will be produced, and the reaction will shift to the right. N_2 and H_2 concentration will decrease. NH_3 concentration will increase.

A flash animation with audio that demonstrates Le Chatelier's principle is at http://www.mhhe.com/physsci/chemistry/essentialchemistry/flash/lechv17.swf.

Introduction to reaction rates
The rate of any process is measured by its change per unit time. The speed of a car is measured by its change in position with time using units of miles per hour. The speed of a chemical reaction is usually measured by a change in the concentration of a reactant or product with time using units of **molarity per second** (M/s). The molarity of a chemical (see **Skill 4.1b**) is represented in mathematical equations using brackets.

The **average reaction rate** is the change in concentration either reactant or product per unit time during a time interval:

$$\text{Average reaction rate} = \frac{\text{Change in concentration}}{\text{Change in time}}$$

Reaction rates are positive quantities. Product concentrations increase and reactant concentrations decrease with time, so a different formula is required depending on the identity of the component of interest:

$$\text{Average reaction rate} = \frac{\left[\text{product}\right]_{final} - \left[\text{product}\right]_{initial}}{\text{time}_{final} - \text{time}_{iniial}}$$

$$= \frac{\left[\text{reactant}\right]_{initial} - \left[\text{reactant}\right]_{final}}{\text{time}_{final} - \text{time}_{iniial}}$$

The **reaction rate** at a given time refers to the **instantaneous reaction rate**. This is found from the absolute value of the **slope of a curve of concentration vs. time**. An estimate of the reaction rate at time t may be found from the average reaction rate over a small time interval surrounding t. For those familiar with calculus notation, the following equations define reaction rate, but calculus is not needed for this skill:

$$\text{Reaction rate at time } t = \frac{d[\text{product}]}{dt} = -\frac{d[\text{reactant}]}{dt}.$$

Effect of reaction conditions on reaction rates

Kinetic molecular theory (See **Competency 3.1**) may be applied to reaction rates in addition to physical constants like pressure. **Reaction rates increase with reactant concentration** because more reactant molecules are present and more are likely to collide with one another in a certain volume at higher concentrations. For ideal gases, the concentration of a reactant is its molar density, and this varies with pressure and temperature as discussed in **Skill 3.1a**.

Kinetic molecular theory also predicts that **reaction rate increase with temperature** because of two reasons:
1) More reactant molecules will collide with each other per second.
2) These collisions will each occur at a higher energy that is more likely to overcome the activation energy (see **Skill 2.2b**) of the reaction.

Skill 2.2b-Interpret a diagram showing activation energy along the reaction pathway

During a chemical reaction, only a fraction of the collisions between the appropriate reactant molecules convert them into product molecules. This occurs for two reasons:

1) Not all collisions occur with a **sufficiently high energy** for the reaction to occur.
2) Not all collisions **orient the molecules properly** for the reaction to occur.

The **activation energy**, E_a, of a reaction is the **minimum energy to overcome the barrier to the formation of products**. This is the minimum energy needed for the reaction to occur.

At the scale of individual molecules, a reaction typically involves a very small period of time when old bonds are broken and new bonds are formed. During this time, the molecules involved are in a **transition state** between reactants and products. A threshold of maximum energy is crossed when the arrangement of molecules is in an unfavorable intermediate between reactants and products known as the **activated complex**. Formulas and diagrams of activated complexes are often written within brackets to indicate they are transition states that are present for extremely small periods of time.

The activation energy, E_a, is the difference between the energy of reactants and the energy of the activated complex. The energy change during the reaction, ΔE, is the difference between the energy of the products and the energy of the reactants. The activation energy of the reverse reaction is $E_a - \Delta E$. These energy levels are represented in an **energy diagram** such as the one shown below for $NO_2 + CO \square \quad NO + CO_2$. This is an exothermic reaction because products are lower in energy than reactants.

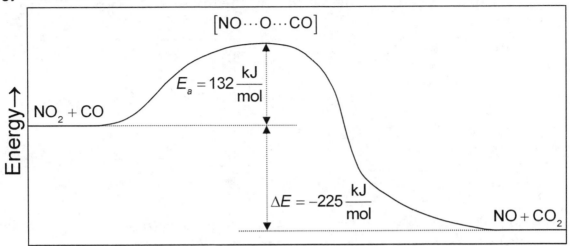

Reaction pathway$\rightarrow$

An energy diagram is a conceptual tool, so there is some variability in how its axes are labeled. The y-axis of the diagram is usually labeled energy (E), but it is sometimes labeled "enthalpy (H)" or (rarely) "free energy (G)." There is an even greater variability in how the x-axis is labeled. The terms "reaction pathway," "reaction coordinate," "course of reaction," or "reaction progress" may be used on the x-axis, or the x-axis may remain without a label.

The energy diagrams of an endothermic and exothermic reaction (See **Skill 5.1a**) are compared below.

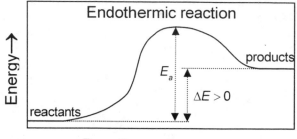

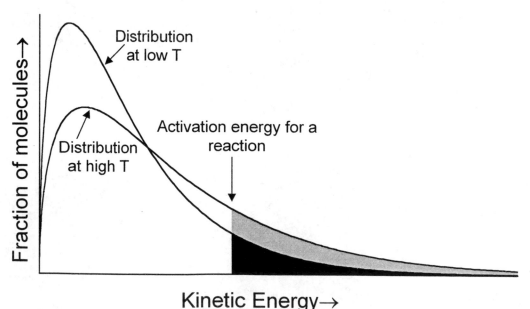

The rate of most simple reactions **increases with temperature** because a **greater fraction of molecules have the kinetic energy** required to overcome the reaction's activation energy. The chart below shows the effect of temperature on the distribution of kinetic energies in a sample of molecules. These curves are called **Maxwell-Boltzmann distributions**. The shaded areas represent the fraction of molecules containing sufficient kinetic energy for a reaction to occur. This area is larger at a higher temperature; so more molecules are above the activation energy and more molecules react per second.

http://www.mhhe.com/physsci/chemistry/essentialchemistry/flash/activa2.swf provides an animated audio tutorial on energy diagrams.

Skill 2.2c-Identify and predict the role of catalysts on the reaction rate

A **catalyst** is a material that increases the rate of a chemical reaction without changing itself permanently in the process. Catalysts provide an alternate reaction mechanism for the reaction to proceed in the forward and in the reverse direction. Therefore, **catalysts have no impact on the chemical equilibrium** of a reaction. They will not make a less favorable reaction more favorable.

Catalysts reduce the activation energy of a reaction. This is the amount of energy needed for the reaction to begin (see **Skill 2.2b**). Molecules with such low energies that they would have taken a long time to react will react more rapidly if a catalyst is present. **A catalyst increases the rate of both the forward and reverse reactions by lowering the activation energy** for the reaction. Catalysts provide a different activated complex for the reaction at a lower energy state. The impact of a catalyst may be represented on an energy diagram as shown below.

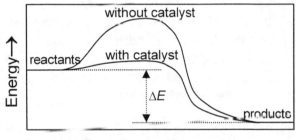

Reaction pathway→

There are two types of catalysts: **Homogeneous catalysts** are in the same physical phase as the reactants. Biological catalysts are called **enzymes**, and most are homogeneous catalysts. A typical homogenous catalytic reaction mechanism involves an initial reaction with one reactant followed by a reaction with a second reactant and release of the catalyst:

$$A + C \rightarrow AC$$

$$B + AC \rightarrow AB + C$$

Net reaction: $A + B \xrightarrow{\text{catalyst C}} AB$

Heterogeneous catalysts are present in a different physical state from the reactants. A typical heterogeneous catalytic reaction involves a solid surface onto which molecules in a fluid phase temporarily attach themselves in such a way to favor a rapid reaction. Catalytic converters in cars utilize heterogeneous catalysis to break down harmful chemicals in exhaust.

Skill 2.2d-Write and calculate an equilibrium constant expression for a given reaction

In **Skill 2.2a**, we saw how the concentrations of reactants and products at equilibrium remain constant because the forward and reverse reactions take place at the same rate. We also saw how this equilibrium responds to a perturbation in one concentration by altering every concentration in a well-defined way until equilibrium is reestablished. In the present skill, we will present a mathematical expression that relates these concentrations and defines the law that governs equilibrium.

Consider the general balanced reaction:
$$mA + nB \rightleftharpoons pR + qS$$
where m, n, p, and q are stoichiometric coefficients and A, B, R, and S are chemical species. An **equilibrium expression** relating the concentrations of chemical species at equilibrium is determined by the equation:

$$K_{eq} = \frac{[R]^p [S]^q}{[A]^m [B]^n}$$

where K_{eq} is a constant value called the **equilibrium constant**. Product concentrations raised to the power of their stoichiometric coefficients are placed in the numerator and reactant concentrations raised to the power of their coefficients are placed in the denominator. Every reaction has a unique value of K_{eq} that varies only with temperature. Alternate subscripts are often given to the equilibrium constant. K_c or K with no subscript is often used instead of K_{eq} to represent the equilibrium constant. Other subscripts are used for specific situations.

Example: Write the equilibrium expression for the reaction $2HI(g) \rightleftharpoons H_2(g) + I_2(g)$.

Solution: $K_{eq} = \dfrac{[H_2][I_2]}{[HI]^2}$.

The units associated with equilibrium constants in the expression above are molarity raised to the power of an integer that depends on the stoichiometric coefficients of the reaction, but it is common practice to write these constants as dimensionless values. Multiplying or dividing the equilibrium expression by 1 M as needed achieves these dimensionless values. **The equilibrium expression for a reaction written in one direction is the reciprocal of the expression for the reaction in the reverse direction**.

For a heterogeneous equilibrium (a chemical equilibrium with components in different phases) , reactants or products may be pure liquids or solids. The concentration of a pure liquid or solid in moles/liter cannot change. It is a constant property of the material, and these constants are incorporated into the equilibrium constant.

Therefore the concentrations of pure liquids and solids are absent from equilibrium expressions for heterogeneous equilibria.

Example: Write the equilibrium expression for the redox reaction between copper and silver: $Cu(s) + 2Ag^+(aq) \rightleftharpoons Cu^{2+}(aq) + 2Ag(s)$.

Solution: $K_{eq} = \dfrac{\left[Cu^{2+}\right]}{\left[Ag^+\right]^2}$. The solids do not appear in the equilibrium expression.

Skill 2.2e-Know that equilibrium is established when the reaction rates of the forward and reverse reactions are equal

This is a fundamental concept of equilibrium as described in **Skill 2.2a**. It's also important to know the converse statement. If the forward and reverse reactions are *unequal* then equilibrium is *not* established.

Domain 3: Kinetic Molecular Theory, Competency 3.1: Gases and Their Properties

Skill 3.1a-Solve problems using the ideal gas law and use the ideal gas law to predict pressure-volume, pressure-temperature, and volume-temperature relationships

These relationships were found by experimental observation and may be explained by the kinetic molecular theory described in **Skill 3.1b**.

Boyle's law states that the volume of a fixed amount of gas at constant temperature is inversely proportional to the gas pressure, or:

$$V \propto \frac{1}{P}.$$

Gay-Lussac's law states that the pressure of a fixed amount of gas in a fixed volume is proportional to absolute temperature, or:

$$P \propto T.$$

Charles's law states that the volume of a fixed amount of gas at constant pressure is directly proportional to absolute temperature, or:

$$V \propto T.$$

The **combined gas law** uses the above laws to determine a proportionality expression that is used for a constant quantity of gas:

$$V \propto \frac{T}{P}.$$

The combined gas law is often expressed as an equality between identical amounts of an ideal gas at two different states ($n_1 = n_2$):

$$\frac{P_1 V_1}{T_1} = \frac{P_2 V_2}{T_2}.$$

Avogadro's hypothesis states that equal volumes of different gases at the same temperature and pressure contain equal numbers of molecules. **Avogadro's law** states that the volume of a gas at constant temperature and pressure is directly proportional to the quantity of gas, or:

$$V \propto n \text{ where } n \text{ is the number of moles of gas.}$$

Avogadro's law and the combined gas law yield $V \propto \frac{nT}{P}$. The proportionality constant

R--the **ideal gas constant**--is used to express this proportionality as the **ideal gas law**:

$$PV = nRT.$$

The ideal gas law is useful because it contains all the information of Charles's, Avogadro's, Boyle's, and the combined gas laws in a single expression.

Solving ideal gas law problems is a straightforward process of algebraic manipulation. **Errors commonly arise from using improper units**, particularly for the ideal gas constant R. An absolute temperature scale (see **Skill 3.1d**) must be used—never °C— and is usually reported using the Kelvin scale, but volume and pressure units often vary from problem to problem.

If pressure is given in atmospheres and volume is given in liters, a value for R of **0.08206 L-atm/(mol-K)** is used. If pressure is given in pascal (newtons/m^2) and volume in m^3, then the SI value for R of **8.314 J/(mol-K)** may be used because a joule is defined as a newton-meter or a pascal-m^3. A value for R of **8.314 Pa- m^3/(mol-K)** is identical to the ideal gas constant using joules.

The ideal gas law may also be rearranged to determine gas molar density in moles per unit volume (molarity):

$$\frac{n}{V} = \frac{P}{RT}.$$

Gas density d in grams per unit volume is found after multiplication by the molecular weight M:

$$d = \frac{nM}{V} = \frac{PM}{RT}.$$

Molecular weight may also be determined from the density of an ideal gas:

$$M = \frac{dV}{n} = \frac{dRT}{P}.$$

Example: Determine the molecular weight of an ideal gas that has a density of 3.24 g/L at 800 K and 3.00 atm.

Solution: $M = \dfrac{dRT}{P} = \dfrac{\left(3.24\ \dfrac{g}{L}\right)\left(0.08206\ \dfrac{\text{L-atm}}{\text{mol-K}}\right)(800\ K)}{3.00\ \text{atm}} = 70.9\ \dfrac{g}{mol}.$

Tutorials for gas laws may be found online at: http://www.chemistrycoach.com/tutorials-6.htm. A flash animation tutorial for problems involving a piston may be found at http://www.mhhe.com/physsci/chemistry/essentialchemistry/flash/gasesv6.swf.

Skill 3.1b-Relate pressure, volume, and temperature to the kinetic theory of atoms and molecules in gases

The relationship between **kinetic energy** and **intermolecular forces** determines whether a collection of molecules will be a gas, liquid, or solid (see **Skill 12.1d**). In a gas, the energy of intermolecular forces is much weaker than the kinetic energy of the molecules. Kinetic molecular theory is usually applied for gases and is best applied by imagining ourselves shrinking down to become a molecule and picturing what happens when we bump into other molecules and into container walls.

Gas **pressure** results from molecular collisions with container walls. The **number of molecules** striking an **area** on the walls and the **average kinetic energy** per molecule are the only factors that contribute to pressure. A higher **temperature** increases speed and kinetic energy. There are more collisions at higher temperatures, but the average distance between molecules does not change, and thus density does not change in a sealed container.

Kinetic molecular theory explains why the pressure and temperature of gases behave the way they do by making a few assumptions, namely:

1) The energies of intermolecular attractive and repulsive forces may be neglected.
2) The average kinetic energy of the molecules is proportional to absolute temperature.
3) Energy can be transferred between molecules during collisions and the collisions are elastic, so the average kinetic energy of the molecules doesn't change due to collisions.
4) The volume of all molecules in a gas is negligible compared to the total volume of the container.

Strictly speaking, molecules also contain some kinetic energy by rotating or experiencing other motions. The motion of a molecule from one place to another is called **translation**. Translational kinetic energy is the form that is transferred by collisions, and kinetic molecular theory ignores other forms of kinetic energy because they are not proportional to temperature.

The following table summarizes the application of kinetic molecular theory to an increase in container volume, number of molecules, and temperature:

Effect of an **increase** in one variable with other two constant	Impact on gas: − = decrease, **0** = no change, **+** = increase						
	Average distance between molecules	Density in a sealed container	Average speed of molecules	Average translational kinetic energy of molecules	Collisions with container walls per second	Collisions per unit area of wall per second	Pressure (P)
Volume of container (V)	+	−	**0**	**0**	−	−	−
Number of molecules	−	+	**0**	**0**	+	+	+
Temperature (T)	**0**	**0**	+	+	+	+	+

Additional details on the kinetic molecular theory may be found at http://hyperphysics.phy-astr.gsu.edu/hbase/kinetic/ktcon.html. An animation of gas particles colliding is located at http://comp.uark.edu/~jgeabana/mol_dyn/.

Skill 3.1c-Know and use STP to solve gas law problems

Many problems are given at "**standard temperature and pressure**" or "**STP**." Standard conditions are *exactly* **1 atm** (101.325 kPa) and **0 °C (273.15 K)**. At STP, one mole of an ideal gas has a volume of:

$$V = \frac{nRT}{P}$$

$$= \frac{(1 \text{ mole})\left(0.08206 \ \frac{\text{L-atm}}{\text{mol-K}}\right)(273 \text{ K})}{1 \text{ atm}} = 22.4 \text{ L}.$$

The value of 22.4 L is known as the **standard molar volume of any gas at STP**.

Skill 3.1d-Convert between Kelvin and Celsius temperature scales

Temperature in Kelvin is found from:
$$T \text{ (in K)} = T(\text{in } ^\circ C) + 273.15$$

Zero Kelvin (0 K or **absolute zero**) corresponds to –273.15 °C, but **the size of a Kelvin is the same as a degree Celsius**.

Examples: Normal body temperature of 37 °C corresponds to 310. K. A fever that raises body temperature by 2 °C to 39 °C increases body temperature by 2 K to 312 K.

Skill 3.1e-Recognize the significance of absolute zero

The significance of absolute zero is that it permits the development of **an absolute temperature scale**. According to the kinetic molecular theory, **there would be no kinetic energy at a temperature of absolute zero**, zero Kelvin (0 K). There would be **no movement** of molecules. Molecules would be unable to sample different states, so there would also be **zero entropy**.

In reality, it is impossible to achieve a temperature of absolute zero, but this temperature may be approached. We also cannot strictly say that all movement would stop because the Heisenberg Uncertainty Principle (See **Skill 1.2a**) states that the exact position and momentum of particles cannot be found at the same time. At absolute zero, molecules have the least amount of kinetic energy and motion permitted by the laws of physics. However, this level of "being strict" is mostly important to physicists and often isn't mentioned in high school chemistry where the kinetic molecular theory is applied.

According to the ideal gas law, $PV = nRT$, **a volume of gas will have zero pressure and a gas at a certain pressure will have zero volume at absolute zero**. In reality, gases do not exist at such low temperatures. All gases will liquefy or solidify before approaching absolute zero.

Skill 3.1f-Solve problems using Dalton's law of partial pressures and Graham's Laws of diffusion

For mixtures of gases in a container, each gas exerts a **partial pressure** that it would have if it were present in the container alone. **Dalton's law** of partial pressures states that the total pressure of a gas mixture is simply the sum of these partial pressures:

$$P_{total} = P_1 + P_2 + P_3 + \ldots$$

Dalton's law may be applied to the ideal gas law:

$$P_{total}V = (P_1 + P_2 + P_3 + \ldots)V = (n_1 + n_2 + n_3 + \ldots)RT .$$

Effusion occurs when gas escapes through a tiny opening into a vacuum or into a region at lower pressure. **Graham's law** states that the rate of effusion (r) for a gas is inversely proportional to the square root of its molecular weight (M):

$$r \propto \frac{1}{\sqrt{M}} .$$

Graham's law may be used to compare the ratios of effusion rates and molecular weights for two different gases:

$$\frac{r_1}{r_2} = \sqrt{\frac{M_2}{M_1}} .$$

Graham's law uses the same two expressions above to describe the dependence of the **diffusion** rate on molecular weight.

Domain 4: Solution Chemistry, Competency 4.1: Solutions

Skill 4.1a-Recognize and identify solutes and solvents

When two or more pure materials mix in a homogeneous way (with their molecules intermixing on a molecular level), the mixture is called a **solution**. Heterogeneous combinations of materials are called **mixtures**. Dispersions of small particles that are larger than molecules are called **colloids**. Liquid solutions are the most common, but any two phases may form a solution. When a pure liquid and a gas or solid form a liquid solution, the pure liquid is called the **solvent** and the non-liquids are called **solutes**. When all components in the solution were originally liquids, then the one present in the greatest amount is called the solvent and the others are called solutes. Solutions with water as the solvent are called **aqueous** solutions. The amount of solute in a solvent is called its **concentration**. A solution with a small concentration of solute is called **dilute**, and a solution with a large concentration of solute is called **concentrated**.

Particles in solution are free to move about and collide with each other, vastly increasing the likelihood that a reaction will occur compared with particles in a solid phase. Aqueous solutions may react to produce an insoluble substance that will fall out of solution as a solid or gas **precipitate** in a **precipitation reaction**. Aqueous solution may also react to form **additional water**, or a different chemical in aqueous solution.

Solubility rules for ionic compounds
Given a cation and anion in aqueous solution, we can determine if a precipitate will form according to some common **solubility rules**.

1) Salts with NH_4^+ or with a cation from group 1 of the periodic table are soluble in water.
2) Nitrates (NO_3^-), acetates ($C_2H_3O_2^-$), chlorates (ClO_3^-), and perchlorates are soluble.
3) Cl^-, Br^-, and I^- salts are soluble except with Ag^+, Hg_2^{2+}, and Pb^{2+}.
4) Sulfates (SO_4^{2-}) are soluble except with Ca^{2+}, Ba^{2+}, Ag^+, Hg_2^{2+}, and Pb^{2+}.
5) Hydroxides (OH^-) are <u>insoluble</u> except with cations from rule 1 and with Ca^{2+}, Sr^{2+}, and Ba^{2+}.
6) Sulfides (S^{2-}), sulfites (SO_3^{2-}), phosphates (PO_4^{3-}), and carbonates (CO_3^{2-}) are insoluble except with cations from rule 1.

Skill 4.1b-Calculate concentration in terms of molarity, parts per million, and percent composition

The **molarity** (abbreviated M) of a solute in solution is defined as the number of moles of solute in a liter of solution.

$$\text{Molarity} = \frac{\text{moles solute}}{\text{volume of solution in liters}}$$

Molarity is the most frequently used concentration unit in chemical reactions because it reflects the number of solute moles available. By using Avogadro's number (see Skill 1.5a), the number of molecules in a flask--a difficult image to conceptualize in the lab--is expressed in terms of the volume of liquid in the flask—a straightforward image to visualize and actually manipulate. Molarity is useful for dilutions because the moles of solute remain unchanged if more solvent is added to the solution:

$$(\text{Initial molarity})(\text{Initial volume}) = (\text{molarity after dilution})(\text{final volume})$$

or

$$M_{initial}V_{initial} = M_{final}V_{final}$$

Mass percentage is frequently used to represent every component of a solution (possibly including the solvent) as a portion of the whole in terms of mass.

$$\text{Mass percentage of a component} = \frac{\text{mass of component in solution}}{\text{total mass of solution}} \times 100\%.$$

Current California state standards (as of 2006) may mislabel mass percentage as "percent composition." A concentration may be measured by a mass percentage, but, as described below, "percent composition" is usually a term applied to the elemental composition of a single compound, not to the solute composition of a solution.

Parts per million (or ppm) in solution usually refers to a dilute component of a solution as a portion of the whole in terms of mass. A solute present in one part per million would amount to one gram in one million grams of solution. This is also one mg of solute in one kg of solution.

$$\text{Parts per million of a component} = \frac{\text{mass of solute}}{\text{total mass of solution}} \times 10^6$$
$$= \frac{\text{number of mg of solute}}{\text{number of kg of solution}}$$

Strictly speaking, the expression above is a **"ppm by mass."** Parts per million is also sometimes used for ratios of moles or volumes.

A **mole fraction** is used to represent a component in a solution as a portion of the entire number of moles present. If you were able to pick out a molecule at random from a solution, the mole fraction of a component represents the probability that the molecule you picked would be that particular component. Mole fractions for all components must sum to one, and mole fractions are just numbers with no units.

$$\text{Mole fraction of a component} = \frac{\text{moles of component}}{\text{total moles of all components}}$$

The **percent composition** of a substance is the **percentage by mass of each element**. It is not a measure of concentration, but current California state standards may mislabel mass percentage as percent composition. Chemical composition is used to verify the purity of a compound in the lab. An impurity will make the actual composition vary from the expected one.

To determine percent composition from a formula, do the following:
1) Write down the **number of atoms each element contributes** to the formula.
2) Multiply these values by the molecular weight of the corresponding element to determine the **grams of each element in one mole** of the formula.
3) Add the values from step 2 to obtain the **formula mass**.
4) Divide each value from step 2 by the formula weight from step 3 and multiply by 100% to obtain the **percent composition**.

The first three steps are the same as those used to determine formula mass (see **Skill 1.5a**), but we use the intermediate results to obtain the composition.

Example: What is the chemical composition of ammonium carbonate $(NH_4)_2CO_3$?

Solution:
1) One $(NH_4)_2CO_3$ contains 2 N, 8 H, 1 C, and 3 O.

2) $$\frac{2 \text{ mol N}}{\text{mol } (NH_4)CO_3} \times \frac{14.0 \text{ g N}}{\text{mol N}} = 28.0 \text{ g N/mol } (NH_4)CO_3$$

$$8(1.0) = 8.0 \text{ g H/mol } (NH_4)CO_3$$
$$1(12.0) = 12.0 \text{ g C/mol } (NH_4)CO_3$$
$$3(16.0) = 48.0 \text{ g O/mol } (NH_4)CO_3$$

Sum is $\overline{96.0 \text{ g } (NH_4)CO_3/\text{mol } (NH_4)CO_3}$

3)

4) $\%N = \dfrac{28.0 \text{ g N/mol } (NH_4)_2CO_3}{96.0 \text{ g } (NH_4)_2CO_3/\text{mol } (NH_4)_2CO_3} = 0.292 \text{ g N/g } (NH_4)_2CO_3 \times 100\% = 29.2\%$

$\%H = \dfrac{8.0}{96.0} \times 100\% = 8.3\%$ $\%C = \dfrac{12.0}{96.0} \times 100\% = 12.5\%$ $\%O = \dfrac{48.0}{96.0} \times 100\% = 50.0\%$

Skill 4.1c-Describe the dissolving process at the molecular level

As more solid solute particles (circles in the figure to the right) dissolve in a liquid solvent (grey background), the concentration of solute increases, and the chance that dissolved solute (grey circles) will collide with the remaining undissolved solid (white circles) also increases. A collision may result in the solute particle reattaching themselves to the solid. This process is called **crystallization**, and is the opposite of the solution process. Particles in the act of dissolving or crystallizing are half-shaded in the figure. An animation of the solution process may be found here: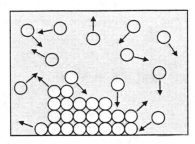
http://www.mhhe.com/physsci/chemistry/essentialchemistry/flash/molvie1.swf.

Equilibrium occurs (see **Competency 2.2**) when no additional solute will dissolve because the rates of crystallization and solution are equal.

$$\text{Solute} + \text{Solvent} \underset{\text{crystallize}}{\overset{\text{dissolve}}{\rightleftharpoons}} \text{Solution}$$

A solution at equilibrium with undissolved solute is a **saturated** solution. The amount of solute required to form a saturated solution in a given amount of solvent is called the **solubility** of that solute. If less solute is present, the solution is called **unsaturated**. It is also possible to have more solute than the equilibrium amount, resulting in a solution that is termed **supersaturated**.

Pairs of liquids that mix in all proportions are called **miscible**. Liquids that don't mix are called **immiscible**.

Intermolecular forces in the solution process
Solutions tend to form when the intermolecular attractive forces between solute and solvent molecules are about as strong as those that exist in the solute alone or in solvent alone. NaCl dissolves in water because:

1) The water molecules interact with the Na^+ and Cl^- ions with sufficient strength to overcome the attraction between them in the crystal.

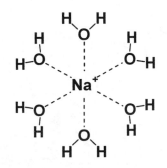

2) Na^+ and Cl^- ions interact with the water molecules with sufficient strength to overcome the attraction water molecules have for each other in the liquid.

The intermolecular attraction between solute and solvent molecules is known as **solvation**. When the solvent is water, it is known as **hydration**. The figure to the left shows a hydrated Na^+ ion.

Polar and nonpolar solutes and solvents

A nonpolar liquid like heptane (C_7H_{16}) has intermolecular bonds with relatively weak London dispersion forces. Heptane is immiscible in water because the attraction that water molecules have for each other via hydrogen bonding is too strong. Unlike Na^+ and Cl^- ions, heptane molecules cannot break these bonds. Because bonds of similar strength must be broken and formed for solvation to occur, nonpolar substances tend to be soluble in nonpolar solvents, and ionic and polar substances are soluble in polar solvents like water. Polar molecules are often called **hydrophilic** and non-polar molecules are called **hydrophobic**. This observation is often stated as "**like dissolves like**." Network solids (e.g., diamond) are soluble in neither polar nor nonpolar solvents because the covalent bonds within the solid are too strong for these solvents to break.

Electrolytes

All NaCl is present in solution as ions. Compounds that are completely ionized in water are called **strong electrolytes** because these solutions easily conduct electricity. Most salts are strong electrolytes. Other compounds (including many acids and bases) may dissolve in water without completely ionizing. These are referred to as **weak electrolytes** (see **Competency 4.2**) and their state of ionization is at equilibrium with the larger molecule (see **Competency 2.2**). Those compounds that dissolve with no ionization (e.g., glucose, $C_6H_{12}O_6$) are called **nonelectrolytes**.

Skill 4.1d-Explain how factors such as temperature, pressure, and surface area affect the dissolving process

Gas solubility

Pressure does not dramatically alter the solubility of solids or liquids, but kinetic molecular theory predicts that **increasing the partial pressure of a gas will increase the solubility of the gas** in a liquid. If a substance is distributed between gas and solution phases and pressure is exerted, more gas molecules will impact the gas/liquid interface per second, so more will dissolve until a new equilibrium is reached at a higher solubility. **Henry's law** describes this relationship as a direct proportionality:

$$\text{Solubility of gas in liquid (in } \frac{\text{mol solute}}{\text{L solution}}) \propto P_{gas}$$

Carbonated drinks are bottled under high CO_2 pressure, permitting the gas to dissolve into aqueous solution. When the bottle is opened, the partial pressure of CO_2 in the gas phase rapidly decreases to the value in the atmosphere, and the gas bubbles out of solution. When the bottle is closed again, CO_2 gas pressure builds until a saturated solution at equilibrium is again obtained. The solubility of gases in a liquid also increases in the bloodstream of deep-sea divers when they experience high pressures. If they return to atmospheric pressure too rapidly, large bubbles of nitrogen gas will form in their blood and cause a potentially lethal condition known as **the bends** or **decompression sickness**. The diver must enter a hyperbaric (high pressure) chambers to redissolve the nitrogen back into the blood.

Increasing temperature will decrease the solubility of a gas in a liquid because kinetic energy opposes intermolecular attractions and permits more molecules to escape from the liquid phase. The vapor pressure of a pure liquid increases with temperature for the same reason. Greater kinetic energy will favor material in the gas phase.

Liquid and solid solubility

For solid and liquid solutes, the impact of temperature depends on whether the solution process requires or releases heat. Endothermic and exothermic reactions will be discussed in more detail in **Competency 5.1**. The following brief analysis is applicable for the effect of temperature on solutions.

Three processes occur when a solution is formed:
1) Solute particles are separated from each other, and heat is required to break these bonds.
2) Solvent particles are separated from each other to create space for solute particles, and heat is required to break these bonds also.
3) Solute and solvent particles interact with each other forming new bonds (see **Skill 4.1c**), and releasing heat.

If the heat required for the first two processes is greater than the heat released by the third, then the entire reaction may be written as an endothermic process:

$$\text{Solute} + \text{Solvent} + \text{Heat} \longrightarrow \text{Solution}$$

and according to Le Chatelier's principle (see **Competency 2.2**), **solubility will increase with increasing temperature for an endothermic solution process**. This occurs for most salts in water, including NaCl. There is a large increase for potassium nitrate—KNO_3.

However, heat is released when many solutes enter solution, and the entire reaction is exothermic:

$$Solute + Solvent \rightleftharpoons Solution + Heat.$$

Solubility will decrease with increasing temperature for an exothermic solution process. This is the case for cerium(III) sulfate—$Ce_2(SO_4)_3$—in water.

Summary
The following table summarizes the impact of temperature and pressure on solubility:

Effect on solution of an **increase** in one variable with the other constant	− = decrease, **0** = no/small change, **+** = increase, **++** = strong increase				
	Gas solute in liquid solvent			Solid and liquid solutes	
	Average kinetic energy of molecules	Collisions of gas with liquid interface	Solubility	Solubility for an endothermic heat of solution	Solubility for an exothermic heat of solution
Pressure	**0**	**++**	**+**	**0**	**0**
Temperature	**+**	**+**	**−**	**+**	**−**

Impact of surface area
From the diagram in **Skill 4.1c**, it is apparent that dissolution will only take place at the surface of a solute where the solvent molecules contact the solute. When this surface area is increased, the solute dissolves more rapidly. **The rate of solution is increased by surface area, but the solubility remains unchanged**. Solubility is the amount of solute that will saturate a solution, and this depends only on pressure, temperature, and the identity of the solute and solvent.

Granulated sugar, for example, will dissolve more rapidly in water than a sugar cube. This is because it takes very little time for water to dissolve through relatively thin layers of sugar in a small grain before reaching the center of each grain. This is in contrast to the sugar in the center of a sugar cube. The sugar in the center of a cube cannot dissolve for until the thicker layers of sugar around it has dissolved away into solution. However, the solubility of sugar in water does not depend on whether sugar cubes or granulated sugar is used.

Skill 4.1e-Describe various methods for separation of solutions (e.g., chromatography, distillation)

Chromatography

Chromatography is a method for **separating mixtures** from a solution by passing the sample through a stationary material. The instrument is called a **chromatograph**. Different components of the mixture travel at different rates. After the separation, the time that component took to emerge from the instrument (or its location within the stationary phase) is found with a detector. The result is a **chromatogram** like the one shown below. The **identity of an unknown** peak is found by comparing its location on the chromatogram to standards. The **concentration** of a component is found from signal strength or peak area by comparison to calibration curves of known concentrations.

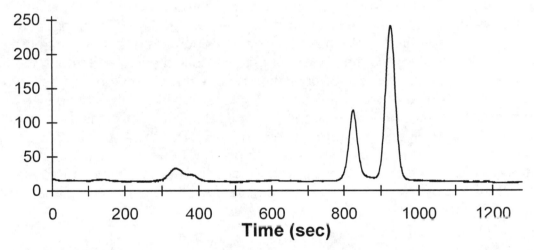

In **paper chromatography** and **thin layer chromatography (TLC)**, the sample rises up by capillary action through a solid phase.

In **gas chromatography (GC)**, the sample is vaporized and forced through a column filled with a packing material. GC is often used to separate and determine the concentration of **low molecular weight volatile organic** compounds.

In **liquid chromatography (LC)**, the sample is a liquid. It is either allowed to seep through an open column using the force of gravity or it is forced through a closed column under pressure. The variations of liquid chromatography depend on the identity of the packing material. For example, an ion-exchange liquid chromatograph contains a material with a charged surface. The mixture components with the opposite charge interact with this packing material and spend more time in the column. LC is often used to separate **large organic polymers** like proteins.

Extraction

Compounds in solution are often separated based on their **solubility differences**. During **liquid-liquid extraction** (also called **solvent extraction**), a second solvent immiscible to the first is added to the solution in a **separatory funnel** (shown at right). Usually one solvent is nonpolar and the other is a polar solvent like water. The two solvents are immiscible and separate from each other after the mixture is shaken to allow solute exchange. One layer contains the compound of interest, and the other contains impurities to be discarded. The solutions in the two layers are separated from each other by draining liquid through the stopcock.

Distillation

Liquids in solution are often separated based on their **boiling point differences**. During simple **distillation**, the solution is placed in a round-bottom flask called the **distillation flask** or **still pot**, and boiling stones are added. The apparatus shown below is assembled (note that clamps and stands are not show), and the still pot is heated using a heating mantle. Hot vapor during boiling escapes through the **distillation head**, enters the **condenser**, and is cooled and condensed back to a liquid. The vapor loses its heat to water flowing through the outside of the condenser. The condensate or **distillate** falls into the **receiving flask**. The apparatus is open to the atmosphere through a vent above the receiving flask. The distillate will contain a higher concentration of material with the lower boiling point. The less volatile component will achieve a high concentration in the still pot. Head temperature is monitored during the process. Distillation may also be used to remove a solid from a pure liquid by boiling and condensing the liquid.

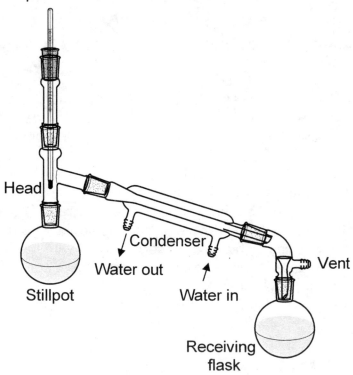

Competency 4.2: Acid and Bases

Skill 4.2a-Distinguish between strong and weak acids and bases based on degree of dissociation and their chemical properties

It was recognized centuries ago that many substances could be divided into the two general categories. **Acids** have a sour taste (as in lemon juice), dissolve many metals, and turn litmus paper red. **Bases** have a bitter taste (as in soaps), feel slippery, and turn litmus paper blue. The chemical reaction between an acid and a base is called **neutralization**. The products of neutralization reactions are neither acids nor bases. Litmus paper is an example of an **acid-base indicator**, a substance that changes color when changing from an acid to a base. Definitions of acids and bases are discussed in **Skill 4.2c**.

Strong and weak acids and bases
Strong acids and bases are strong electrolytes (see **Skill 4.1c**), and weak acids and bases are weak electrolytes, so **strong acids and bases completely dissociate in water**, but weak acids and bases do not.

Examples: $HCl(aq) + H_2O(l) \rightarrow H_3O^+(aq) + Cl^-(aq)$ goes to completion. HCl is a strong acid. $HF(aq) + H_2O(l) \rightleftharpoons F^-(aq) + H_3O^+(aq)$ is an equilibrium reaction. Some HF and some F^- are present in solution. HF is a weak acid.

The aqueous dissociation constants K_a and K_b quantify acid and base strength. K_a and K_b are two examples of special equilibrium constants. Larger values for these constants indicate a stronger acid or base.

The **acid-dissociation constant**, K_a, is the equilibrium constant for the ionization of a weak acid to a hydrogen ion and its conjugate base:

$$HX(aq) \rightleftharpoons H^+(aq) + X^-(aq) \qquad K_a = \frac{[H^+][X^-]}{[HX]}.$$

Polyprotic acids (see **Skill 4.2c**) have unique values for each dissociation: K_{a1}, K_{a2}, etc.

The **base-dissociation constant**, K_b, is the equilibrium constant for the addition of a proton to a weak base by water to form its conjugate acid and an OH^- ion. In these reactions, it is water that is dissociating as a result of reaction with the base:

$$\text{weak base}(aq) + H_2O(l) \rightleftharpoons \text{conjugate acid}(aq) + OH^-(aq)$$

$$K_b = \frac{[\text{conjugate acid}][OH^-]}{[\text{weak base}]}.$$

The concentration of water is nearly constant and is incorporated into the dissociation constant. For ammonia (the most common weak base), the equilibrium reaction and base-dissociation constant are:

$$NH_3(aq) + H_2O(l) \rightleftharpoons NH_4^+(aq) + OH^-(aq)$$

$$K_b = \frac{\left[NH_4^+\right]\left[OH^-\right]}{\left[NH_3\right]}$$

Another way of looking at acid dissociation is that strong acids transfer protons more readily than H_3O^+ transfers protons, so they protonate water, the conjugate base (see **Skill 4.2c**) of H_3O^+. In general, **if two acid/base conjugate pairs are present, the stronger acid will transfer a proton to the conjugate base of the weaker acid**.

Acid and base **strength is not related to safety**. Weak acids like HF may be extremely corrosive and dangerous.

The most **common strong acids and bases** are listed in the following table:

Strong acid		Strong base	
HCl	Hydrochloric acid	LiOH	Lithium hydroxide
HBr	Hydrobromic acid	NaOH	Sodium hydroxide
HI	Hydroiodic acid	KOH	Potassium hydroxide
HNO_3	Nitric acid	$Ca(OH)_2$	Calcium hydroxide
H_2SO_4	Sulfuric acid	$Sr(OH)_2$	Strontium hydroxide
$HClO_4$	Perchloric acid	$Ba(OH)_2$	Barium hydroxide

A flash animation tutorial demonstrating the difference between strong and weak acids is located at
http://www.mhhe.com/physsci/chemistry/essentialchemistry/flash/acid13.swf.

Chemical trends in acid and base strength
The strongest acid in a polyprotic series is always **the acid with the most protons** (e.g. H_2SO_4 is a stronger acid than HSO_4^-). The strongest acid in a series with the same central atom is always **the acid with the central atom at the highest oxidation number** (e.g. $HClO_4$ > $HClO_3$ > $HClO_2$ > $HClO$ in terms of acid strength. See **Skill 2.1d**.). The strongest acid in a series with different central atoms at the same oxidation number is usually **the acid with the central atom at the highest electronegativity** (e.g. the K_a of HClO > HBrO > HIO). This electronegativity trend stretches across the periodic table for oxides as discussed in **Skill 1.1c**.

Skill 4.2b-Calculate pH and hydrogen ion concentration in solutions including buffer solutions

The $H^+(aq)$ ion

In acid-base systems, **"protonated water" or "$H^+(aq)$" are shorthand for a mixture of water ions**. For example, HCl reacting in water may be represented as a dissociation:
$$HCl(aq) \rightarrow H^+(aq) + Cl^-(aq).$$
The same reaction may be described as the transfer of a proton to water to form H_3O^+:
$$HCl(aq) + H_2O(l) \rightarrow Cl^-(aq) + H_3O^+(aq).$$

H_3O^+ is called a **hydronium ion**. Its Lewis structure is shown below to the left. In reality, the hydrogen bonds in water are so strong that H^+ ions exist in water as a mixture of species in a hydrogen bond network. Two of them are shown below at center and to the right. Hydrogen bonds are shown as dashed lines.

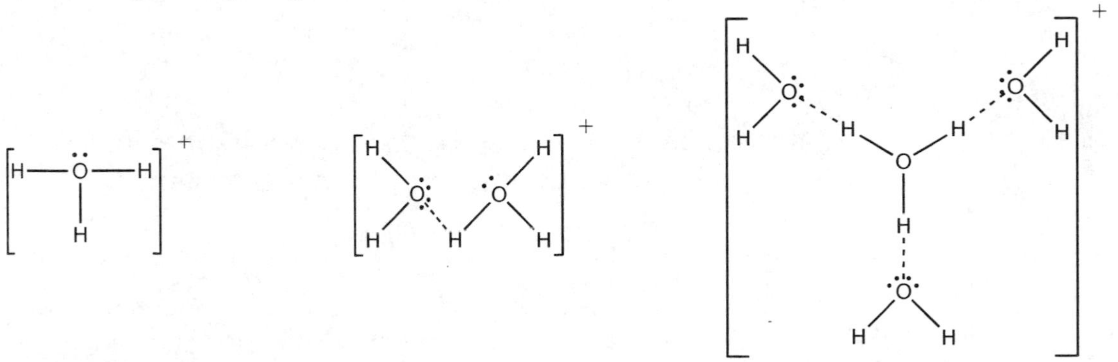

Ion-product constant, K_w

The **ion-product constant for water**, K_w is the equilibrium constant for the dissociation of H_2O. Water molecules may donate protons to other water molecules in a process known as autoionization:
$$2H_2O(l) \rightleftharpoons H_3O^+(aq) + OH^-(aq)$$
The above equation may be rewritten as the following reaction that defines K_w. As with K_b (see **Skill 4.2a**), the concentration of water is nearly constant.
$$H_2O(l) \rightleftharpoons H^+(aq) + OH^-(aq)$$
$$K_w = [H^+][OH^-] = 1.0 \times 10^{-14} \text{ at } 25°C.$$

Pure water at equilibrium has an equal concentration of the two ions: $[H^+] = [OH^-]$.

Therefore $K_w = [H^+]^2 = 1.0 \times 10^{-14}$. Solving for $[H^+]$ yields $\mathbf{[H^+] = 1.0 \times 10^{-7}}$ **M for pure water**.

The **product of K_a for an acid and K_b for its conjugate base will always be K_w.** This is demonstrated below for the weak acid, HF and its conjugate base, F^-:

$$HF(aq) \rightleftharpoons H^+(aq) + F^-(aq) \qquad K_a = \frac{[H^+][F^-]}{[HF]}.$$

$$F^-(aq) + H_2O(l) \rightleftharpoons HF(aq) + OH^-(aq) \qquad K_b = \frac{[HF][OH^-]}{[F^-]}$$

Multiplication of K_a and K_b yields:
$$K_a \times K_b = \left(\frac{[H^+][F^-]}{[HF]}\right)\left(\frac{[HF][OH^-]}{[F^-]}\right)$$
$$= [H^+][OH^-] = K_w$$

Definition of pH and pK_a

The concentration of $H^+(aq)$ ions is often expressed in terms of pH. **The pH of a solution is the negative base-10 logarithm of the hydrogen-ion molarity.**

$$pH = -\log[H^+] = \log\left(\frac{1}{[H^+]}\right).$$

A ten-fold increase in $[H^+]$ decreases the pH by one unit. $[H^+]$ may be found from pH using the expression:

$$[H^+] = 10^{-pH}.$$

Because $[H^+] = 10^{-7}$ M for pure water, **the pH of a neutral solution is 7.** In an **acidic solution**, $[H^+] > 10^{-7}$ M and **pH < 7.** In a basic solution, $[H^+] < 10^{-7}$ M and **pH > 7.**

Example: An aqueous solution has an H^+ ion concentration of 4.0×10^{-9}. Is the solution acidic or basic? What is the pH of the solution?

Solution: The solution is basic because $[H^+] < 10^{-7}$ M.

$$pH = -\log[H^+] = -\log 4 \times 10^{-9}$$
$$= 8.4.$$

The negative base-10 log is a convenient way of representing other small numbers used in chemistry by placing the letter "p" before the symbol. Values of K_a are often represented as pK_a, with $pK_a = -\log K_a$.

Buffer solutions

A **buffer solution** is a solution that **resists a change in pH** after addition of small amounts of an acid or a base. Buffer solutions require the presence of an acid to neutralize an added base and also the presence of a base to neutralize an added acid. These two components present in the buffer also must not neutralize each other! A **conjugate acid-base pair is present in buffers** to fulfill these requirements (see **Skill 4.2c**).

Buffers are prepared by mixing together **a weak acid or base and a salt of the acid or base** that provides the conjugate.

Consider the buffer solution prepared by mixing together acetic acid—$HC_2H_3O_2$—and sodium acetate—$C_2H_3O_2^-$ containing Na^+ as a spectator ion (See **Skill 2.1b**). The equilibrium reaction for this acid/conjugate base pair is:

$$HC_2H_3O_2 \ \square \quad C_2H_3O_2^- + H^+.$$

If H^+ ions from a strong acid are added to this buffer solution, Le Chatelier's principle (see **Skill 2.2a**) predicts that the reaction will shift to the left and much of this H^+ will be consumed to create more $HC_2H_3O_2$ from $C_2H_3O_2^-$. If a strong base that consumes H^+ is added to this buffer solution, Le Chatelier's principle predicts that the reaction will shift to the right and much of the consumed H^+ will be replaced by the dissociation of $HC_2H_3O_2$. The net effect is that **buffer solutions prevent large changes in pH that occur when an acid or base is added to pure water** or to an unbuffered solution.

The amount of acid or base that a buffer solution can neutralize before dramatic pH changes begins to occur is called its **buffering capacity**. Blood and seawater both contain several conjugate acid-base pairs to buffer the solution's pH and decrease the impact of acids and bases on living things.

An excellent flash animation with audio to explain the action of buffering solutions is found at http://www.mhhe.com/physsci/chemistry/essentialchemistry/flash/buffer12.swf.

Calculating pH and H^+ concentration

The pH and $[H^+]$ of a **solution containing a strong acid or strong base** may be found using stoichiometry alone for a strong acid, and stoichiometry together with K_w for a base.

Example: What is the pH of a solution of 0.020 M $Ca(OH)_2$?

Solution: $Ca(OH)_2$ is a strong base according to the table in **Skill 4.2a**, so it completely dissociates:

$$Ca(OH)_2(aq) \rightarrow Ca^{2+}(aq) + 2OH^-(aq).$$

The stoichiometry (see **Skill 2.1b**) of the dissociation may be used to determine $[OH^-]$:

$$\frac{0.020 \text{ mol } Ca(OH)_2}{L} \times \frac{2 \text{ mol } OH^-}{1 \text{ mol } Ca(OH)_2} = \frac{0.040 \text{ mol } OH^-}{L} = 0.040 \text{ M } OH^-.$$

Using the ion-product constant of water, we may find $[H^+]$:

$$K_w = 1.0 \times 10^{-14} = \left[H^+\right]\left[OH^-\right] = \left[H^+\right](0.040).$$

$$\text{Therefore, } \left[H^+\right] = \frac{1.0 \times 10^{-14}}{0.040} = 2.5 \times 10^{-13} \text{ M}.$$

Finally, we determine the pH of the solution from its hydrogen ion concentration:

$$pH = -\log\left[H^+\right] = -\log\left(2.5 \times 10^{-13}\right) = 12.6.$$

The pH and $[H^+]$ of a **solution containing a weak acid or weak base** may be found using K_a or K_b (together with K_w for a base). If more than 5% of the electrolyte is ionized, the quadratic equation should be used. A review of the quadratic equation in the context of chemical equilibrium may be found at http://www.chem.tamu.edu/class/fyp/mathrev/mr-quadr.html.

Example: $K_a = 3.0 \times 10^{-8}$ for hypochlorous acid, HClO. What is the pH of a solution of 0.50 M HClO?

Solution: The dissociation $HClO(aq) \rightleftharpoons H^+(aq) + ClO^-(aq)$ has the equilibrium constant:

$$K_a = \frac{\left[H^+\right]\left[ClO^-\right]}{\left[HClO\right]} = 3.0 \times 10^{-8}.$$

There is only HClO at 0.50 M initially. Let $x = \left[H^+\right]$ at equilibrium. We may then arrange the initial and equilibrium concentrations into a table based on what is consumed and produced according to reaction stoichiometry:

	$HClO(aq)$	$\rightleftharpoons$	$H^+(aq)$	+	$ClO^-(aq)$
Initial:	0.50 M		0 M		0 M
Equilibrium:	$(0.50 - x)$ M		x M		x M

Sustitution into the equilibrium constant gives us:

$$K_a = \frac{\left[H^+\right]\left[ClO^-\right]}{\left[HClO\right]} = \frac{(x)(x)}{0.50 - x} = 3.0 \times 10^{-8}.$$

The expression $\dfrac{x^2}{0.50 - x} = 3.0 \times 10^{-8}$ may be rearranged to yield the quadratic:

$$x^2 + 3.0 \times 10^{-8} x - 1.5 \times 10^{-8} = 0$$

and we could solve for x using the quadratic formula:

$$x = \frac{-b \pm \sqrt{b^2 - 4ac}}{2a}$$ where $a = 1$, $b - 3.0 \times 10^{-8}$, and $c = -1.5 \times 10^{-8}$

However, it will usually be safe to estimate that x (the H^+ concentration) is sufficiently small to avoid doing this. For this example, we require that x is less than 5% of 0.50 M (i.e., $x < 0.05 \times 0.50$ M or 2.5×10^{-2} M).

In that case $0.50 - x$ is roughly 0.50, and the expression $\dfrac{x^2}{0.50 - x} = 3.0 \times 10^{-8}$ simplifies to:

$$\frac{x^2}{0.50} = 3.0 \times 10^{-8}.$$

Solving for x gives us:

$$x = \sqrt{1.5 \times 10^{-8}} = 1.2 \times 10^{-4} \text{ M } H^+.$$

This value is less than 2.5×10^{-2} M, so the quadratic equation was not needed.

Finally, we determine the pH: $pH = -\log(1.2 \times 10^{-4}) = 3.9$.

The pH and [H⁺] of **a buffer solution may be estimated using the Henderson-Hasselbalch equation**:

$$pH = pK_a + \log\left(\frac{[\text{base}]}{[\text{acid}]}\right).$$

The logarithm is in numerical-base-10. This is also called the **buffer equation**.

Expressed in terms of H^+ concentration and K_a, the Henderson-Hasselbalch equation is:

$$-\log\left[H^+\right] = -\log K_a + \log\left(\frac{[\text{base}]}{[\text{acid}]}\right).$$

Many assumptions are required to use these equations, but other methods of calculating the pH of buffers are too difficult to appear on an examination and are beyond the scope of high school chemistry. Therefore, if you are asked for the pH of a buffer solution on the teacher certification exam, you can use the buffer equation with confidence.

Example: A solution contains 0.050 M acetic acid, $HC_2H_3O_2$, and 0.020 M of acetate ion supplied by sodium acetate, $NaC_2H_3O_2$. The K_a of acetic acid is 1.8×10^{-5}. What is the pH of the solution?

Solution: $HC_2H_3O_2$ is a weak acid, and its dissociation reaction is:

$$HC_2H_3O_2 \; \square \quad C_2H_3O_2^- + H^+.$$

Sodium acetate provides the conjugate base, so we know we have a buffer problem with Na^+ as a spectator ion. The pKa may be found from:

$$pK_a = -\log K_a = -\log\left(1.8 \times 10^{-5}\right) = 4.8.$$

From the Henderson-Hasselbalch equation:

$$pH = pK_a + \log\left(\frac{[\text{base}]}{[\text{acid}]}\right) = 4.8 + \log\left(\frac{0.02}{0.05}\right) = 4.8 + (-0.4)$$

$$= 4.4$$

A comprehensive set of lectures on pH calculation is presented at:
http://www.chembuddy.com/?left=pH-calculation&right=toc.

Skill 4.2c-Use Arrhenius, Brønsted-Lowry, and Lewis acid-base definitions appropriately to characterize acids and bases and in acid-base reactions

Arrhenius definition of acids and bases
Svante **Arrhenius** proposed in the 1880s that **acids form H^+ ions and bases form OH^- ions in water**. The net ionic reaction for neutralization between an Arrhenius acid and base always produces water as shown below for nitric acid and sodium hydroxide:

$$HNO_3(aq) + NaOH(aq) \rightarrow NaNO_3(aq) + H_2O(l)$$

$$H^+(aq) + NO_3^-(aq) + Na^+(aq) + OH^-(aq) \rightarrow NO_3^-(aq) + Na^+(aq) + H_2O(l) \text{ (complete ionic)}$$

$$H^+(aq) + OH^-(aq) \rightarrow H_2O(l) \text{ (net ionic)}$$

Brønsted-Lowry definition of acids and bases
In the 1920s, Johannes **Brønsted** and Thomas **Lowry** recognized that **acids can transfer a proton to bases** regardless of whether an OH^- ion accepts the proton. In an equilibrium reaction, the direction of proton transfer depends on whether the reaction is read left to right or right to left, so **Brønsted acids and bases exist in conjugate pairs with and without a proton**. Acids that are able to transfer more than one proton are called **polyprotic acids**.

Examples:
1) In the reaction:

$$HF(aq) + H_2O(l) \rightleftharpoons F^-(aq) + H_3O^+(aq),$$

HF transfers a proton to water. Therefore HF is the Brønsted acid and H_2O is the Brønsted base. But in the reverse direction, hydronium ions transfer a proton to fluoride ions. H_3O^+ is the conjugate acid of H_2O because it has an additional proton, and F^- is the conjugate base of HF because it lacks a proton.

2) In the reaction:

$$NH_3(aq) + H_2O(l) \rightleftharpoons NH_4^{'}(aq) + OH^-(aq),$$

water transfers a proton to ammonia. H_2O is the Brønsted acid and OH^- is its conjugate base. NH_3 is the Brønsted base and NH_4^+ is its conjugate acid.

3) In the reaction:

$$H_3PO_4 + HS^- \rightleftharpoons H_2PO_4^- + H_2S$$

$H_3PO_4/H_2PO_4^-$ is one conjugate acid-base pair and H_2S/HS^- is the other.

4) H_3PO_4 is a polyprotic acid. It may further dissociate to transfer more than one proton:

$$H_3PO_4 \rightleftharpoons H_2PO_4^- + H^+$$

$$H_2PO_4^- \rightleftharpoons HPO_4^{2-} + H^+$$

$$HPO_4^{2-} \rightleftharpoons PO_4^{3-} + H^+$$

Lewis definition of acids and bases

The transfer of a proton from a Brønsted acid to a Brønsted base requires that the base accept the proton. When Lewis diagrams (see **Skill 4.3**) are used to draw the proton donation of Brønsted acid-base reactions, it is always clear that the base must contain an unshared electron pair to form a bond with the proton. For example, ammonia contains an unshared electron pair in the following reaction:

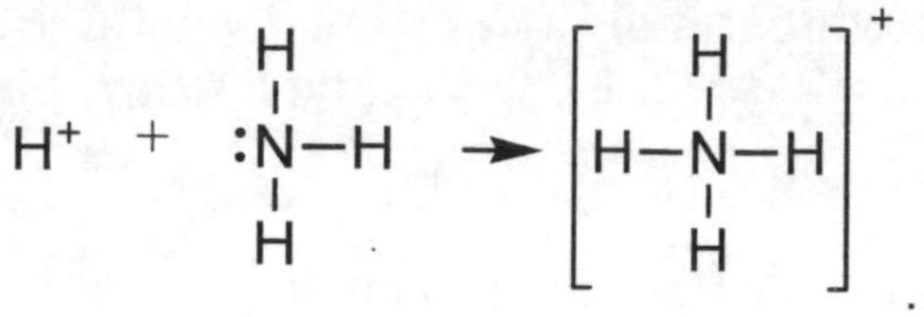

$$H^+ \; + \; :N-H \; \longrightarrow \; \left[H-N-H \right]^+$$

In the 1920s, Gilbert N. **Lewis** proposed that **bases donate unshared electron pairs to acids**, regardless of whether the donation is made to a proton or to another atom. Boron trifluoride is an example of a Lewis acid that is not a Brønsted acid because it is a chemical that accepts an electron pair without involving an H^+ ion:

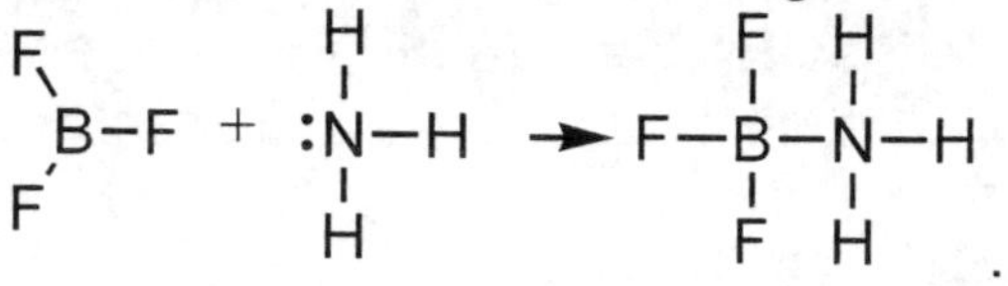

$$B-F \; + \; :N-H \; \longrightarrow \; F-B-N-H$$

The Lewis theory of acids and bases is more general than Brønsted-Lowry theory, but Brønsted-Lowry's definition is used more frequently. The terms "acid" and "base" most often refer to Brønsted acids and bases, and the term "Lewis acid" is usually reserved for chemicals like BF_3 that are not also Brønsted acids.

Summary of definitions

A Lewis base transfers an electron pair to a Lewis acid. A Brønsted acid transfers a proton to a Brønsted base. These exist in conjugate pairs at equilibrium. In an Arrhenius base, the proton acceptor (electron pair donor) is OH^-. All Arrhenius acids/bases are Brønsted acids/bases and all Brønsted acids/bases are Lewis acids/bases. Each definition contains a subset of the one that comes after it.

Domain 5, Competency 5.1: Chemical Thermodynamics

Skill 5.1a-Perform calculations using specific heat, heats of fusion, heats of vaporization, and heat of reaction (enthalpy)

Internal energy and enthalpy
The **internal energy** of a material is the **sum of the total kinetic energy** of its molecules and the **potential energy** of interactions between those molecules. Total kinetic energy includes the contributions from translational motion and other components of motion such as rotation. The potential energy includes **energy stored in the form of resisting intermolecular attractions** between molecules.

The **enthalpy** (*H*) of a material is the **sum of its internal energy and the mechanical work** it can do by driving a piston. We usually don't deal with mechanical work in high school chemistry, so the differences between internal energy and enthalpy are not important. The key concept is that a change in the **enthalpy** of a substance is the total **energy** change caused by **adding/removing heat** at constant pressure.

When a material is heated and experiences a phase change, **thermal energy is used to break the intermolecular bonds** holding the material together. Similarly, bonds are formed with the release of thermal energy when a material changes its phase during cooling. Therefore, **the energy of a material increases during a phase change that requires heat and decreases during a phase change that releases heat**. For example, the energy of H_2O increases when ice melts and decreases when water freezes.

Heat capacity and specific heat
A substance's molar **heat capacity** is the heat required to **change the temperature of one mole of the substance by one degree**. Heat capacity has units of joules per mol-kelvin or joules per mol-°C. The two units are interchangeable because we are only concerned with differences between one temperature and another. A Kelvin degree and a Celsius are the same size.

The **specific heat** of a substance (also called specific heat capacity) is the heat required to **change the temperature of one gram or kilogram by one degree**. Specific heat has units of joules per mole-gram or joules per mole-kilogram.

These terms are used to solve thermochemistry problems involving a change in temperature by applying the formula:
$q = n \times C \times \Delta T$ where $q \Rightarrow$ heat added (positive) or evolved (negative)

$\qquad n \Rightarrow$ amount of material

$\qquad C \Rightarrow$ molar heat capacity if n is in moles, specific heat if n is a mass

$\qquad \Delta T \Rightarrow$ change in temperature $T_{final} - T_{initial}$

Heats of fusion, vaporization, and sublimation

A substance's **heat of fusion** (ΔH_{fusion}) is the heat required to **change one mole from a solid to a liquid** by freezing. This is also the heat released from the substance when it changes from a liquid to a solid (melts).

A substance's **heat of vaporization** ($\Delta H_{vaporization}$) is the heat required to **change one mole of a substance from a liquid to a gas** or the heat released by condensation.

A substance's heat of sublimation ($\Delta H_{sublimation}$) is the heat required to change one mole directly from a solid to a gas by sublimation or the heat released by deposition.

These three values are also called enthalpies or "latent heats" of fusion, vaporization, and sublimation. They have units of joules per mole, and are negative values when heat is released.

$$\text{Solid} \xrightarrow[\text{melting}]{\Delta H_{fusion}} \text{Liquid} \xrightarrow[\text{vaporization}]{\Delta H_{vaporization}} \text{Gas} \qquad \text{Solid} \xrightarrow[\text{sublimation}]{\Delta H_{sublimation}} \text{Gas}$$

$$\text{Gas} \xrightarrow[\text{condensation}]{-\Delta H_{vaporization}} \text{Liquid} \xrightarrow[\text{freezing}]{-\Delta H_{fusion}} \text{Solid} \qquad \text{Gas} \xrightarrow[\text{deposition}]{-\Delta H_{sublimation}} \text{Solid}$$

These terms are used to solve thermochemistry problems involving a change of phase by applying the formula:

$$q = n \times \Delta H_{change}$$

where $q \Rightarrow$ heat added (positive) or evolved (negative)

$n \Rightarrow$ amount of material

$\Delta H_{change} \Rightarrow$ enthalpy of fusion, vaporization, or sublimation for heat added

$\Rightarrow$ −(enthalpy of fusion, vaporization, or sublimation) for heat evolved

Example: What is the change in energy of 10 g of gold at 25 °C when it is heated beyond its melting point to 1300 °C. You will need the following data for gold:

Solid heat capacity: 28 J/mol-K

Molten heat capacity: 20 J/mol-K

Enthalpy of fusion: 12.6 kJ/mol

Melting point: 1064 °C

Solution: First determine the number of moles used: $10 \text{ g} \times \dfrac{1 \text{ mol}}{197 \text{ g}} = 0.051 \text{ mol}$.

There are then three steps. 1) Heat the solid. 2) Melt the solid. 3) Heat the liquid. All three require energy so they will be positive numbers.

1) Heat the solid: $q_1 = n \times C \times \Delta T = 0.051 \text{ mol} \times 28 \dfrac{\text{J}}{\text{mol-K}} \times (1064 \text{ °C} - 25 \text{ °C})$

$= 1.48 \times 10^3 \text{ J} = 1.48 \text{ kJ}$

2) Melt the solid: $q_2 = n \times \Delta H_{fusion} = 0.051 \text{ mol} \times 12.6 \dfrac{\text{kJ}}{\text{mol}}$

$= 0.64 \text{ kJ}$

3) Heat the liquid:

$q_3 = n \times C \times \Delta T = 0.051 \text{ mol} \times 20 \dfrac{\text{J}}{\text{mol-K}} \times (1300 \text{ °C} - 1064 \text{ °C})$

$= 2.4 \times 10^2 \text{ J} = 0.24 \text{ kJ}$

The sum of the three processes is the total change in energy of the gold:

$q = q_1 + q_2 + q_3 = 1.48 \text{ kJ} + 0.64 \text{ kJ} + 0.24 \text{ kJ} = 2.36 \text{ kJ}$

$= 2.4 \text{ kJ}$

<u>Heat of reaction</u>
When a chemical reaction takes place, the enthalpies of the products will differ from the enthalpies of the reactants. There is an energy change for the reaction ΔH_{rxn}, determined by **the sum of the products minus the sum of the reactants**:
$$\Delta H_{rxn} = H_{product\ 1} + H_{product\ 2} + \ldots - \left(H_{reactant\ 1} + H_{reactant\ 2} + \ldots\right).$$
The enthalpy change for a reaction is commonly called the **heat of reaction**.

If the enthalpies of the products are greater than the enthalpies of the reactants then ΔH_{rxn} **is positive** and the reaction is **endothermic**. Endothermic reactions **absorb heat** from their surroundings. The simplest endothermic reactions break chemical bonds.

If the enthalpies of the products are less than the enthalpies of the reactants then ΔH_{rxn} **is negative** and the reaction is **exothermic**. Exothermic reactions **release heat** into their surroundings. The simplest exothermic reactions form new chemical bonds.

The heat absorbed or released by a chemical reaction often has the impact of changing the temperature of the reaction vessel and of the chemicals themselves. The measurement of these heat effects is known as **calorimetry**.

The enthalpy change of a reaction ΔH_{rxn} **is equal in magnitude but has the opposite sign to the enthalpy change for the reverse reaction**. If a series of reactions lead back to the initial reactants then the net energy change for the entire process is zero.

When a reaction is composed of substeps, the **total enthalpy change will be the sum of the changes for each step**. Even if a reaction in reality contains no substeps, we may still write any number of reactions in series that lead from the same reactants to the same products and their sum will be the heat of the reaction of interest. The ability to add together these enthalpies to form ultimate products from initial reactants is known as **Hess's Law**. It is used to determine one heat of reaction from others:
$$\Delta H_{net\ rxn} = H_{rxn\ 1} + H_{rxn\ 2} + \ldots$$

A **standard** thermodynamic value occurs with all components at 25 °C and 100 kPa. This *thermodynamic standard state* is slightly different from the *standard temperature and pressure* (STP) often used for gas law problems (0 °C and 1 atm=101.325 kPa). Standard properties of common chemicals are listed in tables.

The **heat of formation** ΔH_f of a chemical is the heat required (positive) or emitted (negative) when elements react to form the chemical. It is also called the enthalpy of formation. The **standard heat of formation** ΔH_f° is the heat of formation with all reactants and products at 25 °C and 100 kPa.

Elements in their **most stable form** are assigned a value of ΔH_f° = 0 kJ/mol. Different forms of an element in the same phase of matter are known as **allotropes**.

Example: The heat of formation for carbon as a gas is: ΔH_f° for $C(g) = 718.4 \ \dfrac{kJ}{mol}$. C in

the solid phase exists in three allotropes. A C_{60} *buckyball* (one face is shown to the left), contains C atoms linked with aromatic bonds and arranged in the shape of a soccer ball. C_{60} was discovered in 1985. *Diamond* (below left) contains single C–C bonds in a three dimensional network. The most stable form at 25 °C is *graphite* (below right). Graphite is composed of C atoms with aromatic bonds in sheets.

$$\Delta H_f^\circ \text{ for } C_{60}(buckminsterfullerene \text{ or } buckyball) = 38.0 \ \frac{kJ}{mol}$$

$$\Delta H_f^\circ \text{ for } C_\infty (diamond) = 1.88 \ \frac{kJ}{mol}$$

$$\Delta H_f^\circ \text{ for } C_\infty (graphite) = 0 \ \frac{kJ}{mol}.$$

Heat of combustion ΔH_c (also called enthalpy of combustion) is the heat of reaction when a chemical **burns in O_2** to form completely oxidized products such as **CO_2 and H_2O**. It is also the heat of reaction for **nutritional molecules that are metabolized** in the body. The standard heat of combustion ΔH_c° takes place at 25 °C and 100 kPa. **Combustion is always exothermic**, so the negative sign for values of ΔH_c is often omitted. If a combustion reaction is used in Hess's Law, the value must be negative.

Example: Determine the standard heat of formation ΔH_f° for ethylene:

$$2C(graphite) + 2H_2(g) \rightarrow C_2H_4(g).$$

Use the heat of combustion for ethylene:

$$\Delta H_c^\circ = 1411.2 \frac{kJ}{mol\ C_2H_4} \quad \text{for} \quad C_2H_4(g) + 3O_2(g) \rightarrow 2CO_2(g) + 2H_2O(l)$$

and the following two heats of formation for CO_2 and H_2O:

$$\Delta H_f^\circ = -393.5 \frac{kJ}{mol\ C} \quad \text{for} \quad C(graphite) + O_2(g) \rightarrow CO_2(g)$$

$$\Delta H_f^\circ = -285.9 \frac{kJ}{mol\ H_2} \quad \text{for} \quad H_2(g) + \frac{1}{2}O_2(g) \rightarrow H_2O(l).$$

Solution: Use Hess's Law after rearranging the given reactions so they cancel to yield the reaction of interest. Combustion is exothermic, so ΔH for this reaction is negative. We are interested in C_2H_4 as a product, so we take the opposite (endothermic) reaction. The given ΔH are multiplied by stoichiometric coefficients to give the reaction of interest as the sum of the three:

$$2CO_2(g) + 2H_2O(l) \rightarrow C_2H_4(g) + 3O_2(g) \qquad \Delta H = 1411.2 \frac{kJ}{mol\ reaction}$$

$$2C(graphite) + 2O_2(g) \rightarrow 2CO_2(g) \qquad \Delta H = -787.0 \frac{kJ}{mol\ reaction}$$

$$2H_2(g) + O_2(g) \rightarrow 2H_2O(l) \qquad \Delta H = -571.8 \frac{kJ}{mol\ reaction}$$

_____

$$2C(graphite) + 2H_2(g) \rightarrow C_2H_4(g) \qquad \Delta H_f^\circ = 52.4 \frac{kJ}{mol}$$

Skill 5.1b-Interpret phase diagrams

Whether a substance exists as a gas, liquid, or solid depends on the nature of its intermolecular attractive forces and on its temperature and pressure. This information is often visualized as a **phase diagram** for the substance.

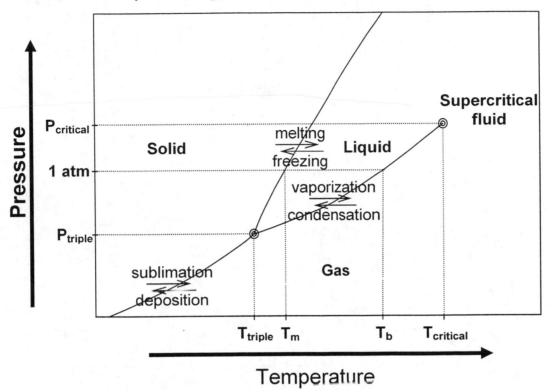

A region on the phase diagram represents each phase. Solid lines dividing these regions are located at conditions under which two phases may exist at equilibrium (see competency 6) and a phase change may occur. All three phases may coexist at the **triple point** of a substance. The triple point pressure of CO_2 is greater than 1 atm, so dry ice sublimates at atmospheric pressure with no liquid phase. **Vapor pressure** at a given temperature is the pressure of the phase transition line to a gas at that temperature. **Normal melting point** (T_m) and **normal boiling point** (T_b) are defined at 1 atm. Note that freezing point and melting point refer to an identical temperature approached from different directions, but they represent the same concept. At temperatures and pressures above the **critical point**, the substance becomes too dense with too much kinetic energy for a gas-liquid interface to form. Matter under these conditions forms a **supercritical fluid** with properties of gases and of liquids.

The phase diagram for water (shown below) is unusual. The solid/liquid phase boundary slopes to the left with increasing pressure because the melting point of water decreases with increasing pressure. Note that the normal melting point of water is lower than its triple point. The diagram is not drawn to a uniform scale. Many anomalous properties of water are discussed here: http://www.lsbu.ac.uk/water/anmlies.html.

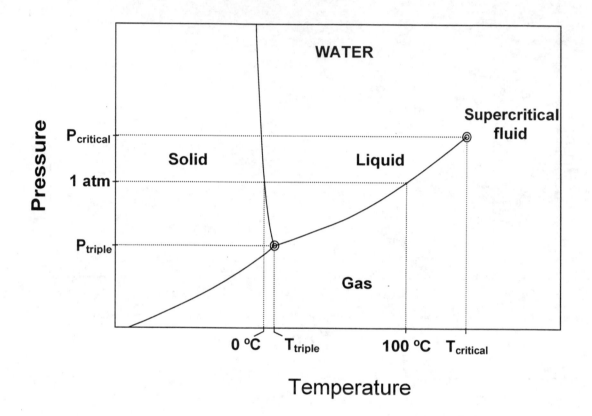

Domain 6, Competency 6.1: Organic Chemistry and Biochemistry

Skill 6.1a-Explain the bonding characteristics of carbon

Also see **Skill 12.1p**. Carbon has a **great affinity for covalent bonding** with a wide variety of other atoms. Carbon also readily bonds to other carbon atoms to form polymers. **Carbon has four valence electrons** (see **Skill 1.1b**). It may share these electrons with four other atoms in single bonds to fulfill the octet rule (see **Skill 1.3b**). Bonding to four different atoms permits carbon to form compounds that are mirror images of of each other. Carbon also readily forms double and triple bonds. Carbon compounds containing oxygen and nitrogen are polar due to electronegativity differences (see **Skill 1.3a**), and these **polar regions of specific chemical activity are known as functional groups**. This leads to a wide variety of possible molecules. **Organic compounds contain carbon,** and they have their own branch of chemistry because of the huge number of carbon compounds in nature, including nearly all the molecules in living things (see **Skill 6.1d**).

Carbon is able to form sp, sp^2, and sp^3 hybridized atomic orbitals and σ and π molecular orbitals (see **Skill 1.3c**). For example, in CH_4, the electron density of the four sp^3 orbitals of C each overlap with an s orbital of H to form four σ bonds. In C_2H_4 (an alkene), two sp^2 orbitals on each C overlap with H, the remaining sp^2 orbitals overlap with each other in a σ bond, and the p orbitals (drawn as shaded shapes) overlap with each other above and beneath the carbons in a π bond (also drawn as shaded shapes). In CO_2, the C atom has two sp hybrid orbitals and two p orbitals. These form one σ bond and one π bond with the two unfilled p orbitals on each O atom. In C_2H_2 (an alkyne), a triple bond forms with one σ and two π.

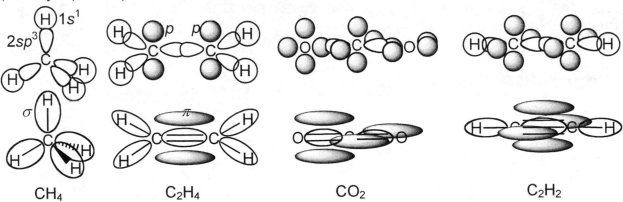

| CH_4 | C_2H_4 | CO_2 | C_2H_2 |

Molecules with double bonds next to each other and aromatic molecules based on benzene (see **Skill 6.1c**) contain **more than two π orbitals on adjacent atoms**. The bonds and the entire molecules are described as being **conjugated**. Electrons in these molecules are free to move from one bond to the next **on the same molecule** and so are **delocalized**. In **Skill 1.3a**, we saw electron delocalization extending throughout the entire substance in materials with metallic bonds.

Benzene (C_6H_6) has the following resonance forms:

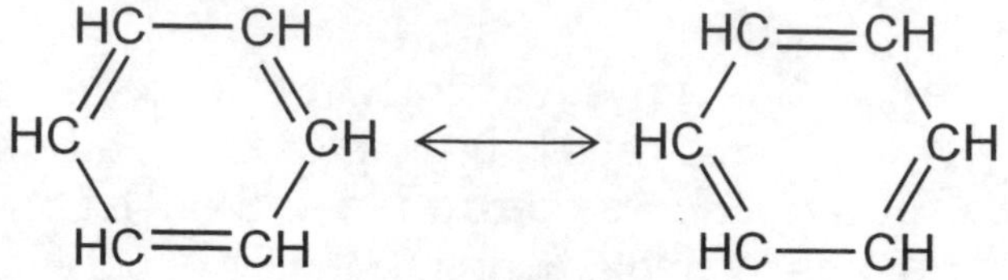

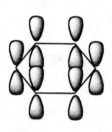

Each carbon atom in benzene bonds to three atoms, so their electrons are in three sp^2 orbitals and one p orbital as we've seen for C_2H_4. The p orbitals are shown as the shaded shapes below on the left (only the C-C bonds are shown). The p atomic orbitals combine to form molecular orbitals with delocalized electrons as shown in the bonding π molecular orbital below to the right.

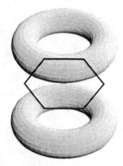

 Aromatic molecules are often drawn with a circle in the center of their benzene rings (shown to the left) to show delocalized π electrons. The atoms of a benzene molecule are all located in the same plane. This is in contrast to molecules that contain only σ bonds as shown to the right for cyclohexane, C_6H_{12}.

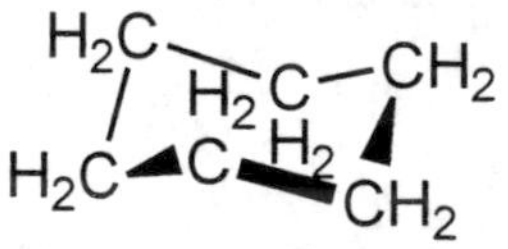

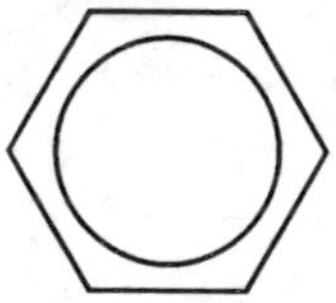

Skill 6.1b-Recognize the chemical structure of various organic functional groups (i.e., alcohols, ketones, ethers, amines, esters, aldehydes, and organic acids) and provide examples of reactions involving these groups

Several functional groups utilize oxygen.

Class of molecule	Functional group	Structure	Affix	Example
Alcohol	Hydroxyl ──OH	primary $R-CH_2-OH$ secondary R_1R_2CH-OH tertiary $R_1R_2R_3C-OH$	–ol	H_3C-CH_2-OH ethanol
Ether	Oxy	R_1-O-R_2	–oxy–	$H_3C-O-CH_2-CH_3$ methoxyethane or ethyl methyl ether
Aldehyde	Carbonyl	$R-C(=O)-H$	–al	$O=CH-CH_2-CH_3$ propionaldehyde or propanal
Ketone		$R_1-C(=O)-R_2$	–one	$H_3C-C(=O)-CH_3$ acetone
Carboxylic acid	Carboxyl	$R-C(=O)-OH$	–oic acid	$HC(=O)-OH$ formic acid or methanoic acid

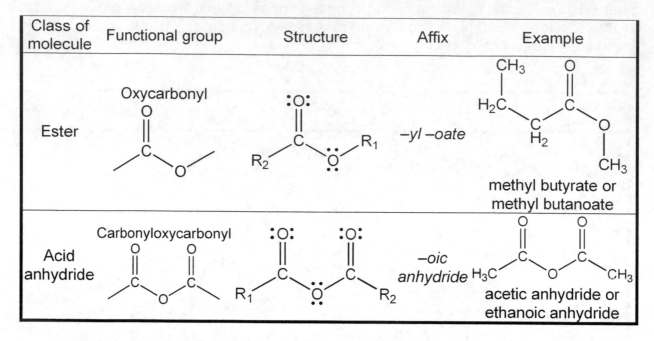

Class of molecule	Functional group	Structure	Affix	Example
Ester	Oxycarbonyl		−yl −oate	methyl butyrate or methyl butanoate
Acid anhydride	Carbonyloxycarbonyl		−oic anhydride	acetic anhydride or ethanoic anhydride

One way to memorize the derivatives utilizing oxygen is to divide them into pairs with a hydrogen atom in the first element of the pair replaced by a hydrocarbon in the second element. These pairs are:

1) alcohol/ether.
2) aldehyde/ketone.
3) carboxylic acid/ester.

Derivatives utilizing other atoms are also common.

Class of molecule	Functional group	Structure	Affix	Example
Nitrile	Cyanide —C≡N	R—C≡N:	–nitrile	H_3C—C≡N acetonitrile or ethanonitrile
Amine	Amino —N—	**primary** R—N̈—H with H below; **secondary** R_1—N̈—H with R_2 below; **tertiary** R_1—N̈—R_3 with R_2 below	–amine	H_3C—$\overset{H_2}{C}$—NH_2 ethanamine
Amide	Aminocarbonyl	**primary** R—C(=O)—N with H, H; **secondary** R_2—C(=O)—N with R_1, H; **tertiary** R_3—C(=O)—N with R_2, R_1	–amide	H_3C—$\overset{H_2}{C}$—C(=O)—NH_2 propionamide or propanamide
Alkyl halide	Halide —X (where X is F, Cl, Br, or I)	R—Ẍ:	fluoro– chloro– bromo– iodo–	Br on CH; H_3C—CH—$\overset{H_2}{C}$—CH_3 2-bromobutane

Examples of reaction types are shown in **Skill 2.1c**. A few common reactions in organic chemistry are listed below:

Esterification occurs when a carboxylic acid and an alcohol react to **form an ester**:

$$H_3C\text{-}COOH \ + \ HO\text{-}CH_2\text{-}CH_3 \ \rightarrow \ H_3C\text{-}COO\text{-}CH_2\text{-}CH_3 \ + \ H_2O$$

acetic acid + ethanol → ethyl acetate + water

Hydrolysis is a reaction in which **a molecule is split into two parts by reacting with water**. An example of a hydrolysis reaction is the reverse of the esterification reaction above.

Decarboxylation is any chemical reaction that **removes a carboxyl (-COOH) group from a compound, producing CO$_2$** in the process. Decarboxylation will convert a carboxylic acid into a hydrocarbon:

$$H_3C\text{-}COOH \ \rightarrow \ CH_4 \ + \ CO_2$$

acetic acid → methane + carbon dioxide

Skill 6.1c-Inventory the ten simplest hydrocarbons that contain single bonds, multiple bonds, and benzene rings

There is no uniform agreement on what constitutes the "simplest set of hydrocarbons", but a general introduction to naming rules for hydrocarbons will help you inventory any simple hydrocarbon you encounter.

Organic compounds that **contain only carbon and hydrogen** are called **hydrocarbons**. Hydrocarbon molecules may be divided into the classes of **cyclic** and **open-chain** depending on whether they contain a ring of carbon atoms. Open-chain molecules may be divided into **branched** or **straight-chain** categories.

Hydrocarbons are also divided into classes called **aliphatic** and **aromatic**. Aromatic hydrocarbons are related to benzene and are always cyclic. Aliphatic hydrocarbons may be open-chain or cyclic. Aliphatic cyclic hydrocarbons are called **alicyclic**. Aliphatic hydrocarbons are one of three types: alkanes, alkenes, and alkynes.

Alkanes
Alkanes contain only single bonds. Alkanes have the maximum number of hydrogen atoms possible for their carbon backbone, so they are called **saturated**. Alkenes, alkynes, and aromatics are **unsaturated** because they have fewer hydrogens.

Straight-chain alkanes are also called **normal alkanes**. These are the simplest hydrocarbons. They consist of a linear chain of carbon atoms.

The names of these molecules contain the suffix *–ane* and a **root based on the number of carbons in the chain** according to the table on the following page. The first four roots, *meth–*, *eth–*, *prop–*, and *but–* have historical origins in chemistry, and the remaining alkanes contain common Greek number prefixes. Alkanes have the general formula C_nH_{2n+2}.

A single molecule may be represented in multiple ways. Methane and ethane in the table are shown as three-dimensional structures with dashed wedge shapes attaching atoms behind the page and thick wedge shapes attaching atoms in front of the page.

Number of carbons	Name	Formula	Structure
1	Methane	CH_4	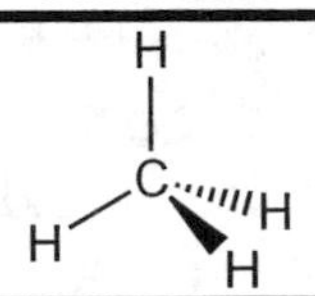
2	Ethane	C_2H_6	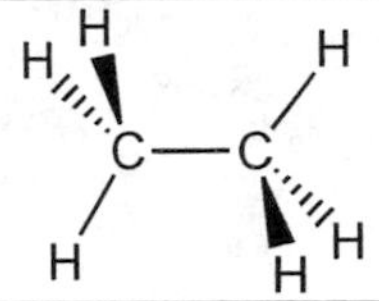
3	Propane	C_3H_8	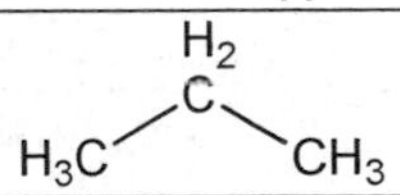
4	Butane	C_4H_{10}	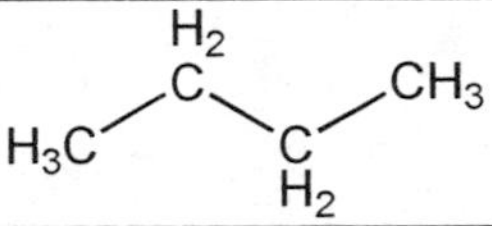
5	Pentane	C_5H_{12}	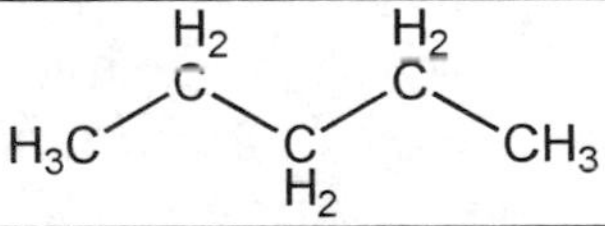
6	Hexane	C_6H_{14}	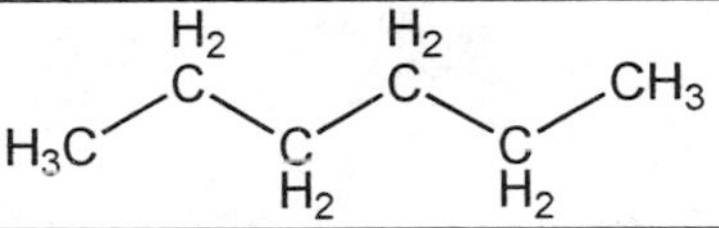
7	Heptane	C_7H_{16}	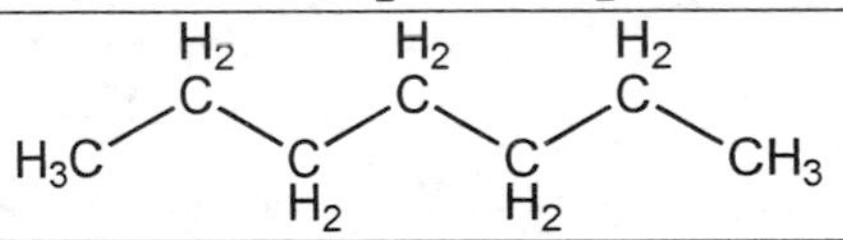
8	Octane	C_8H_{18}	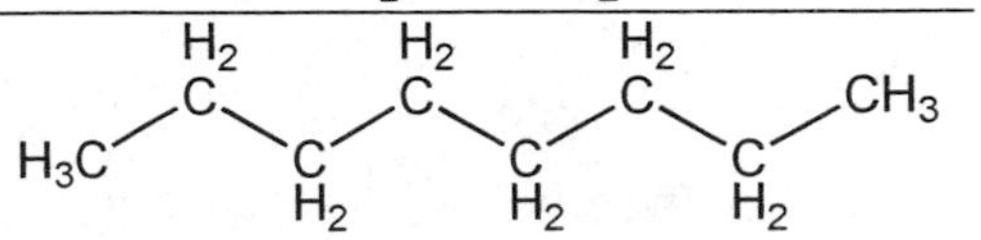

Additional ways that pentane might be represented are:

n-pentane (the *n* represents a *normal* alkane)

$CH_3CH_2CH_2CH_2CH_3$

$CH_3(CH_2)_3CH_3$

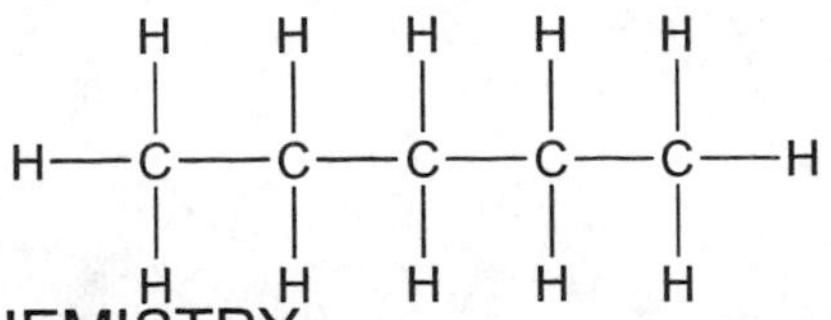

If one hydrogen is removed from an alkane, the residue is called an **alkyl** group. The −*ane* suffix is replaced by an −*yl*− infix when this residue is used as **functional group**. Functional groups are used to systematically build up the names of organic molecules.

Branched alkanes are named using a four-step process:

1) Find the longest continuous carbon chain. This is the parent hydrocarbon.
2) Number the atoms on this chain beginning at the end near the first branch point, so the lowest locant numbers are used. Number functional groups from the attachment point.
3) Determine the numbered locations and names of the substituted alkyl groups. Use *di*−, *tri*−, and similar prefixes for alkyl groups represented more than once. Separate numbers by commas and groups by dashes.
4) List the locations and names of alkyl groups in alphabetical order by their name (ignoring the *di*−, *tri*− prefixes) and end the name with the parent hydrocarbon.

Example—Name the following hydrocarbon:

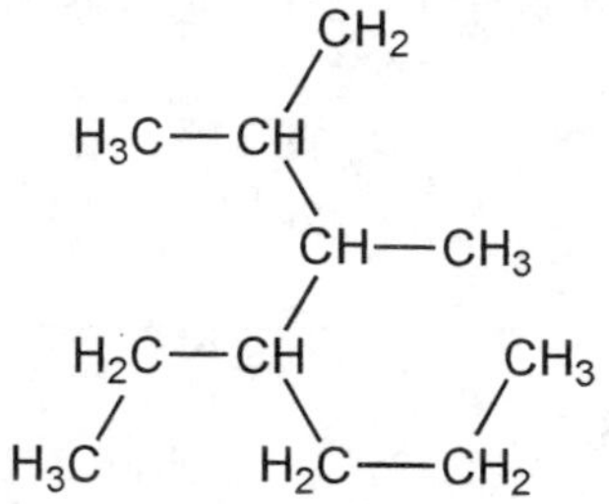

Solution—
1) The longest chain is seven carbons in length, as shown by the bold lines below. This molecule is a heptane.
2) The atoms are numbered from the end nearest the first branch as shown:

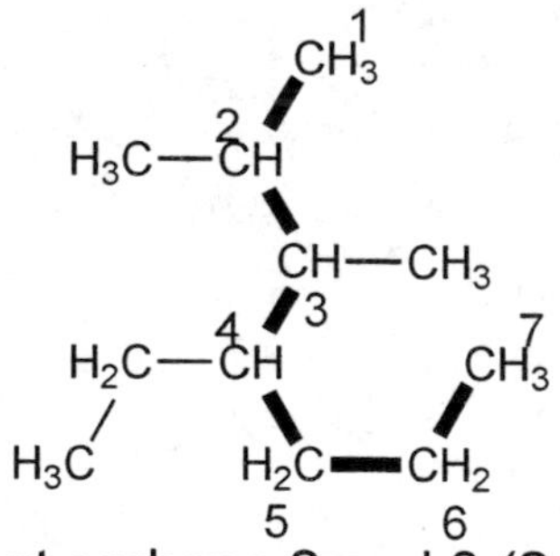

3) Methyl groups are located at carbons 2 and 3 (2,3-dimethyl), and an ethyl group is located at carbon 4.
4) "Ethyl" precedes "methyl" alphabetically. The hydrocarbon name is: 4-ethyl-2,3-dimethylheptane.

The following branched alkanes have accepted common names:

Structure	Systematic name	Common name
	2-methylpropane	isobutane
	2-methylbutane	isopentane
	2,2-dimethylpropane	neopentane

The following alkyl groups have accepted common names. The systematic names assign a locant number of 1 to the attachment point:

Structure	Systematic name	Common name
	1-methylethyl	isopropyl
	2-methylpropyl	isobutyl
	1-methylpropyl	*sec*-butyl
	1,1-dimethylethyl	*tert*-butyl

Alkenes

Alkenes contain one or more double bonds. Alkenes are also called olefins. The suffix used in the naming of alkenes is –*ene*, and the number roots are those used for alkanes of the same length.

A number preceding the name shows the location of the double bond for alkenes of length four and above. Alkenes with one double bond have the general formula C_nH_{2n}. Multiple double bonds are named using –*diene*, –*triene*, etc. The infix –*enyl*– is used for functional groups after a hydrogen is removed from an alkene. Ethene and propene have the common names **ethylene** and **propylene**. The ethenyl group has the common name **vinyl** and the 2-propenyl group has the common name **allyl**.

Examples:

$H_2C\!=\!\!=\!CH_2$ is ethylene or ethene. $H_2C\!=\!\!=\!CH$ is a vinyl or ethenyl group.

is propylene or propene. is an allyl or 2-propenyl group.

is 2-hexene.

is 2-methyl-1,3-butadiene (common name: isoprene).

Note that isoprene contains two adjacent double bonds, so it is a **conjugated** molecule (see **Skill 6.1a**).

Alkynes and alkenynes

Alkynes contain one or more triple bonds. They are named in a similar way to alkenes. The suffix used for alkynes is –*yne*. Ethyne is often called **acetylene**. Alkynes with one triple bond have the general formula C_nH_{2n-2}. Multiple triple bonds are named using –*diyne*, –*triyne*, etc. The infix –*ynyl*– is used for functional groups composed of alkynes after the removal of a hydrogen atom.

Hydrocarbons with **both double and triple bonds are known as alkenynes.** The locant number for the double bond precedes the name, and the locant for the triple bond follows the infix –*en*– and precedes the suffix –*yne*.

Examples: $HC\equiv CH$ is acetylene or ethyne.

$HC\equiv C-CH_2-CH_3$ is 1-butyne.

$HC\equiv C-C\equiv C-CH_3$ is 1,3-pentadiyne.

is a 4-hexynyl group.

is 1-buten-3-yne. This compound has the common name of vinylacetylene

Cycloalkanes, –enes, and –ynes

Alicyclic hydrocarbons use the prefix *cyclo*– before the number root for the molecule. The structures for these molecules are often written as if the molecule lay entirely within the plane of the paper even though in reality, these rings dip above and below a single plane. When there is more than one substitution on the ring, numbering begins with the first substitution listed in alphabetical order.

Examples:

is cyclopropane

is methylcyclohexane.

is 1,3-cyclohexadiene.

is 1-ethyl-3-propylcyclobutane.

Aromatic hydrocarbons

Aromatic hydrocarbons are structurally related to benzene or made up of benzene molecules fused together. These molecules are called **arenes** to distinguish them from alkanes, alkenes, and alkynes. All atoms in arenes lie in the same plane. In other words, aromatic hydrocarbons are flat. Aromatic molecules have electrons in delocalized π orbitals that are free to migrate throughout the molecule. See **Skill 6.1a** for a description of the molecular geometry of arenes.

Substitutions onto the benzene ring are named in alphabetical order using the lowest possible locant numbers. The prefix *phenyl–* may be used for C_6H_5- (benzene less a hydrogen) attached as a functional group to a larger hydrocarbon residue. Arenes in general form aryl functional groups. A phenyl group may be represented in a structure by the symbol Ø. The prefix *benzyl–* may used for $C_6H_5CH_2-$ (methylbenzene with a hydrogen removed from the methyl group) attached as a functional group.

Examples:

is benzene.

is 2-isopropyl-1,4-dimethylbenzene.

is 3-phenyloctane or (1-ethylhexyl)benzene.

The most often used common names for aromatic hydrocarbons are listed in the following table. Naphthalene is the simplest molecule formed by fused benzene rings.

Structure	Systematic name	Common name
	methylbenzene	toluene
	1,2-dimethylbenzene	*ortho*-xylene or *o*-xylene
	1,3-dimethylbenzene	*meta*-xylene or *m*-xylene
	1,4-dimethylbenzene	*para*-xylene or *p*-xylene
	ethenylbenzene	styrene
		naphthalene

Skill 6.1d-Understand the differences in structure and properties between amino acids and their polymers and between sugars and their polymers

Proteins
Proteins play a role in nearly every process in living organisms and are the most important and diverse molecules in living things. **Amino acids form the building blocks of proteins**. Amino acids contain both an amine and a carboxylic acid (See **Skill 6.1b**).

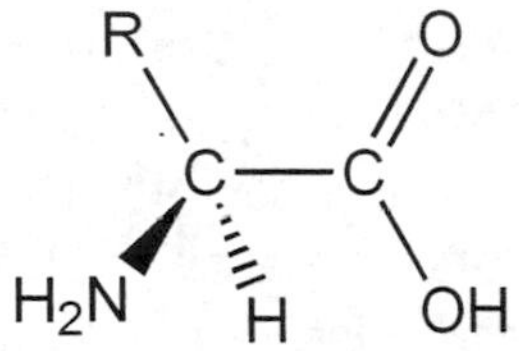

Each of the 20 different common amino acids uses a different **side chain** for R. Side chains may be nonpolar or polar. The polar side chains may be acidic or basic. Side chains may also be aromatic or aliphatic.

The carbonyl carbon atom of one amino acid bonds to the amine nitrogen of another to form an amide group. This bond is called a peptide bond:

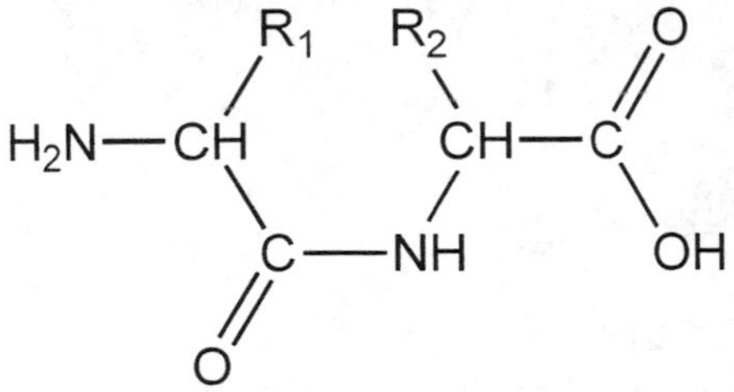

The molecule to the left is a **dipeptide** because it contains two amino acids. Many amino acids strung together form a **polypeptide**, and the term **protein** is used for these larger chains.

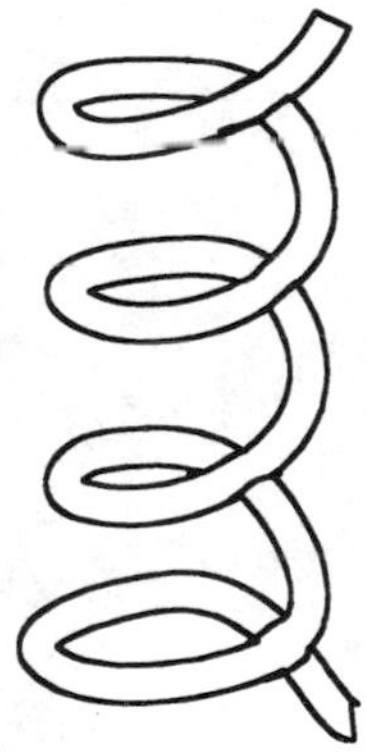

Interactions among specific sequences of side chains give each protein a certain shape with unique chemical properties. A common shape found within many proteins is an α-**helix** shown to the right. Physical properties of the protein follow from the way individual protein molecules interact with water and with each other.

A protein called **keratin** is insoluble in water but binds to other keratin molecules to form hard structures. Proteins like keratin are known as **structural proteins** or **fibrous proteins**. Keratin is the main component in hair and fingernails. A different protein called **insulin** is soluble in water and achieves a certain shape as an individual molecule. Proteins like insulin are known as **globular proteins**. Insulin in the bloodstream regulates glucose metabolism.

Globular proteins called **enzymes** act as catalysts to increase the rate of biochemical reactions. The names of enzymes often end with the suffix –*ase*. Many other protein names end with the suffix –*in*. Heating a protein or changing its chemical environment may cause it to lose its shape without breaking any covalent bonds. This loss of structure is called **denaturation**.

Carbohydrates

Monosaccharides (also known as **simple sugars**) **form the building blocks of carbohydrates**. The empirical formula for simple sugars is CH_2O. The name *carbohydrate* is derived from "hydrate of carbon" based on this formula. The names of monosaccharides use the suffix *–ose*. A monosaccharide contains multiple hydroxyl groups and may be an **aldose** or a **ketose** depending on whether it contains an aldehyde or a ketone group (see **Skill 6.1b**).

Organisms use the bonds in carbohydrates to store energy in chemical form. The most important monosaccharide is glucose. Glucose is a **hexose** because it contains six carbon atoms. Like all **hexoses**, glucose has the formula $C_6H_{12}O_6$. It is also an aldose. Like many monosaccharides, the carbonyl group of glucose may react with one of its hydroxyl groups. This creates an **equilibrium between open chain and ring forms**. These two forms of glucose are shown below:

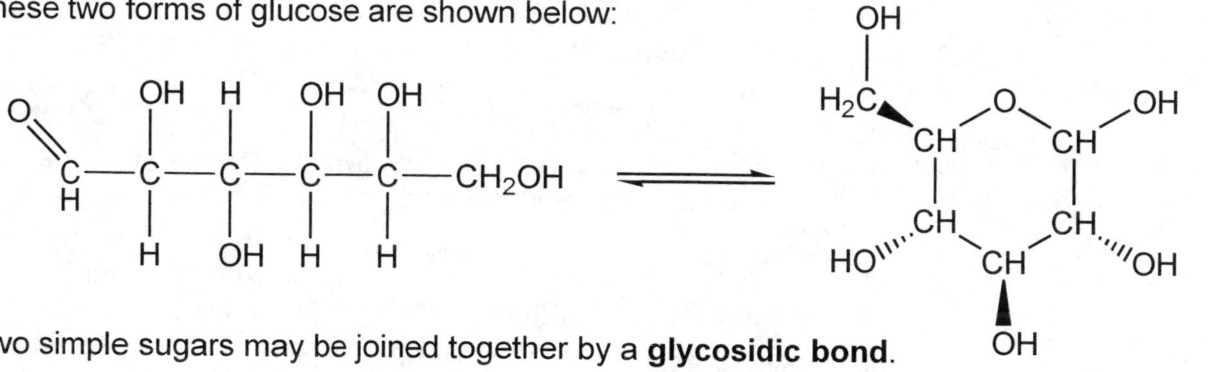

Two simple sugars may be joined together by a **glycosidic bond**.

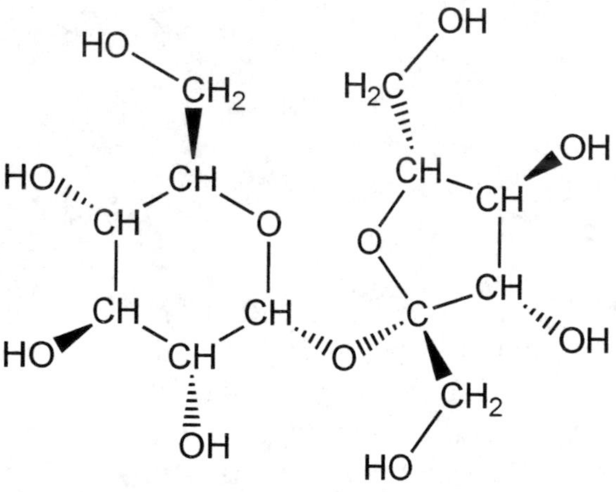

The molecule to the left is the **disaccharide** sucrose. Many sugars linked together form a **polysaccharide**, and the term **complex carbohydrate** is used for these structures. More than two glycosidic bonds may attach to a simple sugar, so **complex carbohydrates often contain branch-like structures. This is in contrast to proteins where building blocks are strung together in a linear fashion**.

glucose complex carbohydrates.

Starch and **cellulose** are two examples of

For information about lipids and nucleic acids, see **Skill 12.1o**.

Domain 7, Competency 7.1: Nuclear Processes

Skill 7.1a-Understand how mass-energy relationships in nuclear reactions and radioactive decay requires the relationship $E = mc^2$

The energies of nuclear reactions and radioactive decays can only be considered with the aid of **Einstein's equation relating mass and energy**:

$$E = mc^2$$

where: $E \Rightarrow$ Energy in Joules

$m \Rightarrow$ Mass in kg

$c \Rightarrow$ Speed of light (2.998×10^8 m/s)

A very large amount of energy is associated with small quantities of mass. A more useful equation determines the impact of a change in mass on energy:

$$\Delta E = c^2 \Delta m$$

The mass changes of energetic chemical reactions are too small to measure. It's a safe assumption that mass is conserved for chemical reactions. However, in nuclear reactions, we can obtain values for the masses of reactants and products.

Example: How much energy is released by one gram of Uranium-235 undergoing the fission reaction:

$$^{235}_{92}U + ^{1}_{0}n \rightarrow ^{141}_{56}Ba + ^{92}_{36}Kr + 3^{1}_{0}n ?$$

The atomic masses (see **Skill 2.1a**) of the components are: uranium-235 = 235.0439 u, barium-141 = 140.9140 u, krypton-92 = 91.9218 u, and the atomic mass of a neutron is 1.00867 u.

Solution: The total mass of the 2 reacting particles is:

235.0439 u + 1.00867 u = 236.0526 u.

The total mass of the 5 product particles is:

140.9140 u + 91.9218 u + 3×1.00867 u = 235.8618 u.

The change in mass when one atom of ^{235}U experiences this fission is:

235.8618 u − 236.0526 u = −0.1908 u

The change in mass when one mole of ^{235}U undergoes fission is found by recognizing that the conversion from u to grams and atoms to moles both require Avogadro's number:

$$\frac{-0.1908 \text{ u mass change}}{\text{atom of } ^{235}_{92}U} \times \frac{6.022 \times 10^{23} \text{ atoms}}{\text{mol } ^{235}_{92}U} \times \frac{1 \text{ g mass change}}{6.022 \times 10^{23} \text{ u mass change}}$$

$$= -0.1908 \frac{\text{g mass change}}{\text{mol } ^{235}_{92}U}$$

Einstein's equation requires mass change in kg, and we are interested in the fission of one gram of uranium:

$$-0.1908 \; \frac{\text{g mass change}}{\text{mol } {}^{235}_{92}\text{U}} \times \frac{1 \text{ mol } {}^{235}_{92}\text{U}}{235.0439 \text{ g } {}^{235}_{92}\text{U}} \times \frac{1 \text{ kg mass change}}{1000 \text{ g mass change}}$$

$$= -8.118 \times 10^{-7} \; \frac{\text{kg mass change}}{\text{g } {}^{235}_{92}\text{U}}$$

This value may be used in Einstein's equation to obtain the number of joules:

$$\Delta E = c^2 \Delta m = \left(2.998 \times 10^8 \; \frac{\text{m}}{\text{s}} \right)^2 \left(-8.118 \times 10^{-7} \text{ kg} \right)$$

$$= 7.296 \times 10^{10} \text{ J}$$

This is a large number for one gram of material. One gram of uranium fission supplies more energy than 500 gallons of gasoline combustion or 10000 kg of exploding TNT.

Skill 7.1b-Compare and contrast alpha, beta, and gamma decay, and the relative kinds of damage to matter caused by α-, β-, and γ- rays

Types of radiation
Some nuclei are unstable and emit particles and electromagnetic radiation. These emissions from the nucleus are known as **radioactivity**; the unstable isotopes are known as **radioisotopes**; and the nuclear reactions that spontaneously alter them are known as **radioactive decay**. Particles commonly involved in nuclear reactions are listed in the following table:

Particle	Neutron	Proton	Electron	Alpha particle	Beta particle	Gamma rays
Symbol	${}^{1}_{0}\text{n}$	${}^{1}_{1}\text{p}$ or ${}^{1}_{1}\text{H}$	${}^{0}_{-1}\text{e}$	${}^{4}_{2}\alpha$ or ${}^{4}_{2}\text{He}$	${}^{0}_{-1}\beta$ or ${}^{0}_{-1}\text{e}$	${}^{0}_{0}\gamma$

Nuclear equations are balanced by equating the sum of mass numbers on both sides of a reaction equation and the sum of atomic numbers on both sides of a reaction equation.

The electron is assigned an atomic number of −1 to account for the conversion during radioactive decay of a neutron to a proton and an emitted electron called a **beta particle**:

$$ {}^{1}_{0}\text{n} \rightarrow {}^{1}_{1}\text{p} + {}^{0}_{-1}\text{e} .$$

Sulfur-35 is an isotope that decays by beta emission:

$$ {}^{35}_{16}\text{S} \rightarrow {}^{35}_{17}\text{Cl} + {}^{0}_{-1}\text{e} .$$

In most cases nuclear reactions result in a **nuclear transmutation** from one element to another. Transmutation was originally connected to the mythical "philosopher's stone" of alchemy that could turn cheaper elements into gold. When Frederick Soddy and Ernest Rutherford first recognized that radioactive decay was changing one element into another, Soddy remembered saying, "Rutherford, this is transmutation!" Rutherford replied, "Soddy, don't call it transmutation. They'll have our heads off as alchemists."

Large isotopes often decay by **alpha particle** emission:

$$^{238}_{92}U \rightarrow \ ^{234}_{90}Th + ^{4}_{2}He \ .$$

Gamma rays are high-energy electromagnetic radiation (see **Skill 1.2b**), and gamma radiation is almost always emitted when other radioactive decay occurs. Gamma rays usually aren't written into nuclear equations because neither the mass number nor the atomic number is altered. One exception is the annihilation of an electron by a positron, an event that only produces gamma radiation:

$$^{0}_{-1}e + ^{0}_{1}e \rightarrow 2 ^{0}_{0}\gamma \ .$$

When two nuclei collide, they sometimes stick to each other and synthesize a new nucleus. This **nuclear fusion** was first demonstrated by the synthesis of oxygen from nitrogen and alpha particles:

$$^{14}_{7}N + ^{4}_{2}He \rightarrow \ ^{17}_{8}O + ^{1}_{1}H \ .$$

Fusion is also used to create new heavy elements, causing periodic tables to grow out of date every few years. In 2004, the name roentgenium was approved (in honor of Wilhelm Roentgen, the discoverer of X-rays) for the element first synthesized in 1994 by the following reaction:

$$^{209}_{83}Bi + ^{64}_{28}Ni \rightarrow \ ^{272}_{111}Rg + ^{1}_{0}n \ .$$

A heavy nucleus may also split apart into smaller nuclei by **nuclear fission** as described in **Skill 7.1a**.

Damage to matter caused by radiation

Non-ionizing radiation does not carry enough energy to remove electrons from atoms, and it generally does not cause damage unless it is damage done by heating the material it contacts. Because quantum-events are all-or-nothing, a large amount of non-ionizing radiation is generally harmless, and we can safely live in a world full of lightning flashes and radio waves.

Ionizing radiation carries enough energy to remove an electron, thus turning an atom into an ion. These events can be very damaging to life because they alter the chemistry of important molecules like DNA. Very high exposure can cause radiation poisoning.

Alpha particles are high-energy helium nuclei. They **are the most destructive form of ionizing radiation.** They carry so much energy because of their charge and large mass, but **they can be stopped by a thin sheet of paper.** Alpha emitting radiation is harmful to life if it is inhaled or ingested. Most smoke detectors use alpha-emitting isotopes in a sealed container.

Beta particles are high-energy electrons. They are less harmful to matter than alpha rays because they are less energetic, but they can penetrate further into matter. A thin sheet of aluminum will stop a typical beta particle.

High energy EM radiation (e.g., some ultraviolet, all X-rays, and especially **gamma rays**—see **Skill 1.2b**) is a form of ionizing radiation. Because photons have no mass, gamma rays are less ionizing than alpha or beta particles, but gamma rays can penetrate through matter, so protection against them requires thicker shielding.

Skill 7.1c-Perform calculations involving half-life

The **half-life** of a reaction is the **time required to consume half the reactant.** The rate of radioactive decay for an isotope is usually expressed as a half-life. Solving these problems is straightforward if the given amount of time is an exact multiple of the half-life. For example, the half-life of ^{233}Pa is 27.0 days. This means that of 200 grams of ^{233}Pa will decay according to the following table:

Day	Number of half-lives	^{233}Pa remaining	^{233}Pa decayed since day 0
0	0	200 g	0 g
27.0	1	100 g	100 g
54.0	2	50.0 g	150.0 g
81.0	3	25.0 g	175.0 g
108.0	4	12.5 g	187.5 g

Regardless of whether the given amount of time is an exact multiple of the half-life, the following equation may be used:

$$A_{remaining} = A_{initially} \left(\frac{1}{2}\right)^{\frac{t}{t_{halflife}}}$$

where: $A_{remaining} \Rightarrow$ amount remaining

$A_{initially} \Rightarrow$ amount initially

$t \Rightarrow$ time

$t_{halflife} \Rightarrow$ half-life

Skill 7.1d-Contrast the benefits and hazards of the use of radiation and radioactivity

Two important benefits of the use of radiation are in the fields of medicine and power generation.

Medicine

Medicine uses **X-rays** as a diagnostic tool and radioisotopes for **diagnostic radiology** and for **radiotherapy**. In diagnostic radiology, a radioisotope is introduced into the body and its location is monitored with a **gamma camera** or other imaging equipment. **Different isotopes are localized to different tissues at specific rates**. Abnormalities in internal organs and bone structure and function are found using these techniques. The isotopes typically emit only gamma rays because alpha and beta radiation are more likely to harm the patient. **Technetium-99m is a commonly used isotope for diagnostic radiology**. Many radioisotopes are used in diagnostic medicine outside the body for blood tests.

Radiotherapy uses radiation as part of **cancer treatment to destroy tumors**. Rapidly growing tumors are more vulnerable to radiation damage from β particles than non-malignant tissue. Radiotherapy works by damaging the DNA of these cells. The radioactive source may be outside the body (external radiotherapy) or introduced into the body. Isotopes used for internal radiotherapy may be injected into the body as a liquid or introduced temporarily through a catheter in a sealed container.

Cobalt-60 was a common isotope for external radiotherapy, but it has mostly been replaced by linear accelerators that provide high-energy electrons (β particles) without a dangerous isotope source. It is still used to irradiate some foods to destroy bacteria. **Iodine-131 is used to combat diseases of the thyroid** and of several types of cancer. A list of isotopes used in nuclear medicine may be found at http://www.cbvcp.com/nmrc/mia.html.

Power generation

Nuclear power currently provides 17% of the world's electricity. Heat is generated by **nuclear fission of uranium-235 or plutonium-239**. This heat is then converted to electricity by boiling water and forcing the steam through a turbine. Fission of ^{235}U and ^{239}Pu occurs when **a neutron strikes the nucleus and breaks it apart into smaller nuclei and additional neutrons**. One possible fission reaction (also, see **Skill 7.1a**) is:

$$_{0}^{1}n + {}_{92}^{235}U \rightarrow {}_{56}^{141}Ba + {}_{36}^{92}Kr + 3{}_{0}^{1}n$$

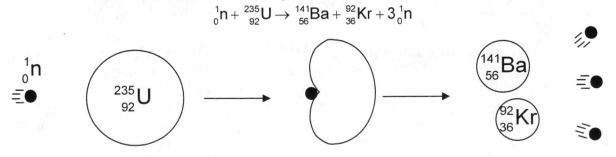

Gamma radiation, kinetic energy from the neutrons themselves, and the decay of the fission products (^{141}Ba and ^{92}Kr in the example above) all produce heat. The neutrons produced by the reaction strike other uranium atoms and produce more neutrons and more energy in a **chain reaction**. If enough neutrons are lost, the chain reaction stops and the process is called **subcritical**. If the mass of uranium is large enough so that one neutron on average from each fission event triggers another fission, the reaction is said to be **critical**. If the mass is larger than this so that few neutrons escape, the reaction is called **supercritical**. The chain reaction then multiplies the number of fissions and the violent explosion of an atomic bomb will take place if the process is not stopped. The concentration of **fissile material** in nuclear power plants is sufficient for a critical reaction to occur but too low for a supercritical reaction to take place.

The alpha decay of **Plutonium-238 is used as a heat source for localized power generation** in space probes and in heart pacemakers from the 1970s.

The most promising nuclear reaction for producing power by **nuclear fusion** is:

$$^{2}_{1}H + ^{3}_{1}H \rightarrow ^{4}_{2}He + ^{1}_{0}n$$

Hydrogen-2 is called **deuterium** and is often represented by the symbol D. Hydrogen-3 is known as **tritium** and is often represented by the symbol T. Nuclear reactions between very light atoms similar to the reaction above are the energy source behind the sun and the hydrogen bomb.

Hazards

Radioactive contamination is the uncontrolled distribution of radioactive material in an environment. The hazards of ionizing radiation were first studied in detail after the **atomic bombs dropped on Hiroshima and Nagasaki in 1945**. The worst nuclear accident in history was the **Chernobyl nuclear power plant disaster in 1986**.

Acute exposure of large doses may cause **radiation poisoning** or **radiation burns**. Chronic exposure may result in **cancer or mutations in one's children** due damage to DNA. Organs with rapidly dividing cells such as bone marrow, intestines, and gonads are most vulnerable. Some effects do not appear until several years have passed. Other organisms in the environment are just as vulnerable as humans to this danger. Because of these risks, radioactive materials are shipped in shielded containers. The risks for medical and food-processing applications that utilize radioactivity are known to be very small compared to the potential benefits, but this is considered by many to be a controversial topic.

Current opinion is that **there is a small risk to human health from even low levels of exposure** to ionizing radiation, but there is also a known quantity of **natural background radiation** that the human species has always encountered. In 1984, an employee at a nuclear power plant began to set off radiation alarms while walking *into* the plant. An investigation found that his home contained high levels of **radon gas** from natural minerals. Radon tests are now routinely performed in many homes.

Chemistry Domains for Science Subtest II (119) and Specialized Subtest IV (125)

This book follows the California numbering system for labeling all chemistry Subject Matter Requirement (SMR) Domains. Domains 1 through 7 in the previous section are refered to as Chemistry Domains. Domains 11 and 12 in this section are refered to as General Chemistry Domains enumerated within the broader scope of general science.

Domain 11, Competency 11.1: Heat Transfer and Thermodynamics

Skill 11.1a-Know the principle of conservation of energy and apply it to energy transfers

Energy is **the driving force for change**. Energy has units of joules (J). Energy is one of the most fundamental concepts in our world. We use it to move people and things from place to place, to heat and light our homes, to entertain us, to produce food and goods and to communicate with each other. It is not a substance but rather the ability possessed by things.

The principle of conservation of energy states that **energy is neither created nor destroyed**. Any time something happens, energy is being transferred from one place to another or one form to another. None of the energy is lost or gained. Einstein's equation, $E = mc^2$ (see **Skill 7.1a**) is viewed by physicists as representing the interconversion of mass and energy, not as the creation of energy from mass.

A few forms of energy are listed below:

Thermal energy is the energy that a substance has due to the **kinetic energy of its molecules** moving about chaotically. The flow of thermal energy from one body to another is called heat (see **Skill 11.1b**).

Chemical energy is the energy that bonds atoms and molecules together (see **Competency 1.3**).

Nuclear energy is contained in the nucleus of an atom (see **Skill 7.1a**).

Mechanical kinetic energy is the energy of moving objects.

Gravitational potential energy is the energy an object has when it is elevated so it may be released and fall.

Electrical Kinetic energy is the energy of electrons in motion along a circuit. The movement of electrons creates an electric current which generates electricity

Here are some examples of how energy is transformed to do work:

1. Stoves transform the chemical energy of fuel into heat.
2. Hydroelectric plants transform the kinetic energy of falling water into electrical energy
3. A flashlight converts chemical energy stored in batteries to light energy (electromagnetic radiation) and heat.

In every case, **the total amount of energy is not changed by the process**. For example, if 2.0×10^6 J of energy is lost from falling water in a hydroelectric plant that produces 1.5×10^6 J of electrical energy, the remaining 5×10^5 J did not disappear. This energy most likely was converted from the falling water into a **form of energy that is less useful** than electrical energy (such as thermal energy that heats up the equipment).

Skill 11.1b-Discuss how the transfer of energy as heat is related to changes in temperature

Heat is a method of transferring energy. Technically, heat is not a form of energy. The type of energy transferred by heat is called **thermal energy, the energy that a substance has due to the kinetic energy of its molecules**. Heat has units of Joules. Heat can not be directly measured. Heat must be calculated.

Heat and temperature are not the same thing. Temperature is a measure of **the average kinetic energy of molecular motion** in a substance. We sense temperature as a measure of "hotness."

A liter of boiling water will transfer more heat than a milliliter of boiling water even though they are both at a temperature of 100 ºC. The liter of water contains more thermal energy because there are more molecules present; the temperatures are identical because the average kinetic energy per molecule is the same. Temperature and density are **intensive properties**, meaning that it does not depend on the amount of material. Volume, mass, and heat content are **extensive properties** because more material will give a higher value for these properties.

Skill 11.1c-Diagram the direction of heat flow in a system

When two objects are in thermal contact, **heat flows from a higher to a lower temperature**. In the example to the right, a spoon at room temperature was placed in a hot cup of coffee. Heat will flow from the tea to the spoon (shown by the right diagonal arrow). Heat will also flow from the tea into the air (shown by the small vertical arrows).

In chemistry, we imagine the transfer of heat as a transfer of kinetic energy between atoms, similar to the transfer of kinetic energy between balls on a pool table. When a faster ball strikes a slower one, the fast ball slows down and the slow ball speeds up. Heat flow from a higher to a lower temperature as analogous to regions where many balls are moving quickly and transferring their kinetic energy to regions where many balls are moving slowly. **Thermal equilibrium** is achieved eventually when the two objects have the same temperature. In the example above, thermal equilibrium will occur when the tea, spoon, and room are all at the same temperature.

An **exothermic** chemical or physical process (such as lighting a match) produces heat and creates a heat flow from the system to its surroundings, raising the temperature of the surrounding environment. An **endothermic** process (such as melting an ice cube in a glass of water) requires heat and creates a heat flow from the surroundings into the system, lowering the temperature of the surrounding environment. See **Skill 5.1a**.

Skill 11.1d-Describe the methods of heat transfer by conduction, convection, and radiation, and provide examples for each

Heat transfer occurs in one of three ways: conduction, convection and radiation.

Conduction is the transfer of heat **directly from one object to another**. Conduction most easily and often occurs in solids but fluids may also transfer energy through conduction. For example, the metal spoon in a hot cup of coffee described in the previous skill will become warm because the hot coffee molecules touch and transfer their thermal energy to the spoon's atoms, warming the spoon's atoms.

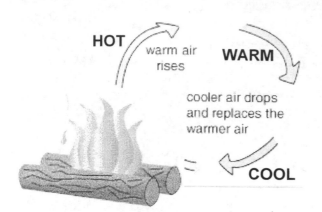

HOT

warm air rises

WARM

cooler air drops and replaces the warmer air

COOL

Convection is the transfer of heat through the **movement of gases or liquids called currents**. With a fire, for example, hot air rises, cold air flows into the space vacated by the moving hot air. This cold air is warmed by the fire and rises as well. This creates a continuous pattern of warming air. Convection can also lead to circulation in a liquid, as in the heating of a pot of water over a flame. Heated water expands and becomes more buoyant. Cooler, more dense water near the surface descends and patterns of circulation can be formed, though they will not be as regular as suggested in the drawing. The arrows in these drawing represent the **flow of material** carrying high or low temperatures. They are not diagrams showing the flow of heat. For the fire and the stove, arrows indicating heat flow would be from the source of the heat upwards.

COOLER   HOTTER

Radiation is the transfer of energy **via electromagnetic waves** (see **Skill 1.2b**) and is the method used by the sun to transport its energy to earth. Light energy can not reach the earth through conduction or convection. Earth and sun are separated by empty space and are not touching so their atoms do not collide and exchange heat. There are no gases or fluids between the sun and earth to transfer energy via convection. Transfer of heat by radiation occurs at the speed of light and travels great distances even in a vacuum.

A warm or hot object gives off **infrared electromagnetic radiation**, which can be absorbed in another object, heating it up. Electric heaters use radiation to heat a room. If a fan is present, they use both radiation and convection.

Skill 11.1e-Explain how chemical energy in fuel is transformed into heat

Chemical energy is the **energy stored in substances due to the arrangement of atoms** within the substance. When atoms are rearranged during chemical reactions, energy is either released or consumed (see **Skill 5.1a**). It is the energy released from chemical reactions that fuels our economy and powers our bodies. Most of the electricity produced on the planet comes from chemical energy released by the burning of petroleum, coal and natural gas. ATP is the molecule used by our body to carry chemical energy form cell to cell.

The energy in molecules is located in the **bonds between the atoms** in the molecule (see **Competency 1.3**). To break these bonds requires energy. Once broken apart, the atoms, ions or molecules rearrange themselves to form new substances, making new bonds. Making new bonds releases energy.

If during a chemical reaction, **more energy is needed to break the reactant bonds than released when product bonds form, the reaction is endothermic** and heat is absorbed. The environment becomes colder.

On the other hand, if **more energy is released due to product bonds forming than is needed to break reactant bonds the reaction is exothermic** and the excess energy is released to the environment as heat. The temperature of the environment goes up.

Bond energies
The total energy absorbed or released in the reaction can be determined by **using heats of formation** (see **Skill 5.1a**) or by using **bond energies**. The total energy change of the reaction is equal to the total energy of all of the bonds of the products minus the total energy of all of the bonds of the reactants.

Burning gasoline as a fuel would be a complex example to consider because gasoline is a mixture of hydrocarbons ranging from 5 to 12 carbon atom chains.

Propane (C_3H_8) is a better example to consider of chemical energy stored in fuel. Propane is a common fuel used in heating homes and backyard grills. When burned, the combustion reaction shown below takes place, and excess energy is released and used to cook our food

$$C_3H_8 \ (g) + 5 \ O_2 \ (g) \rightarrow 3 \ CO_2 \ (g) + 4 \ H_2O(l)$$

The total energy of the products is from the bonds found in the carbon dioxide molecules and the water molecules.

or 6 C=O bonds and 8 H-O bonds.

A table of bond energies gives the following information:

C=O   743 kJ/mol   H-O   463 kJ/mol

For these molecules there would be: $(6 \times -743$ kJ/mol$) + (8 \times -463$ kJ/mol$) = -8162$ kJ of energy released when these molecules form. Negative values are used to indicate energy released for this exothermic process of bond formation.

The reactants are these:

$$H-\underset{\underset{H}{|}}{\overset{\overset{H}{|}}{C}}-\underset{\underset{H}{|}}{\overset{\overset{H}{|}}{C}}-\underset{\underset{H}{|}}{\overset{\overset{H}{|}}{C}}-H \qquad + 5 \quad O=O$$

or 2 C-C bonds, 8 C-H bonds, and 5 O=O bonds.

These bonds require the following energy to break:
C-C   348 kJ/ mol   C-H   412 kJ/mol   O=O 498 kJ/mol.

The total energy required for the reactants would be:
$(2 \times 348$ kJ$) + (8 \times 412$ kJ$) + (5 \times 498$ kJ$) = 6482$ kJ of energy required. Positive values are used to indicate energy required for the endothermic process of bond destruction.

The total energy change that occurs during the combustion of propane is found from the sum of the energy released by the formation of the product bonds and the energy required to break the reactant bonds:

-8162 kJ $+ 6482$ kJ $= -1680$ kJ of energy is released for every mole of propane that burns.

Chemical energy transformed into heat for propulsion
Hydrogen burns with oxygen in the propulsion engine of the space shuttle. Very hot water vapor is produced by the exothermic reaction, and this vapor expands with great force to generate the upward thrust needed for launch. This water vapor is at a much higher temperature than the hydrogen and oxygen reactants. This increase in the kinetic energy of atoms is due to the transformation of chemical energy to heat, and results in the kinetic energy of the shuttle itself.

Skill 11.1f-Design and explain experiments to induce a physical change such as freezing, melting, or boiling

For this experiment we will utilize water in two different phases. For freezing, follow this procedure:
1) Fill a large container or beaker with ice water.
2) Put a few ml of water at room temperature into a test tube
3) Clamp the test tube above the ice water and clamp a thermometer to read the temperature of the water in the test tube.
4) Record an initial temperature
5) Lower the test tube with the thermometer inside into the ice bath.
6) Record the temperature of the water in the test tube every 15 seconds until it does not change for 5 minutes. Note the final temperature.
7) Observe that the water in the test tube has frozen solid and the thermometer bulb is encased in ice.

The time course of the cooling will show the temperature of the water in the test tube approach and then achieve 0 °C at which point it will remain constant because the physical change from liquid water to ice has occurred. During the time that this change was taking place, the heat removed from water in the test tube did not cause a further decrease in temperature. Therefore, the average kinetic energy of the molecules remained the same. However, the heat removed from the water in the tube did allow intermolecular attractive forces to form, and these forces crystallized the molecules together into a solid form.

For melting, follow this procedure:
8) Raise up the test tube with the thermometer clamped inside so it is out of the ice water.
9) Record an initial temperature.
10) Discard the ice water.
11) Record the temperature of the of the water in the tube every 15 seconds until it approaches the temperature from step 4.

The time course of the heating will show the temperature of the ice in the tube remain at 0 °C until all the ice melts. During this time, the heat added to the ice from the room is not causing an increase in temperature. Instead it is acting to break the intermolecular attractive forces of the solid so that only liquid remains. Then the added heat from the room will increase water temperature until it returns to room temperature.

A similar protocol is followed for boiling.

If we were able to add heat at a constant rate to ice that had been cooled to –50 °C until it became water vapor at above 100 °C, the **heating curve** of **temperature vs time** would appear like this:

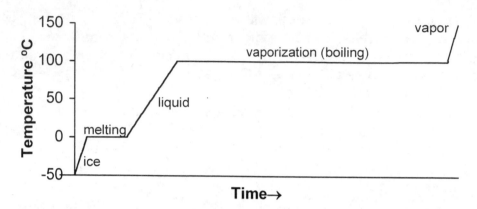

The **sloped regions** indicate periods of time when a **single phase increases in temperature** due to the addition of heat. The flat regions indicate periods of time when two phases are present and the addition of heat serves to **break intermolecular forces** in order to achieve a physical change from one phase to the other.

A similar curve is generated in a simulated experiment at this URL:
http://www.chm.davidson.edu/ChemistryApplets/PhaseChanges/HeatingCurve.html.

Skill 11.1g-Distinguish between physical and chemical changes and provide examples of each

A **physical change** does not create a new substance. **Atoms are not rearranged into different compounds**. The material has the same chemical composition as it had before the change. Changes of state as described in the previous section are physical changes. Frozen water or gaseous water is still H_2O. Taking a piece of paper and tearing it up is a physical change. You simply have smaller pieces of paper.

A **chemical change** is a chemical reaction. It **converts one substance into another** because atoms are rearranged to form a different compound. Paper undergoes a chemical change when you burn it. You no longer have paper. A chemical change to a pure substance alters its properties. Examples of chemical change are listed in **Skill 2.1c**.

Domain 12, Competency 12.1: Structure and Properties of Matter

Skill 12.1a-Identify, describe, and diagram the basic components within an atom (i.e., proton, neutron, and electron)

See Skill 1.2c. Skill 12.1a is required for certification in other branches of science besides chemistry. It is a subset of the content described in Skill 1.2c.

Skill 12.1b-Know that isotopes of any element have different numbers of neutrons but the same number of protons, and that some isotopes are radioactive

The identity of an **element** depends on the **number of protons** in the nucleus of the atom. This value is called the **atomic number** and it is sometimes written as a subscript before the symbol for the corresponding element. Atoms and ions of a given element that differ in number of neutrons have a different mass and are called **isotopes**. A nucleus with a specified number of protons and neutrons is called a **nuclide**, and a nuclear particle, either a proton or neutron, may be called a **nucleon**. The total number of nucleons is called the **mass number** and may be written as a superscript before the atomic symbol.

$$^{14}_{6}C$$ represents an atom of carbon with 6 protons and 8 neutrons.

The **number of neutrons** may be found by **subtracting the atomic number from the mass number**. For example, uranium-235 has 235-92=143 neutrons because it has 235 nucleons and 92 protons.

Different isotopes have different natural abundances and have different nuclear properties, but an atom's chemical properties are almost entirely due to electrons.

Some nuclei are unstable and emit particles and electromagnetic radiation. These emissions from the nucleus are known as **radioactivity**; the unstable isotopes are known as **radioisotopes**; and the nuclear reactions that spontaneously alter them are known as **radioactive decay**. For more information on radioactive isotopes, see **Competency 7.1**.

Skill 12.1c-Differentiate between atoms, molecules, elements, and compounds

A pure substance may be an element (such as carbon in diamond) or a compound (such as carbon dioxide, CO_2). **Compounds may be decomposed into two or more different elements. Elements cannot be decomposed into simpler substances.**

Atoms are the smallest possible unit of an element (see **Competency 1.2**). Carbon atoms may arrange themselves into different pure substances such as graphite and diamond (See **Skill 5.1a**). **Molecules are combinations of tightly bound atoms.** For example, the formula N_2 is a nitrogen molecule, but it is not a compound. It is the element nitrogen. N is a nitrogen atom.

In the kinetic molecular theory of gases (**Competency 3.1**), the distinction between atoms and molecules is not very important. Atoms of argon gas obey the ideal gas law in much the same was as molecules of N_2, so the word "molecule" is used less formally in this subfield to include atomic gases.

Skill 12.1d-Compare and contrast states of matter and describe the role energy plays in the conversion from one state to another

Molecules have **kinetic energy (**they move around), and they also have **intermolecular attractive forces** (they stick to each other). The relationship between these two determines whether a collection of molecules will be a gas, liquid, or solid.

A **gas** has an indefinite shape and an indefinite volume. The kinetic model for a gas is a collection of widely separated molecules, each moving in a random and free fashion, with negligible attractive or repulsive forces between them. Gases will expand to occupy a larger container so there is more space between the molecules. Gases can also be compressed to fit into a small container so the molecules are less separated. **Diffusion** occurs when one material spreads into or through another. Gases diffuse rapidly and move from one place to another.

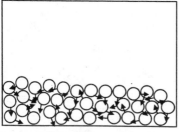

A **liquid** assumes the shape of the portion of any container that it occupies and has a specific volume. The kinetic model for a liquid is a collection of molecules attracted to each other with sufficient strength to keep them close to each other but with insufficient strength to prevent them from moving around randomly. Liquids have a higher density and are much less compressible than gases because the molecules in a liquid are closer together.

Diffusion occurs more slowly in liquids than in gases because the molecules in a liquid stick to each other and are not completely free to move.

A **solid** has a definite volume and definite shape. The kinetic model for a solid is a collection of molecules attracted to each other with sufficient strength to essentially lock them in place. Each molecule may vibrate, but it has an average position relative to its neighbors. If these positions form an ordered pattern, the solid is called **crystalline**. Otherwise, it is called **amorphous**. Solids have a high density and are almost incompressible because the molecules are close together. Diffusion occurs extremely slowly because the molecules almost never alter their position.

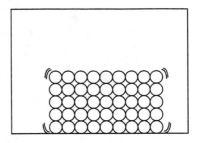

Phase changes occur when the relative importance of kinetic energy and intermolecular forces is altered sufficiently for a substance to change its state.

The transition from gas to liquid is called **condensation** and from liquid to gas is called **vaporization**. The transition from liquid to solid is called **freezing** and from solid to liquid is called **melting**. The transition from gas to solid is called **deposition** and from solid to gas is called **sublimation**.

Heat removed from a substance during condensation, freezing, or deposition permits new intermolecular bonds to form, and heat added to a substance during vaporization, melting, or sublimation breaks intermolecular bonds. During these phase transitions, this **latent heat** is removed or added with **no change in the temperature** of the substance because the heat is not being used to alter the speed of the molecules or the kinetic energy when they strike each other or the container walls. Latent heat alters intermolecular bonds.

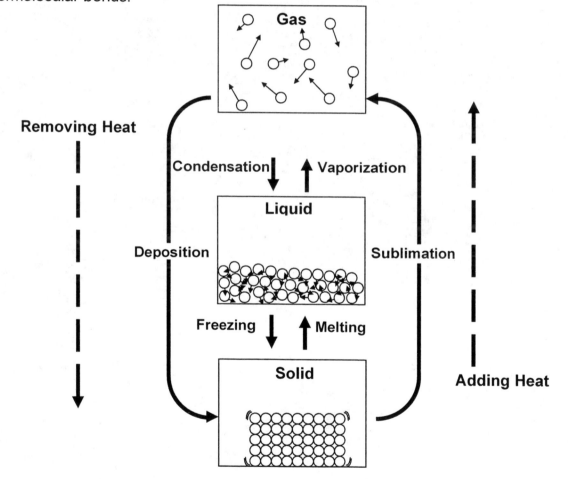

Skill 12.1e-Discuss the physical properties of matter including structure, melting point, boiling point, hardness, density, and conductivity

A **physical property** of matter is a property that can be determined without inducing a chemical change (see **Skill 11.1g**). The elemental percent composition of a substance (see **Skill 4.1b**) requires that the compound be broken down into its elements, and so it is a chemical property, not a physical one.

The term "structure" in chemistry usually refers to a chemical structure, meaning the spatial arrangement of atoms or its representation in a structural formula (see **Skill 6.1c**). This is a chemical property, not a physical property, so the CSET standard may be referring to physical structure in a broader sense. All matter has mass and takes up space with an associated size. Matter experiencing gravity has a weight. Most matter we encounter exists in one of three phases (see **Skill 12.1d**).

Melting point refers to the temperature at which a solid becomes a liquid. **Boiling ponint** refers to the temperature at which a liquid becomes a gas. Melting takes place when there is sufficient energy available to break the intermolecular forces that hold molecules together in a solid. Boiling occurs when there is enough energy available to break the intermolecular forces holding molecules together as a liquid. See **Skill 5.1b** and **Skill 12.1d**.

Hardness describes how difficult it is to scratch or indent a substance. The hardest natural substance is diamond.

Density measures the mass of a unit volume of material. See **Skill 12.1g**.

Electrical conductivity measures a material's ability to conduct an electric current. The high conductivity of metals is due to the presence of metallic bonds (see **Skill 1.3a**). The high conductivity of electrolyte solutions is due to the presence of ions in solution (see **Skill 4.1c**).

See **Skill 1.3d** for a list of additional physical properties.

Skill 12.1f-Recognize that all chemical substances are characterized by a unique set of physical properties

As a corollary to this statement, remember that two unknown pure substances that have different properties cannot be the same substance. Pure water at 1 atm will always have a boiling point of 100 °C. If a chemical substance has a different boiling point, it cannot be water.

Skill 12.1g-Define and calculate density, and predict whether an object will sink or float in a fluid

Density is a measure of mass per unit of volume. Units of g/cm^3 are commonly used. SI base units of kg/m^3 are also used. One g/cm^3 is equal to one thousand kg/m^3. Density (ρ) is calculated from mass (m) and volume (V) using the formula:

$$\rho = \frac{m}{V}.$$

The above expression is often manipulated to determine the mass of a substance if its volume and density are known ($m = \rho V$) or the volume of a substance if its mass and density are known ($V = m / \rho$).

The density of water at 4 °C is 1.000 g/cm^3. If an object is denser than the fluid in which it is immersed, it will sink. If it is less dense than the fluid, it will float. Ice floats on water because the solid phase of H$_2$O at 0 °C is less dense than the liquid phase. The solid phase for most other substances would sink at its melting point because the solid is more dense than the liquid.

Skill 12.1h-Explain that chemical changes in materials result in the formation of a new substance corresponding to the rearrangement of the atoms in molecules

A chemical change by definition (see **Skill 11.1g**) must rearrange atoms to form a new molecule. The idea that chemical changes are due to the rearrangement of atoms in molecules formed the basis of Dalton's atomic theory (see **Skill 1.2a**).

Skill 12.1i-Explain and apply principles of conservation of matter to chemical reactions, including balancing chemical equations

See Skill 2.1b. Skill 12.1i is required for certification in other branches of science besides chemistry. It is a subset of the content described in Skill 2.1b.

Skill 12.1j-Distinguish among acidic, basic, and neutral solutions by their observable properties

It was recognized centuries ago that many substances could be divided into the two general categories. **Acids** have a sour taste (as in lemon juice), dissolve many metals, and turn litmus paper red. **Bases** have a bitter taste (as in soaps), feel slippery, and turn litmus paper blue. The chemical reaction between an acid and a base is called **neutralization**. The products of neutralization reactions are neither acids nor bases. Litmus paper is an example of an **acid-base indicator**, a substance that changes color when changing from an acid to a base.

Skill 12.1k-Describe the construction and organization of the periodic table

The first periodic table was developed in 1869 by Dmitri Mendeleev. Mendeleev arranged the elements in order of increasing atomic mass into **columns of similar physical and chemical properties**. He then **predicted the existence and the properties of undiscovered elements** to fill the gaps in his table. These interpolations were treated with skepticism until three of Mendeleev's theoretical elements were discovered and were found to have the properties he predicted.

In the modern periodic table shown before Skill 1.1a, **elements are arranged in numerical order by atomic number** (see **Skill 1.2c**). The elements in a **column are known as a group**, and groups are numbered from 1 to 18. Older numbering styles used roman numerals and letters. **Elements with similar properties are called a family** or a **chemical series**. The modern table, like Mendeleev's, places elements with similar properties into columns. Families are called **group names** when they correspond to a single column. Individual families are discussed in detail in **Skill 1.1a.** and the final subsection of **Skill 1.1b**. **A row of the periodic table is known as a period**. Periods of the known elements are numbered from 1 to 7.

The periodic table is also organized to correspond to electron configurations within the atom. The table may be divided into blocks corresponding to the subshell of the orbital filled most recently by an electron using the building-up rule (See **Skill 1.1b**). Elements in the same column have similar properties because they have the same valence (outermost) electron configurations. These are the electrons that are most important in determining chemical properties.

Skill 12.1I-Based on position in the periodic table, predict which elements have characteristics of metals, semimetals, nonmetals, and inert gases

Elements in the periodic table are divided into the two categories of **metals** and **nonmetals** with a jagged line separating the two as shown in the figure. Elements near the line exhibit some properties of each and are called **metalloids** or **semimetals**.

The most metallic element is francium at the bottom left of the table, and the most nonmetallic is fluorine. The metallic character of elements within a group increases with period number. This means that **within a column, the more metallic elements are at**

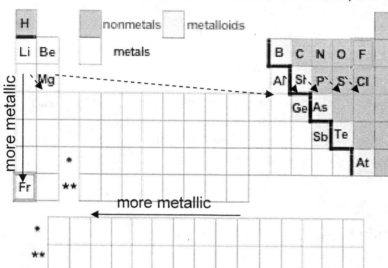

the bottom. The metallic character of elements within a period decreases with group number. Therefore, **within a row, the more metallic elements are on the left**. Among the main group atoms (see **Skill 1.1b**), **elements diagonal to each other** as indicated by the dashed arrows **have similar properties** due to a similar metallic character. The **noble gases** (group 18 elements) are nonmetals and are exceptions to the diagonal rule. Noble gases are **nearly chemically inert**. The heavier noble gases form a number of compounds with oxygen and fluorine such as KrF_2 and XeO_4

Physical properties relating to metallic character are summarized in the following table:

Element	Electrical/thermal conductivity	Malleable/ductile as solids?	Lustrous?	Melting point of oxides, hydrides, and halides
Metals	High	Yes	Yes	High
Metalloids	Intermediate. Altered by dopants (semiconductors)	No (brittle)	Varies	Varies (oxides). Low (hydrides, halides)
Nonmetals	Low (insulators)	No	No	Low

A summary of additional properties is provided in the final figure of **Skill 1.1c**.

Malleable materials can **be beaten into sheets**. **Ductile** materials can **be pulled into wires**. **Lustrous** materials **have a shine**. Oxides, hydrides, and halides are compounds with O, H, and halogens respectively.

Measures of intermolecular attractions other than melting point (see **Skill 1.3d**) are also higher for metal oxides, hydrides, and halides than for the nonmetal compounds. A dopant is a small quantity of an intentionally added impurity. The controlled movement of electrons in doped silicon semiconductors carries digital information in computer circuitry.

Skill 12.1m-Explain chemical reactivity using position on the periodic table

The most powerful chemical reactions between elements occur between metals and non-metals. This also corresponds to reactions between the most and least electronegative elements (see **Skill 1.3a**). Therefore, **in a reaction with a metal, the most reactive elements are the most nonmetallic elements** or compounds containing those elements. These elements are also the most electronegative. **In a reaction with a nonmetal, the most reactive elements are the most metallic** or least electronegative elements. The reactivity of elements may be described by a **reactivity series**: an ordered list with chemicals that react strongly at one end and nonreactive chemicals at the other. The following reactivity series is for metals reacting with oxygen:

Metal	K	Na	Ca	Mg	Al	Zn	Fe	Pb	Cu	Hg	Ag	Au
Reaction with O_2	Burns violently		Burns rapidly					Oxidizes slowly			No reaction	

Skill 12.1n-Predict and explain chemical bonding using elements' positions in the periodic table

There is a **periodicity in oxidation numbers** as shown in the table below for examples of oxides with the maximum oxidation number. Remember that an element may occur in different compounds in several different oxidation states.

Group	1	2	13	14	15	16	17	18
Oxide with maximum oxidation number	Li_2O	BeO	B_2O_3	CO_2	N_2O_5		Cl_2O_7	XeO_4
	Na_2O	MgO	Al_2O_3	SiO_2	P_2O_5	SO_3	Br_2O_7	
Oxidation number	+1	+2	+3	+4	+5	+6	+7	+8

They are called "oxidation numbers" because oxygen was the element of choice for reacting with materials when modern chemistry began, and the result was Mendeleev arranging his first table to look similar to this one.

Skill 12.1o-Recognize that inorganic and organic compounds (e.g., water, salt, carbohydrates, lipids, proteins, nucleic acids) are essential to processes within living systems

In the beginning of the 18th century, chemists thought that compounds from living organisms were so complex that they could only have been made through a transcendent "life-force." This hypothesis was called **vitalism**. Chemists named these compounds "organic" and tended to study only inorganic compounds. In 1828, Friedrich **Wöhler** synthesized the organic compound urea using the carbon in silver cyanide, proving that the vitalism hypothesis was wrong. Organic chemistry today refers to the chemistry of compounds containing carbon. For detailed information on amino acids, proteins, sugars, and polysaccharides, see **Skill 6.1d**.

Lipids

Lipids typically have **large hydrocarbons** as part of their structure and are **insoluble in water**. Animal fats and vegetable oils are **complex lipids** called **triacylglycerides**. These molecules contain three ester groups.

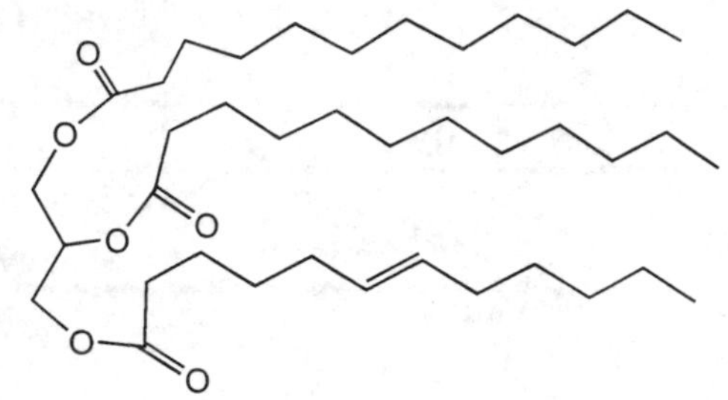

Fats such as the molecule above may be broken apart to yield **glycerol** and long-chain carboxylic acids (see **Skill 6.1b**) known as **fatty acids**. Glycerol is shown to the right and two fatty acids are shown below.

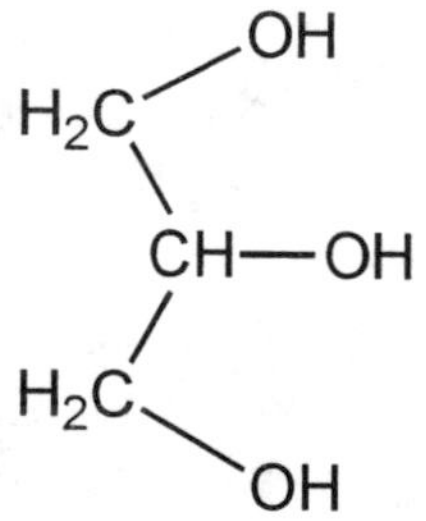

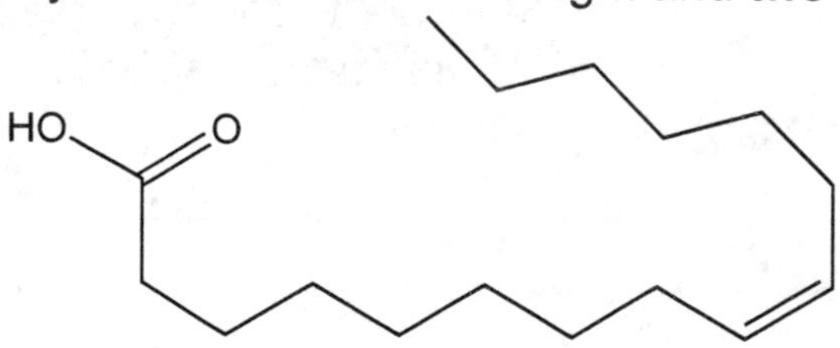

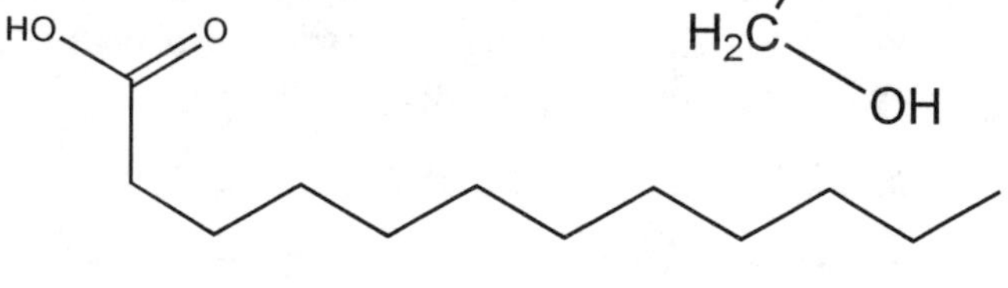

Classes of hydrocarbons are often applied to the corresponding fatty acid. **Saturated fat** refers to fatty acids containing a hydrocarbon chain with only single bonds as shown above on the right. **Unsaturated fat** refers to fatty acids containing one or more alkene group. If one alkene linkage is present on the hydrocarbon, it is **monounsaturated**. If more than one is present, it is **polyunsaturated**. Unsaturated fats are also described as *cis*– or *trans*– and may be conjugated. The molecule above on the left is a monounsaturated *cis*-fatty acid. Unsaturated fat in processed food is often converted to saturated fat by **hydrogenation**.

Simple lipids such as cholesterol (shown below) do not contain ester groups:

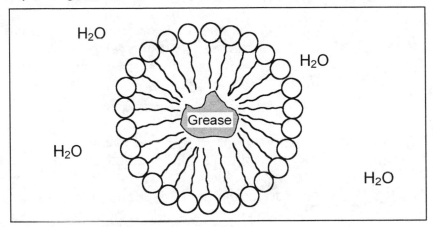

Many lipids like the fatty acids above have a long non-polar hydrocarbon "tail" region and a small polar "head" region. In water, the hydrocarbon is **hydrophobic** and the polar region is **hydrophilic**. See **Skill 4.1c** for a review of these terms.

Soaps and synthetic **detergents** clean materials because their molecules have these two regions. When they are dispersed in water, the hydrophilic heads face the water in an attempt to dissolve, but the hydrophobic tails are attracted to each other and surround any grease particulates. These spherical clusters are called **micelles**. The net effect is to disperse grease in water where it can be washed away.

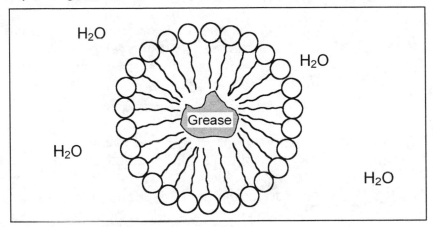

Lipid molecules in the membranes of cells form a **lipid bilayer** by lining up tail-to-tail in order to separate the space inside the cell from the extracellular environment.

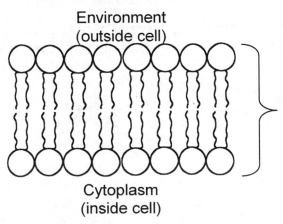

Nucleic Acids

Nucleotides form the building blocks of nucleic acids. A nucleotide is made up of a phosphate, a sugar, and an amine "base." An example is shown below:

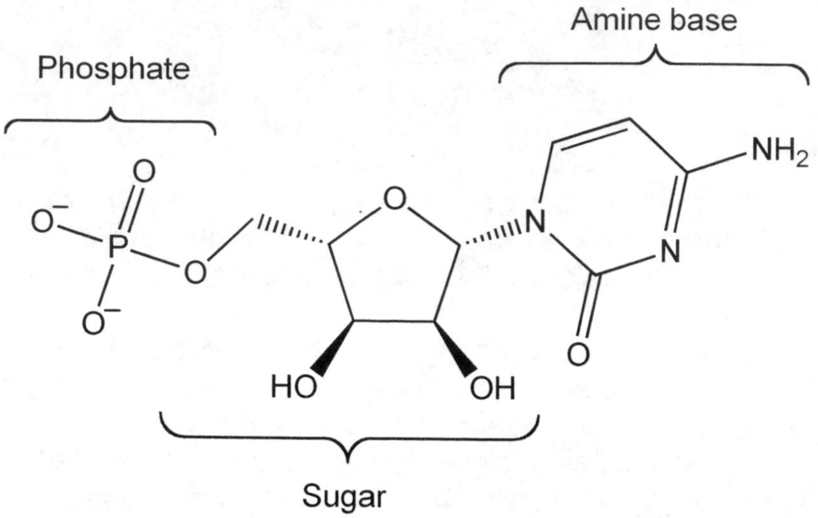

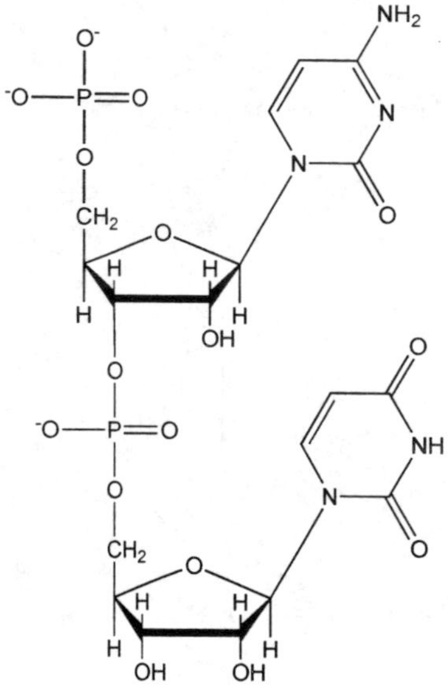

Living things use nucleic acids to carry genetic information based on the identity of the amine base present. This information is used to determine the amino acid sequence of every protein in the organism and it provides a blueprint for how the organism is made.

The phosphate of one nucleotide may form a covalent bond with the sugar residue of another to form a **dinucleotide** as shown on the left. Sugar-phosphate groups link to each other to form a helix "backbone" with the amine bases protruding outwards. Many nucleotides linked together in this way form **ribonucleic acid (RNA)** if the sugar is ribose and **deoxyribonucleic acid (DNA)** if the sugar is ribose lacking a hydroxyl group.

Amine bases on one nucleic acid molecule may form hydrogen bonds with bases on a second strand. For DNA, these two strands form the familiar **double-helix**.

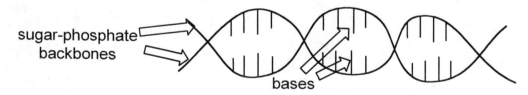

Skill 12.1p-Explain the central role of carbon in living system chemistry

Carbon is almost unique among elements in its ability to form long molecular chains and rings that may also include nitrogen, oxygen, halogens, and many other atoms. These molecules may be large enough to bend and fold into distinct shapes with non-polar and polar regions. The polar regions may contain positive charges, negative charges, or hydrogen-bond-forming atoms that are all able to interact with neighboring molecules in specific ways. These interactions perform a wide variety of functions such as altering the shape and composition of molecules. For more detailed information, see **Skill 6.1a**.

Part II: Subject Matter Skills and Abilities Applicable to the Content Domains in Science (all CSET exams)

Domain 1. Investigation and Experimentation

Skill 1.1 Question Formulation

The first step in scientific inquiry is posing a question to be answered. Next, one forms a hypothesis, and then conducts an experiment to test the hypothesis. Comparison between the predicted and observed results is the next step. Conclusions are then formed based on the analysis and it is determined whether the hypothesis is correct or incorrect. If incorrect, the next step is to form a new hypothesis and the process is repeated.

Let's use the following everyday situation as an example. Through the course of making breakfast, you bring three eggs from the refrigerator over to the stove. Your hands are full and you accidentally drop an egg on the floor, which immediately shatters all over the tile floor. As you clean up the mess you wonder if you had carried the eggs in their cardboard container, would they have broken if dropped? Similarly, if dropped would they have broken on a softer surface, for example linoleum?

a. Formulate and evaluate a viable hypothesis

Once the question is formulated take an educated guess about the answer to the problem or question. For our scientist above, a plausible hypothesis might be that even if dropped, the egg would not have broken if it had been enclosed in its protective cardboard box.

b. Recognize the value and role of observation prior to question formulation

The scientist conducting our imaginary egg experiment made observations prior to the experiment. He knows that eggshells are fragile, and that their interior is liquid. He also noted that his floor was made of tile, a hard surface, and that the broken egg had not been protected. His observations, however general they may have seemed, led him to create a viable question and an educated guess (hypothesis) about what he expected. While scientists often have laboratories set up to study a specific thing, it is likely that along the way they will find an unexpected result. It is always important to be open-minded and to look at all of the information. An open-minded approach to science provides room for more questioning, and, hence, more learning.

c. Recognize the iterative nature of questioning

The question stage of scientific inquiry involves repetition. By repeating the experiment you can discover whether or not you have reproducibility.

If results are reproducible, the hypothesis is valid. If the results are not reproducible, one has more questions to ask.

d. Given an experimental design, identify possible hypotheses that it may test

An experiment is proposed and performed with the sole objective of testing a hypothesis. You discover the aforementioned scientist conducting an experiment with the following characteristics. He has two rows each set up with four stations. The first row has a piece of tile as the base at each station. The second row has a piece of linoleum as the base at each station. The scientist has eight eggs and is prepared to drop one over each station. What is he testing? He is trying to answer whether or not the egg is more likely to break when dropped over one material as opposed to the other. His hypothesis might have been: The egg will be less likely to break when dropped on linoleum.

Skill 1.2 Planning a Scientific Investigation (including Experimental Design)

a. Given a hypothesis, formulate an investigation or experimental design to test that hypothesis

Suppose our junior scientist wants to look at his initial question, "if you had carried the eggs in their cardboard container, would they have broken if dropped?" A sensible hypothesis to this question would be that an egg would be less likely to break if it was dropped in its cardboard container, than if it were unprotected. Because reproducibility is important, we need to set up multiple identical stations, or use the same station for repeatedly conducting the same experiment. Either way it is key that everything is identical. If the scientist wants to study the break rate for one egg in it's container, then it needs to be just one egg dropped each time in an identical way. The investigator should systematically walk to each station and drop an egg over each station and record the results. The first four times, the egg should be dropped without enclosing it in a cardboard carton. This is the control. It is a recreation of what happened accidentally in the kitchen and one would expect the results to be the same- an egg dropped onto tile will break. The next four times, the egg should be dropped nestled within its original, store manufactured, cardboard container. One would expect that the egg would not break, or would break less often under these conditions.

b. Evaluate an experimental design for its suitability to test a given hypothesis

When designing an experiment, one needs to clearly define what one is testing. One also needs to consider the question asked. The more limited the question, the easier it is to set up an experiment to answer it.

Ideally, if an egg were dropped, the egg would be safest when dropped in a protective carton over a soft surface. However, one should not measure multiple variables at once. Studying multiple variables at once makes the results difficult to analyze. How would the investigator discern which variable was responsible for the result? When evaluating experimental design, make sure to look at the number of variables, how clearly they were defined, and how accurately they were measured. Also, was the experiment applicable? Did it make sense and address the hypothesis?

c. Distinguish between variable and controlled parameters

The procedure used to obtain data is important to the outcome. Experiments consist of **controls** and **variables**. A control is the experiment run under normal conditions. The variable includes a factor that is changed. In biology, the variable may be light, temperature, pH, time, etc. The differences in tested variables may be used to make a prediction or form a hypothesis. Only one variable should be tested at a time. One would not alter both the temperature and pH of the experimental subject.
An **independent variable** is one that is changed or manipulated by the researcher. This could be the amount of light given to a plant or the temperature at which bacteria is grown. The **dependent variable** is that which is influenced by the independent variable.

Skill 1.3 Observation and Data Collection

a. Identify changes in natural phenomena over time without manipulating the phenomena (e.g. a tree limb, a grove of trees, a stream, a hill slope).

Scientists identify changes in natural phenomena over time using basic tools of measurement and observation. Scientists measure growth of plants by measuring plant dimensions at different time intervals, changes in plant and animal populations by counting, and changes in environmental conditions by observation. The following are four examples of natural phenomena, and the observation techniques used to measure change in each case.

To identify change in a tree limb, we measure the dimensions (length, circumference) of the limb at different time intervals. In addition, we can study the types and amount of organisms growing on the limb by observing a small sample and applying the observations to make estimations about the entire limb. Finally, we can watch for the presence of disease or bacterial infection by observing the color and consistency of the limb and any changes over time.

To identify change in a grove of trees, we employ similar techniques as used in the observation of a tree limb. First, we measure the size of the trees at different time intervals.

If the grove contains many trees, we may measure only a representative sample of trees and apply the results to make conjectures about the grove population. Finally, we closely monitor the trees for changes that may indicate disease or infection.

To identify change in a stream, we measure and observe characteristics of both the stream itself and the organisms living in it. First, we measure the width and depth of the stream at different time intervals to monitor erosion. Second, we observe the water level at different time intervals to monitor the effect of weather patterns. Finally, using sampling techniques, we observe and measure the types and number of organisms present in the stream and how these characteristics change over time.

To identify change on a hill slope, we measure the angle and dimensions of the slope at different time intervals to monitor the effects of erosion by wind and rain. In addition, we use sampling techniques to make generalizations about the organisms living on the slope. Finally, we can monitor how the types and amounts of vegetation on the slope change in relation to the change in the angle of the slope (i.e. determine which types of plants have the ability to grow in certain conditions).

b. Analyze the locations, sequences, and time intervals that are characteristic of natural phenomena (e.g. locations of planets over time, succession of species in an ecosystem).

One of the main goals of science is the study and explanation of natural phenomena. When studying natural phenomena, scientists describe the characteristic locations, sequences, and time intervals. Examples of natural phenomena studied by scientists include the locations of planets over time and the succession of species in an ecosystem.

The eight planets of the solar system (Pluto was formerly included as a planet but has been removed as of Summer 2006) orbit the sun in a specific sequence. The time it takes to complete an orbit of the Sun is different for each planet. In addition, we can determine the location of each planet in relation to the Sun and to each other using mathematical models and charts.

Mercury orbits closest to the sun, followed by Venus, Earth, Mars, Jupiter, Saturn, Uranus, and Neptune. Neptune is farthest from the Sun for 20 of every 248 years. Planets will never collide because one is always higher than the other, even when their orbits do intersect.

The amount of time a planet takes to complete one orbit of the Sun increases as the distance from the Sun increases. This value, called the sidereal period, ranges from 0.241 years for Mercury to 248.1 years.

The synodic period measures the amount of time it takes for a planet to return to the same point in the sky as observed from Earth. Mercury has the shortest synodic period of 116 days while Mars has the longest of 780 days. The synodic periods of Jupiter, Saturn, Uranus, and Neptune are similar, slightly less than 400 days for each.

Succession of species is the change in the type and number of plants, animals, and microorganisms that occurs periodically in all ecosystems. The two types of succession are primary and secondary. Primary succession describes the creation and subsequent development of a new, unoccupied habitat (e.g. a lava flow). Secondary succession describes the disruption of an existing community (e.g. fire, human tampering, flood) and the response of the community to the disruption. Succession is usually a very long process. New communities often take hundreds or thousands of years to reach a fully developed state (climax community). And, while succession in climax communities is minimal, environmental disruption can easily restart the succession process.

In general, simple organisms (e.g. bacteria, small plants) dominate new communities and prepare the environment for the development of larger, more complex species. For example, the dominant vegetation of an empty field will progress sequentially from grasses to small shrubs to soft wood trees to hard wood trees. We can observe and measure succession in two ways. First, we can measure the changes in a single community over time.

Second, we can observe and compare similar communities at different stages of development. We are limited in the amount of data we can gather using the first method because of the slow nature of the succession process. The techniques used to observe succession include fossil observation, geological study, and environmental sampling.

c. Select and use appropriate tools and technology (e.g. computer-linked probes, spreadsheets, graphing calculators) to perform tests, collect data, analyze relationships, and display data.

Scientists use a variety of tools and technologies to perform tests, collect and display data, and analyze relationships. Examples of commonly used tools include computer-linked probes, spreadsheets, and graphing calculators.

Scientists use computer-linked probes to measure various environmental factors including temperature, dissolved oxygen, pH, ionic concentration, and pressure. The advantage of computer-linked probes, as compared to more traditional observational tools, is that the probes automatically gather data and present it in an accessible format. This property of computer-linked probes eliminates the need for constant human observation and manipulation.

Scientists use spreadsheets to organize, analyze, and display data. For example, conservation ecologists use spreadsheets to model population growth and development, apply sampling techniques, and create statistical distributions to analyze relationships. Spreadsheet use simplifies data collection and manipulation and allows the presentation of data in a logical and understandable format.

Graphing calculators are another technology with many applications to science. For example, biologists use algebraic functions to analyze growth, development and other natural processes. Graphing calculators can manipulate algebraic data and create graphs for analysis and observation. In addition, biologists use the matrix function of graphing calculators to model problems in genetics. The use of graphing calculators simplifies the creation of graphical displays including histograms, scatter plots, and line graphs. Scientists can also transfer data and displays to computers for further analysis. Finally, scientists connect computer-linked probes, used to collect data, to graphing calculators to ease the collection, transmission, and analysis of data.

d. Evaluate the precision, accuracy, and reproducibility of data

Accuracy is the degree of conformity of a measured, calculated quantity to its actual (true) value. Precision also called reproducibility or repeatability and is the degree to which further measurements or calculations will show the same or similar results.

Accuracy is the degree of veracity while precision is the degree of reproducibility. The best analogy to explain accuracy and precision is the target comparison. Repeated measurements are compared to arrows that are fired at a target. Accuracy describes the closeness of arrows to the bull's eye at the target center. Arrows that strike closer to the bull's eye are considered more accurate.

e. Identify and analyze possible reasons for inconsistent results, such as sources of error or uncontrolled conditions

Reproducibility is highly important when considering science. If results are not reproducible, they are usually not given much credit, regardless of the hypothesis. For this reason, we pay close attention to minimizing sources of error. Examples of common sources of error might be contamination or an improperly mixed buffer. In addition, one should remember that scientists are humans, and human error is always a possibility.

All experimental uncertainty is due to either random errors or systematic errors. Random errors are statistical fluctuations in the measured data due to the precision limitations of the measurement device.

Random errors usually result from the experimenter's inability to take the same measurement in exactly the same way to get exactly the same number. Systematic errors, by contrast, are reproducible inaccuracies that are consistently in the same direction. Systematic errors are often due to a problem that persists throughout the entire experiment. Systematic and random errors refer to problems associated with making measurements. Mistakes made in the calculations or in reading the instrument are not considered in error analysis.

f. Identify and communicate sources of unavoidable experimental error.

Unavoidable experimental error is the random error inherent in scientific experiments regardless of the methods used. One source of unavoidable error is measurement and the use of measurement devices. Using measurement devices is an imprecise process because it is often impossible to accurately read measurements. For example, when using a ruler to measure the length of an object, if the length falls between markings on the ruler, we must estimate the true value. Another source of unavoidable error is the randomness of population sampling and the behavior of any random variable. For example, when sampling a population we cannot guarantee that our sample is completely representative of the larger population. In addition, because we cannot constantly monitor the behavior of a random variable, any observations necessarily contain some level of unavoidable error.

g. Recognize the issues of statistical variability and explain the need for controlled tests.

Statistical variability is the deviation of an individual in a population from the mean of the population. Variability is inherent in biology because living things are innately unique. For example, the individual weights of humans vary greatly from the mean weight of the population. Thus, when conducting experiments involving the study of living things, we must control for innate variability. Control groups are identical to the experimental group in every way with the exception of the variable being studied. Comparing the experimental group to the control group allows us to determine the effects of the manipulated variable in relation to statistical variability.

h. Know and evaluate the safety issues when designing an experiment and implement appropriate solutions to safety problems

All science labs should contain the following items of **safety equipment**. Those marked with an asterisk are requirements by state laws.

* fire blanket which is visible and accessible
*Ground Fault Circuit Interrupters (GCFI) within two feet of water supplies
*signs designating room exits
*emergency shower providing a continuous flow of water

*emergency eye wash station which can be activated by the foot or forearm
*eye protection for every student and a means of sanitizing equipment
*emergency exhaust fans providing ventilation to the outside of the building
*master cut-off switches for gas, electric and compressed air. Switches must have
 permanently attached handles. Cut-off switches must be clearly labeled.
*an ABC fire extinguisher
*storage cabinets for flammable materials
-chemical spill control kit
-fume hood with a motor which is spark proof
-protective laboratory aprons made of flame retardant material
-signs which will alert to potential hazardous conditions
-containers for broken glassware, flammables, corrosives, and waste. Containers
 should be labeled.

Students should wear safety goggles when performing dissections, heating, or while using acids and bases. Hair should always be tied back and objects should never be placed in the mouth. Food should not be consumed while in the laboratory. Hands should always be washed before and after laboratory experiments. In case of an accident, eye washes and showers should be used for eye contamination or a chemical spill that covers the student's body. Small chemical spills should only be contained and cleaned by the teacher.

Kitty litter or a chemical spill kit should be used to clean spills. For large spills, the school administration and the local fire department should be notified. Biological spills should also be handled only by the teacher. Contamination with biological waste can be cleaned by using bleach when appropriate.
Accidents and injuries should always be reported to the school administration and local health facilities. The severity of the accident or injury will determine the course of action to pursue.

It is the responsibility of the teacher to provide a safe environment for their students. Proper supervision greatly reduces the risk of injury and a teacher should never leave a class for any reason without providing alternate supervision. After an accident, two factors are considered; **foreseeability** and **negligence**. Foreseeability is the anticipation that an event may occur under certain circumstances. Negligence is the failure to exercise ordinary or reasonable care. Safety procedures should be a part of the science curriculum and a well managed classroom is important to avoid potential lawsuits.

i. Appropriately employ a variety of print and electronic resources (e.g. the World Wide Web) to collect information and evidence as part of a research project.

Scientists use print and electronic resources to collect information and evidence. Gathering information from scientific literature is a necessary element in successful research project design. Scientific journals, a major source of scientific information, provide starting points for experimental design and points of comparison in the interpretation of experimental results. Examples of important scientific journals are *Science*, *Nature*, and *Cell*. Scientists use the World Wide Web to search and access scientific journal articles through databases such as PubMed, JSTOR, and Google Scholar. In addition, the World Wide Web is a rich source of basic background information useful in the design and implementation of research projects. Examples of relevant online resources include scientific encyclopedias, general science websites, and research laboratory homepages.

j. Assess the accuracy validity and reliability of information gathered from a variety of sources

Because people often attempt to use scientific evidence in support of political or personal agendas, the ability to evaluate the credibility of scientific claims is a necessary skill in today's society. In evaluating scientific claims made in the media, public debates, and advertising, one should follow several guidelines.

First, scientific, peer-reviewed journals are the most accepted source for information on scientific experiments and studies. One should carefully scrutinize any claim that does not reference peer-reviewed literature.

Second, the media and those with an agenda to advance (advertisers, debaters, etc.) often overemphasize the certainty and importance of experimental results. One should question any scientific claim that sounds fantastical or overly certain.

Finally, knowledge of experimental design and the scientific method is important in evaluating the credibility of studies. For example, one should look for the inclusion of control groups and the presence of data to support the given conclusions.

Skill 1.4 Data Analysis/Graphing

a. Construct appropriate graphs from data and develop qualitative and quantitative statements about relationships between variables

Graphing is an important skill to visually display collected data for analysis. The two types of graphs most commonly used are the **line graph** and the **bar graph** (histogram).

Line graphs are set up to show two variables represented by one point on the graph. The X-axis is the horizontal axis and represents the dependent variable. Dependent variables are those that would be present independently of the experiment. A common example of a dependent variable is time. Time proceeds regardless of anything else going on. The Y-axis is the vertical axis and represents the independent variable. Independent variables are manipulated by the experiment, such as the amount of light, or the height of a plant. Graphs should be calibrated at equal intervals. If one space represents one day, the next space may not represent ten days. A "best fit" line is drawn to join the points and may not include all the points in the data. Axes must always be labeled. A good title will describe both the dependent and the independent variable. Bar graphs are set up similarly in regards to axes, but points are not plotted. Instead, the dependent variable is set up as a bar where the X-axis intersects with the Y-axis. Each bar is a separate item of data and is not joined by a continuous line.

When drawing conclusions from graphs, one can make quantitative or qualitative statements. Quantitative is derived from quantity (numerical, precise) and qualitative (impressive) is derived from quality. For example, stating that the median is 12 would be a quantitative assessment.

The type of graphic representation used to display observations depends on the data that is collected. **Line graphs** are used to compare different sets of related data or to predict data that has not yet been measured. An example of a line graph would be comparing the rate of activity of different enzymes at varying temperatures. A **bar graph** or **histogram** is used to compare different items and make comparisons based on this data. An example of a bar graph would be comparing the ages of children in a classroom. A **pie chart** is useful when organizing data as part of a whole. A good use for a pie chart would be displaying the percent of time students spend on various after school activities.

b. Recognize the slope of the linear graph as the constant in the relationship y=kx and apply this principle in interpreting graphs constructed from data

Analyzing graphs is a useful method for determining the mathematical relationship between the dependent and independent variables of an experiment. The usefulness of the method lies in the fact that the variables on the axes of a straight-line graph are represented by the expression, $y = m*x + b$, where m=the slope of the line, b=the y intercept of the line. This equation works only if the data fit a straight-line graph. Thus, once the data set has been collected, and modified, and plotted to achieve a straight-line graph, the mathematical equation can be derived.

c. Apply simple mathematical relationships to determine a missing quantity in an algebraic expression, given the two remaining terms (e.g., speed = distance/time, density = mass/volume, force = pressure x area, volume = area x height)

Science and mathematics are related. Science data is strongest when accurate, and is therefore described in terms of units. To acquire proper units, one must apply math skills. Some common examples include speed, density, force, and volume. Let us look at density –

$D = m/v$
Where
D = density g/cm
m = mass in grams
v = volume in cm

One would substitute known quantities for the alphabetical symbols. It is absolutely important to write the appropriate units e.g., g (gram), cm (centimeter) etc. This is fundamental algebra.

The second example is the formula for calculating momentum of an object.

M = mass (kg) times velocity (meters/second)
$M = mv$
The units of momentum are kg (m/s)

d. Determine whether a relationship on a given graph is linear or non-linear and determine the appropriateness of extrapolating the data.

The individual data points on the graph of a linear relationship cluster around a line of best fit. In other words, a relationship is linear if we can sketch a straight line that roughly fits the data points. Consider the following examples of linear and non-linear relationships.

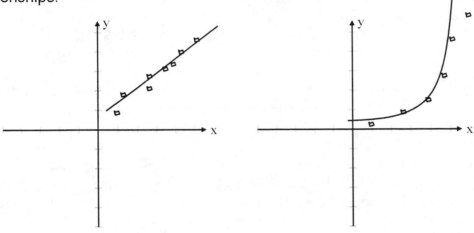

Linear Relationship   Non-Linear Relationship

Note that the non-linear relationship, an exponential relationship in this case, appears linear in parts of the curve. In addition, contrast the preceding graphs to the graph of a data set that shows no relationship between variables.

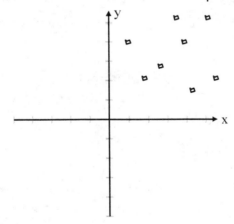

Extrapolation is the process of estimating data points outside a known set of data points. When extrapolating data of a linear relationship, we extend the line of best fit beyond the known values. The extension of the line represents the estimated data points. Extrapolating data is only appropriate if we are relatively certain that the relationship is indeed linear.

For example, the death rate of an emerging disease may increase rapidly at first and level off as time goes on. Thus, extrapolating the death rate as if it were linear would yield inappropriately high values at later times.

Similarly, extrapolating certain data in a strictly linear fashion, with no restrictions, may yield obviously inappropriate results. For instance, if the number of plant species in a forest were decreasing with time in a linear fashion, extrapolating the data set to infinity would eventually yield a negative number of species, which is clearly unreasonable.

e. Solve scientific problems by using quadratic equations and simple trigonometric, exponential, and logarithmic functions.

Scientists use mathematical tools and equations to model and solve scientific problems. Solving scientific problems often involves the use of quadratic, trigonometric, exponential, and logarithmic functions.

Quadratic equations take the standard form $ax^2 + bx + c = 0$. The most appropriate method of solving quadratic equations in scientific problems is the use of the quadratic formula. The quadratic formula produces the solutions of a standard form quadratic equation.

$$x = \frac{-b \pm \sqrt{b^2 - 4ac}}{2a} \quad \text{\{Quadratic Formula\}}$$

One common application of quadratic equations is the description of biochemical reaction equilibriums. Consider the following problem.

Example 1

80.0 g of ethanoic acid (MW = 60g) reacts with 85.0 g of ethanol (MW = 46g) until equilibrium. The equilibrium constant is 4.00. Determine the amounts of ethyl acetate and water produced at equilibrium.

$$CH_3COOH + CH_3CH_2OH = CH_3CO_2C_2H_5 + H_2O$$

The equilibrium constant, K, describes equilibrium of the reaction, relating the concentrations of products to reactants.

$$K = \frac{[CH_3CO_2C_2H_5][H_2O]}{[CH_3CO_2H][CH_3CH_2OH]} = 4.00$$

The equilibrium values of reactants and products are listed in the following table.

	CH₃COOH	CH₃CH₂OH	CH₃CO₂C₂H₅	H₂O
Initial	80/60 = 1.33 mol	85/46 = 1.85 mol	0	0
Equilibrium	1.33 – x	1.85 – x	x	x

Thus, K = $\dfrac{[x][x]}{[1.33-x][1.85-x]} = \dfrac{x^2}{2.46-3.18x+x^2} = 4.00$.

Rearrange the equation to produce a standard form quadratic equation.

$$\frac{x^2}{2.46-3.18x+x^2} = 4.00$$

$$x^2 = 4.00(2.46-3.18x+x^2) = 9.84 - 12.72x + 4x^2$$

$$0 = 3x^2 - 12.72x + 9.84$$

Use the quadratic formula to solve for x.

$$x = \frac{-(-12.72)\pm\sqrt{(-12.72)^2 - 4(3)(9.84)}}{2(3)} = 3.22 \text{ or } 1.02$$

3.22 is not an appropriate answer, because we started with only 3.18 moles of reactants. Thus, the amount of each product produced at equilibrium is 1.02 moles.

Scientists use trigonometric functions to define angles and lengths. For example, field biologists can use trigonometric functions to estimate distances and directions. The basic trigonometric functions are sine, cosine, and tangent. Consider the following triangle describing these relationships.

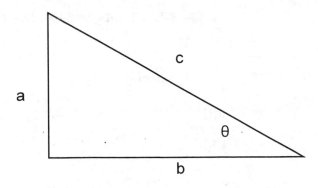

$$\sin\theta = \frac{a}{c}, \cos\theta = \frac{b}{c}, \tan\theta = \frac{a}{b}$$

Exponential functions are useful in modeling many scientific phenomena. For example, scientists use exponential functions to describe bacterial growth and radioactive decay. The general form of exponential equations is $f(x) = Ca^x$ (C is a constant). Consider the following problem involving bacterial growth.

Example 2

Determine the number of bacteria present in a culture inoculated with a single bacterium after 24 hours if the bacterial population doubles every 2 hours. Use $N(t) = N_0 e^{kt}$ as a model of bacterial growth where N(t) is the size of the population at time t, N_0 is the initial population size, and k is the growth constant.

We must first determine the growth constant, k. At t = 2, the size of the population doubles from 1 to 2. Thus, we substitute and solve for k.

$$2 = 1(e^{2k})$$

$$\ln 2 = \ln e^{2k} \qquad \text{Take the natural log of each side.}$$

$$\ln 2 = 2k(\ln e) = 2k \qquad \ln e = 1$$

$$k = \frac{\ln 2}{2} \qquad \text{Solve for k.}$$

The population size at t = 24 is

$$N(24) = e^{(\frac{\ln 2}{2})24} = e^{12\ln 2} = 4096 .$$

Finally, logarithmic functions have many applications to science and biology. One simple example of a logarithmic application is the pH scale. Scientists define pH as follows.

pH = - $\log_{10}$ [H^+], where [H^+] is the concentration of hydrogen ions

Thus, we can determine the pH of a solution with a [H^+] value of 0.0005 mol/L by using the logarithmic formula.

pH = - $\log_{10}$ [0.0005] = 3.3

Skill 1.5 Drawing Conclusions and Communicating Explanations

The state of California needs to ensure that its licensed teachers are capable of the list below. These items are not items that can be explained in essay format; rather they are an accumulation of your years of learning. You will be able to find correlations with these items in other areas of this manual.

a. Draw appropriate and logical conclusions from data
b. Communicate the logical connection among hypotheses, science concepts, tests conducted, data collected, and conclusions drawn from the scientific evidence
c. Communicate the steps and results of an investigation in written reports and oral presentations
d. Recognize whether evidence is consistent with a proposed explanation
e. Construct appropriate visual representations of scientific phenomenon and processes (e.g., motion of Earth's plates, cell structure)
f. Read topographic and geologic maps for evidence provided on the maps and construct and interpret a simple scale map

Domain 2. Nature of Science

Skill 2.1 Scientific Inquiry

a. Distinguish among the terms hypothesis, theory, and prediction as used in scientific investigations

Science may be defined as a body of knowledge that is systematically derived from study, observations, and experimentation. Its goal is to identify and establish principles and theories that may be applied to solve problems. Pseudoscience, on the other hand, is a belief that is not warranted. There is no scientific methodology or application. Some of the more classic examples of pseudoscience include witchcraft, alien encounters or any topic that is explained by hearsay.

Scientific theory and experimentation must be repeatable. It is also possible to be disproved and is capable of change. Science depends on communication, agreement, and disagreement among scientists. It is composed of theories, laws, and hypotheses.

theory - the formation of principles or relationships which have been verified and accepted.

law - an explanation of events that occur with uniformity under the same conditions (laws of nature, law of gravitation).

hypothesis - an unproved theory or educated guess followed by research to best explain a phenomenon. A theory is a proven hypothesis.

Science is limited by the available technology. An example of this would be the relationship of the discovery of the cell and the invention of the microscope. As our technology improves, more hypotheses will become theories and possibly laws. Science is also limited by the data that is able to be collected. Data may be interpreted differently on different occasions. Science limitations cause explanations to be changeable as new technologies emerge.

The first step in scientific inquiry is posing a question to be answered. Next, a hypothesis is formed to provide a plausible explanation. An experiment is then proposed and performed to test this hypothesis. A comparison between the predicted and observed results is the next step. Conclusions are then formed and it is determined whether the hypothesis is correct or incorrect. If incorrect, the next step is to form a new hypothesis and the process is repeated.

b. Evaluate the usefulness, limitations, and interdisciplinary and cumulative nature of scientific evidence as it relates to the development of models and theories as representations of reality

All evidence can be manipulated by the presenter for their own purposes. This is why we stress that one must carefully evaluate resources. For instance, when reading a scientific article: Is it published in a well known journal, does it use controls, does it make sense, is the experiment clearly explained, are the results reproducible? One must also recognize the limitations of research. An experiment is more clearly analyzed if it only has one variable. Would the research still be true if another variable, for example, heat, time, or substrate were changed? One must consider the conditions under which the research was conducted. Were the most advanced technological machines used, or would there be a more applicable way to study the issue? For example, no one realized there was more to know about microscopic life until microscopy became more advanced. We now use scanning electron microscopes (SEM's), making light microscopes somewhat obsolete, and opening our eyes to a whole new level of thoroughness. As technology changes, so too does our knowledge and our awareness of reality. Galileo was a major scientist of his time (often referred to as the father of science) and used mathematics to properly describe scientific events. For all of his great efforts, though, as our machines have grown in power, we have had to rethink some of his theories. His improvements on the telescope enabled him to locate and accurately name many planets, stars, and systems. He was unable, however, to correctly ascertain the orbits of planets and the genesis of tides. Sir Isaac Newton expounded upon previous works, including Galileo's, when creating his laws of physics. Thus, tides were finally explained accurately, through an accumulation of knowledge.

c. Recognize that when observations do not agree with an accepted scientific theory, either the observations are mistaken or fraudulent, or the accepted theory is erroneous or incorrect

Sir Isaac Newton must have sensed that Galileo's tide theory didn't make sense- it didn't hold up to his observations. He had the opportunity, like present day scientists, to review his observations for error, or find a better explanation. One must note, though, that better in this case must be scientifically accurate in order to be impressive to peers specializing in science.

d. Understand that reproducibility of data is critical to the scientific endeavor

In order to have your theory accepted, it must be accurate and clearly derived. This means that another scientist could recreate your experiment from your notes, find similar data, and draw the same conclusions. In this way the validity of science is substantiated.

e. Recognize that science is a self-correcting process that eventually identifies misconceptions and experimental biases

The scientific process encourages periodic reassessment. The conclusion step allows one to examine the hypothesis as it relates to the experimental data. At this point, one can find positive correlations or discord. When results are unexpected, one should revisit all possible sources of error. If an error is not found to explain the results, one can reconsider the hypothesis and also think about other possibilities. This is why experimentation often results in further experimentation.

> **Notice: For those of you using the state of California topical guide, please note that they omit letters f and g. XAMonline has taken that fact into account and properly sequenced the letters.**

f. Recognize that an inquiring mind is at the heart of the scientific method and that doing science involves thinking critically about the evidence presented, the usefulness of models, and the limitations of theories

Science is not merely about creating; it is also about assessment and solutions. Science can be thought of as a loop. One questions something, and creates an experiment to study it. One can learn from this evidence, and then ask more questions. In depth learning involves looking at the experimental data from all angles and continuing to seek knowledge. Learning in depth does not occur by looking at something superficially or by taking someone else's data as 'proof.' Go one step further: analyze the evidence as if you were searching for a problem- maybe there won't be one, but you will be more likely to find it if there is!

g. Recognize that theories are judged by how well they explain observations and predict results and that when they represent new ideas that are counter to mainstream ideas they often encounter vigorous criticism

If a theory explains a phenomenon well, it is worth considering, even if it turns out to be incorrect later on. The problem with this is two fold. First, a person can use a theory to push their own beliefs. This is the case with people seeing what they want to see, and then forming theories based around their opinions. An example would be if a scientist expected certain results, and then found ways to skew the results to match his theory. A theory based upon opinions will soon be seen as transparent and will be dismissed because it has no pertinent data to support it. Even if a theory is developed well, it still may not be readily accepted. A new theory is almost always difficult to introduce to an established community. To have a theory hold up to scrutiny, the author must have accurate data. Second, the author must continue to publicize the information. Just because a theory is not commonplace, does not mean it is incorrect. Novel ideas often become cornerstones in understanding, but it doesn't happen overnight. If the experiment has reproducible results and strong mathematics, people will eventually be swayed.

h. Recognize that when observations, data, or experimental results do not agree, the unexpected results are not necessarily mistakes; to discard the unusual in order to reach the expected is to guarantee that nothing but what is expected will ever be seen

Often, results other than what were expected are from an error. However, this is not always the case. Consider a scientist who has double checked his work multiple times and can find no errors. He cannot explain what has happened except to assume that his theory was wrong. Maybe there is a fundamental scientific phenomenon that has yet to be explained and he couldn't possibly have known. Discoveries can occur in this way. If the scientist were to give up, he and society would lose the opportunity to learn something new. If the scientist opens his mind to the discovery, there are limitless possibilities for learning.

i. Know why curiosity, honesty, openness, and skepticism are so highly regarded in science and how they are incorporated into the way science is carried out

Curiosity fuels research. It prompts the questions that turn into scientific inquiry. Honesty is paramount to the scientific way. To put the research out there, and be true in your report of the findings, is to help mankind and cooperate in scientific endeavors. While antonyms, openness and skepticism are both necessary in the field of research. One should be humble. One should be open to others' ideas, and open to their own unexpected findings, but be critical in evaluation of the work as it was conducted. It is key to incorporate all of these traits and to conduct yourself in a respectable manner.

Skill 2.2 Scientific Ethics

To understand scientific ethics, we need to have a clear understanding of ethics. Ethics is defined as a system of public, general rules for guiding human conduct. The rules are general because they are supposed to all people at all times and they are public because they are not secret codes or practices.

Philosophers have given a number of moral theories to justify moral rules, which range from utilitarianism (a theory of ethics that prescribes the quantitative maximization of good consequences for a population. It is a form of consequentialism. This theory was proposed by Mozi, a Chinese philosopher who lived during BC 471-381), Kantianism (a theory proposed by Immanuel Kant, a German philosopher who lived during 1724-1804, which ascribes intrinsic value to rational beings and is the philosophical foundation of contemporary human rights) to social contract theory (a view of the ancient Greeks which states that the person's moral and or political obligations are dependent upon a contract or agreement between them to form society).

The following are some of the guiding principles of scientific ethics:

1. Scientific Honesty: not to fabricate or misinterpret data for personal gain
2. Caution: to avoid errors and sloppiness in all scientific experimentation
3. Credit: to give credit where credit is due and not to copy
4. Responsibility: only to report reliable information to the public and not to mislead in the name of science
5. Freedom: freedom to criticize old ideas, question new research and freedom to research

a. Understand that honesty is at the core of scientific ethics; first and foremost is the honest and accurate reporting of procedures used and data collected.

Scientists are expected to show good conduct in their scientific pursuits. Conduct here refers to all aspects of scientific activity including experimentation, testing, education, data evaluation, data analysis, data storing, peer review, government funding, the staff, etc.

b. Know that all scientists are obligated to evaluate the safety of an investigation and ensure the safety of those performing the experiment

As a teacher, the safety of your classroom is your responsibility. One should make every effort to ensure students' safety. You will need to be aware of all potential safety concerns. Advance preparation will prepare you to take the necessary precautions related to the specific experiment. You should use the applicable MSDS and check pertinent regulations (at your place of employment as well as on the state/national levels). It will be necessary to take foreseeability and negligence into consideration. I t is the responsibility of the scientist to make sure that all organisms associated with the project are kept safe. This refers to both people and animals.

c. Know the procedures for respectful treatment of all living organisms in experimentation and other investigations

No dissections may be performed on living mammalian vertebrates or birds. Lower order life and invertebrates may be used. Biological experiments may be done with all animals except mammalian vertebrates or birds. No physiological harm may result to the animal. All animals housed and cared for in the school must be handled in a safe and humane manner. Animals are not to remain on school premises during extended vacations unless adequate care is provided. Any instructor who intentionally refuses to comply with the laws may be suspended or dismissed.

Pathogenic organisms must never be used for experimentation. Students should adhere to the following rules at all times when working with microorganisms to avoid accidental contamination:

1.   Treat all microorganisms as if they were pathogenic.
2.   Maintain sterile conditions at all times

Dissection and alternatives to dissection
Animals which were not obtained from recognized sources should not be used. Decaying animals or those of unknown origin may harbor pathogens and/or parasites. Specimens should be rinsed before handling. Latex gloves are desirable. If not available, students with sores or scratches should be excused from the activity. Formaldehyde is likely carcinogenic and should be avoided or disposed of according to district regulations. Students objecting to dissections for moral reasons should be given an alternative assignment. Interactive dissections are available online or from software companies for those students who object to performing dissections. There should be no penalty for those students who refuse to physically perform a dissection.

Skill 2.3 Historical Perspectives

a. Discuss the cumulative nature of scientific evidence as it relates to the development of models and theories

Science is an ongoing process. There was a time when microscopes, telescopes, calculators, and computers did not exist. Their current availability has led to many discoveries. We have had the opportunity to investigate why people become sick, and the mechanisms responsible for their illnesses. We have also broadened our knowledge of physical science- the laws that govern the universe.

With each new breakthrough we either build upon current knowledge, or if the new piece doesn't work with previous thoughts, we reevaluate the validity of all of the information, past and present. For this reason, models and theories are continuously evolving.

b. Recognize that as knowledge in science evolves, when observations do not support an accepted scientific theory, the observations are reconsidered to determine if they are mistaken or fraudulent, or if the accepted theory is erroneous or incomplete (e.g., an erroneous theory is the Piltdown Man fossil; an incomplete theory is Newton's laws of gravity)

When one realizes that their results do not match those previously established, the new results must be reconsidered. At this point, one of four possibilities exist. One should look closely at the new results. The first place for disagreement is the new observations-they may be mistaken. Was there an error in data collection or analysis? Repeating the experiment may yield results that more closely agree with the previous theory. If the results of the follow up experiment are the same, an observer may wonder if the new data is fraudulent (second possibility). Take for example the scientist who fabricates data, but repeatedly insists on its integrity, even though it contradicts previous studies (remember that having a current study contradict a previous one would be acceptable, providing the results were true and reproducible). Another possibility would be a problem with the previously accepted theory. An erroneous theory is one which was created with misinformation. An example of an erroneous theory would be the Piltdown Man fossil. The Piltdown Man fossil consisted of fragments of a skull and jaw bone collected in the early 1900's from a gravel pit at Piltdown, a village in England. The claim was asserted that this discovery was the fossilized remains of an unknown early form of man. In 1953 it was exposed as a forgery, and properly evaluated as the lower jaw bone of an ape combined with the skull of a fully developed, modern man. There is still some debate as to who created the forgery, but it provided quite a stir in the scientific community. The problem with an erroneous theory is that it can be believable, and then future assumptions may be based on its inaccuracy. When theories become entrenched this way it is difficult sometimes to go back and locate the error. This can be seen when studying phylogenies. If Piltdown Man was assumed to come from ancestors, and to have generations below him, the accusation of his being fraudulent sheds new light on the phylogenic tree as it was proposed. A final source for dispute would be that the original theory was incomplete, such as was true with Newton's laws of gravity. Galileo had created an erroneous theory to describe the motion of planets. It was discredited when Sir Isaac Newton established his famous laws of gravity. Newton's concept of gravity held until the beginning of the 20th century, when Einstein proposed his general theory of relativity. The key to Einstein's version is that inertia occurs when objects are in free-fall instead of when they are at rest. The theory of general relativity has been well accepted because of how its predictions have been repeatedly confirmed.

c. Recognize and provide specific examples that scientific advances sometimes result in profound paradigm shifts in scientific theories

A paradigm shift is a change in the underlying assumptions that define a particular scientific theory. Scientific advances, such as increased technology allowing different or more reliable data collection, sometimes result in paradigm shifts in scientific theories.

One classic example of a scientific paradigm shift is the transition from a geocentric (Earth-centered) to heliocentric (Sun-centered) model of the universe. Invention and development of the telescope allowed for greater observation of the planets and the Sun. The theory that the Sun is the center of the universe around which the planets, including the Earth, rotate gained acceptance largely because of the advances in observational technology.

Another example of a paradigm shift is the acceptance of plate tectonics as the explanation for large-scale movements in the Earth's crust. Advances in seismic imaging and observation techniques allowed for the collection of sufficient data to establish plate tectonics as a legitimate geological theory.

d. Discuss the need for clear and understandable communication of scientific endeavors so that they may be reproduced and why reproduction of these endeavors is important

Clear and understandable communication is essential for continuity and progress in science. When scientists complete scientific endeavors, such as research experiments, it is important that they carefully record their methods and results. Such precise communication and record keeping allows other scientists to reproduce the experiments in the future.

Reproduction of scientific endeavors is important because it simplifies the verification process. Because scientific experiments are subject to many sources of error, verification of results is essential. Scientists must verify results from scientific endeavors in order to justify the use of the acquired data in developing theories and future experiments.

In addition, clear communication of scientific endeavors allows scientists to learn from the work of others. Such sharing of information speeds the process of scientific research and development.

Domain 3. Science and Society

Skill 3.1 Science Literacy

a. Recognize that science attempts to make sense of how the natural and the designed world function

Human beings reside at the top of the food web for many reasons including physical dexterity and size, but largely because of brain power. We are thinkers, designed to be curious (as are our friends, the primates). Science is our attempt to understand the world around us, and to live within it. Science is not always accurate, and often theories are inadequate, or believed to be true only to be disproven later. Please remember that science is a man made endeavor, and you and your students should treat it as such.

b. Demonstrate the ability to apply critical and independent thinking to weigh alternative explanations of events

In section 1.3j we demonstrated the importance of assessing the validity of information. One should consider the suggestions given in 1.3j when weighing evidence. Additional information on this subject may be found in Scientific Inquiry: Section 2.1 a-k.

c. Apply evidence, numbers, patterns, and logical arguments to solve problems

Two of the most important aspects of science are data and honesty. In the scientific realm, numbers are stronger than words, so be sure to back up your comments with accurate data and examples. By using the scientific method, you will be more likely to catch mistakes, correct biases, and obtain accurate results. When assessing experimental data utilize the proper tools and mathematical concepts discussed in this guide. For an in depth review of the scientific method please see Domain 1: Investigation and Experimentation.

d. Understand that, although much has been learned about the objects, events and phenomena in nature, there are many unanswered questions, i.e., science is a work in progress

The combination of science, mathematics and technology forms the scientific endeavor and makes science a success. It is impossible to study science on its own without the support of other disciplines like mathematics, technology, geology, physics and other disciplines as well. Science is an ongoing process involving multiple fields and individuals. Technology also plays a role in scientific discoveries- we are limited by technology. We are constantly creating new devices for experimentation, and with each one comes new revelations.

As such, science is constantly developing. The nature of science mainly consists of three important things:

The scientific world view
This includes some very important issues such as – it is possible to understand this highly organized world and its complexities with the help of the latest technology. Scientific ideas are subject to change. After repeated experiments, a theory is established, but this theory could be changed or supported in future. Only laws that occur naturally do not change.

Scientific knowledge may not be discarded but is modified – e.g., Albert Einstein didn't discard the Newtonian principles but modified them in his theory of relativity.
Also, science can't answer all our questions. We can't find answers to questions related to our beliefs, moral values and norms.

Scientific inquiry
Scientific inquiry starts with a simple question. This simple question leads to information gathering, an educated guess otherwise known as hypothesis. To prove the hypothesis, an experiment has to be conducted, which yields data and the conclusion. All experiments must be repeated at least twice to get reliable results. Thus scientific inquiry leads to new knowledge or verifying established theories.

Science requires proof or evidence. Science is dependent on accuracy, not bias or prejudice. In science, there is no place for preconceived ideas or premeditated results. By using their senses and modern technology, scientists will be able to get reliable information.

Science is a combination of logic and imagination. A scientist needs to think and imagine and be able to reason.

Science explains, reasons and predicts. These three are interwoven and are inseparable. While reasoning is absolutely important for science, there should be no bias or prejudice.

Science is not authoritarian, because history has shown that scientific authority has sometimes been proven wrong. Nobody can determine or make decisions for others on any issue.

Scientific enterprise
Science is a complex activity involving various people and places. A scientist may work alone or in a laboratory, classroom or for that matter anywhere. Mostly science is a group activity requiring lot of social skills, such as cooperation, communication of results or findings, consultations, discussions etc.

Science demands a high degree of communication to governments, funding authorities and to the public.

e. Know that the ability of science and technology to resolve societal problems depends on the scientific literacy of a society

The most common definitions of science literacy are: scientific awareness and scientific ways of knowing. In simple terms, scientific literacy is a combination of concepts, history, and philosophy that help us to understand the scientific issues of our time. The aim is to have a society which is aware of scientific developments.

The benefits to any society of being scientifically literate are –

1. To understand current issues
2. To appreciate the role of natural laws in individuals' lives
3. To have an idea of scientific advances

We are living in an age of scientific discoveries and technology. On TV and in the newspapers, we are constantly fed news related to science and technology. Scientific and technological issues are dominating our lives. We need to be scientifically literate to understand these issues. Understanding these debates has become as important as reading and writing. In order to appreciate the world around us and to be able to make informed personal decisions, we need to be scientifically literate.

It is the responsibility of the scientific community and educators to help the public to cope with the fast paced changes that are taking place now in the fields of science and technology.

Scientific literacy is based on the understanding of the most general principles and a broad knowledge of science. A society that is scientifically aware possesses facts and vocabulary sufficient to understand the context of the daily news. If one can understand articles about genetic engineering, the ozone hole, and greenhouse effect as well as sports, politics, arts, or the theater, then one is scientifically literate.

Scientific literacy is different from technological literacy and many times people are not clear about this. A survey indicated that less than 7% of adults, 22% of college graduates and 26% of those with graduate degrees are scientifically literate. These numbers are not encouraging. In order to rectify this problem, more emphasis has been placed on science education in K-12 and at the college level.

Skill 3.2 Diversity

a. Identify examples of women and men of various social and ethnic backgrounds with diverse interests, talents, qualities and motivations who are, or who have been, engaged in activities of science and related fields

Curiosity is the heart of science. Maybe this is why so many diverse people are drawn to it. In the area of zoology one of the most recognized scientists is Jane Goodall. Miss Goodall is known for her research with chimpanzees in Africa. Jane has spent many years abroad conducting long term studies of chimp interactions, and returns from Africa to lecture and provide information about Africa, the chimpanzees, and her institute located in Tanzania.

In the area of chemistry we recognize Dorothy Crowfoot Hodgkin. She studied at Oxford and won the Nobel Prize of Chemistry in 1964 for recognizing the shape of the vitamin B 12.

Have you ever heard of Florence Nightingale? She was a true person living in the 1800's and she shaped the nursing profession. Florence was born into wealth and shocked her family by choosing to study health reforms for the poor in lieu of attending the expected social events. Florence studied nursing in Paris and became involved in the Crimean war. The British lacked supplies and the secretary of war asked for Florence's assistance. She earned her nickname walking the floors at night checking on patients and writing letters to British officials demanding supplies.

In 1903 the Nobel Prize in Physics was jointly awarded to three individuals: Marie Curie, Pierre Curie, and Becquerel. Marie was the first woman ever to receive this prestigious award. In addition, she received the Nobel Prize in chemistry in 1911, making her the only person to receive two Nobel awards in science. Ironically, her cause of death in 1934 was of overexposure to radioactivity, the research for which she was so respected.

Neil Armstrong is an American icon. He will always be symbolically linked to our aeronautics program. This astronaut and naval aviator is known for being the first human to set foot on the Moon.

Sir Alexander Fleming was a pharmacologist from Scotland who isolated the antibiotic penicillin from a fungus in 1928. Flemming also noted that bacteria developed resistance whenever too little penicillin was used or when it was used for too short a period, a key problem we still face today.

Skill 3.3 Science, Technology, and Society

a. Identify and evaluate the impact of scientific advances on society

Society as a whole impacts biological research. The pressure from the majority of society has led to bans and restrictions on human cloning research. Human cloning has been restricted in the United States and many other countries. The U.S. legislature has banned the use of federal funds for the development of human cloning techniques. Some individual states have banned human cloning regardless of where the funds originate.

The demand for genetically modified crops by society and industry has steadily increased over the years. Genetic engineering in the agricultural field has led to improved crops for human use and consumption. Crops are genetically modified for increased growth and insect resistance because of the demand for larger and greater quantities of produce.

With advances in biotechnology come those in society who oppose it. Ethical questions come into play when discussing animal and human research. Does it need to be done? What are the effects on humans and animals? There are no right or wrong answers to these questions. There are governmental agencies in place to regulate the use of humans and animals for research.

Science and technology are often referred to as a "double-edged sword". Although advances in medicine have greatly improved the quality and length of life, certain moral and ethical controversies have arisen. Unforeseen environmental problems may result from technological advances. Advances in science have led to an improved economy through biotechnology as applied to agriculture, yet it has put our health care system at risk and has caused the cost of medical care to skyrocket. Society depends on science, yet is necessary that the public be scientifically literate and informed in order to prevent potentially unethical procedures from occurring. Especially vulnerable are the areas of genetic research and fertility. It is important for science teachers to stay abreast of current research and to involve students in critical thinking and ethics whenever possible.

b. Recognize that scientific advances may challenge individuals to reevaluate their personal beliefs

It is easy to say one is for or against something. Biotechnological advances are reaching new heights. This is both exciting and, to some, it creates anxiety. We are stretching our boundaries and rethinking old standards. Things we never thought possible, such as the human genome project, now seem ordinary, and cloning, once in the realm of science fiction, is now available. These revelations force us to rethink our stance on issues.

It is normal to reevaluate one's beliefs. Reevaluation requires truly thinking about a topic, which in turn allows for recommitment to a topic or, possibly, a new, well thought out, position.

Skill 3.4 Safety

a. Choose appropriate safety equipment for a given activity (e.g., goggles, apron, vented hood)

It is the responsibility of the teacher to provide a safe environment for their students. Proper supervision greatly reduces the risk of injury and a teacher should never leave a class for any reason without providing alternate supervision. After an accident, two factors are considered; **foreseeability** and **negligence**. Foreseeability is the anticipation that an event may occur under certain circumstances. Negligence is the failure to exercise ordinary or reasonable care. Safety procedures should be a part of the science curriculum and a well managed classroom is important to avoid potential lawsuits. Students should wear safety goggles when performing dissections, heating, or while using acids and bases. Hair should always be tied back and objects should never be placed in the mouth. Food should not be consumed while in the laboratory. Hands should always be washed before and after laboratory experiments. In case of an accident, eye washes and showers should be used for eye contamination or a chemical spill that covers the student's body. Small chemical spills should only be contained and cleaned by the teacher. Kitty litter or a chemical spill kit should be used to clean spill. For large spills, the school administration and the local fire department should be notified. Biological spills should also be handled only by the teacher. Contamination with biological waste can be cleaned by using bleach when appropriate.
Accidents and injuries should always be reported to the school administration and local health facilities. The severity of the accident or injury will determine the course of action to pursue.

b. Discuss the safe use, storage, and disposal of commonly used chemicals and biological specimens

All laboratory solutions should be prepared as directed in the lab manual. Care should be taken to avoid contamination. All glassware should be rinsed thoroughly with distilled water before using and cleaned well after use. All solutions should be made with distilled water as tap water contains dissolved particles that may affect the results of an experiment. Unused solutions should be disposed of according to local disposal procedures.

The "Right to Know Law" covers science teachers who work with potentially hazardous chemicals. Briefly, the law states that employees must be informed of potentially toxic chemicals. An inventory must be made available if requested.

The inventory must contain information about the hazards and properties of the chemicals. This inventory is to be checked against the "Substance List". Training must be provided on the safe handling and interpretation of the Material Safety Data Sheet.

The following chemicals are potential carcinogens and not allowed in school facilities: Acrylonitriel, Arsenic compounds, Asbestos, Bensidine, Benzene, Cadmium compounds, Chloroform, Chromium compounds, Ethylene oxide, Ortho-toluidine, Nickle powder, and Mercury.

Chemicals should not be stored on bench tops or heat sources. They should be stored in groups based on their reactivity with one another and in protective storage cabinets. All containers within the lab must be labeled. Suspect and known carcinogens must be labeled as such and segregated within trays to contain leaks and spills.

Chemical waste should be disposed of in properly labeled containers. Waste should be separated based on their reactivity with other chemicals.

Biological material should never be stored near food or water used for human consumption. All biological material should be appropriately labeled. All blood and body fluids should be put in a well-contained container with a secure lid to prevent leaking. All biological waste should be disposed of in biological hazardous waste bags.

Material safety data sheets are available for every chemical and biological substance. These are available directly from the company of acquisition or the internet. The manuals for equipment used in the lab should be read and understood before using them.

c. Assess the safety conditions needed to maintain a science laboratory (e.g., eye wash, shower, fire extinguisher)

All science labs should contain the following items of **safety equipment**. Those marked with an asterisk are requirements by state laws.

* fire blanket which is visible and accessible
*Ground Fault Circuit Interrupters (GCFI) within two feet of water supplies
*signs designating room exits
*emergency shower providing a continuous flow of water
*emergency eye wash station which can be activated by the foot or forearm
*eye protection for every student and a means of sanitizing equipment
*emergency exhaust fans providing ventilation to the outside of the building
*master cut-off switches for gas, electric and compressed air. Switches must have permanently attached handles. Cut-off switches must be clearly labeled.
*an ABC fire extinguisher
*storage cabinets for flammable materials

-chemical spill control kit
-fume hood with a motor which is spark proof
-protective laboratory aprons made of flame retardant material
-signs which will alert potential hazardous conditions
-containers for broken glassware, flammables, corrosives, and waste. Containers
 should be labeled.

d. Read and decode MSDS/OSHA (Material Safety Data Sheet/Occupational Safety and Health Administration) labels on laboratory supplies and equipment

In addition to the safety laws set forth by the government regarding equipment necessary to the lab, OSHA (Occupational Safety and Health Administration) has helped to make environments safer by instituting signs that are bilingual. These signs use pictures rather than/in addition to words and feature eye-catching colors. Some of the best known examples are exit, restrooms, and handicap accessible.

Of particular importance to laboratories are diamond safety signs, prohibitive signs, and triangle danger signs. Each sign encloses a descriptive picture.

As a teacher, you should utilize a MSDS (Material Safety Data Sheet) whenever you are preparing an experiment. It is designed to provide people with the proper procedures for handling or working with a particular substance. MSDS's include information such as physical data (melting point, boiling point, etc.), toxicity, health effects, first aid, reactivity, storage, disposal, protective gear, and spill/leak procedures. These are particularly important if a spill or other accident occurs. You should review a few, available commonly online, and understand the listing procedures.

e. Discuss key issues in the disposal of hazardous materials in either the laboratory or the local community

Hazardous materials should never be disposed of in regular trash. Hazardous materials include many cleansers, paints, batteries, oil, and biohazardous products. Labels which caution one to wear gloves, to never place an item near another item (e.g., fire, electrical outlet), or to always use an item in a well ventilated area, should be taken as signals that the item is hazardous. Disposal of waste down the sink or in regular trash receptacles means that it will eventually enter the water/sewer system or ground, where it could cause contamination. Liquid remains/spills should be solidified using cat litter and then disposed of carefully. Sharps bins are used for the disposal of sharp objects and glass. Red biohazard bags/containers are used for the disposal of biohazard refuse.

f. Be familiar with standard safety procedures such as those outlined in the Science Safety Handbook for California Schools (1999)

In addition to the standard safety precautions covered in this section, the state of California has published a document entitled *Science Safety Handbook for California Schools*. This handbook can be purchased or printed at http://www.cde.ca.gov/pd/ca/sc/documents/scisafebk.pdf#search=%22CA%20science%20safety%20book%20for%20CA%20schools%22.

Bibliography

American Chemical Society (2001) *Chemical Safety for Teachers and Their Supervisors, Grades 7-12*, ed. Jay Young, ACS Board-Council Committee on Chemical Safety. Available at http://membership.acs.org/c/ccs/pubs/chemical_safety_manual.pdf.

American Chemical Society (2002) *Safety in Academic Chemical Laboratories*, 7th ed, 2 vols, ed. Jay Young, ACS Board-Council Committee on Chemical Safety. Available at http://membership.acs.org/c/ccs/pubs/SACL_Students.pdf and http://membership.acs.org/c/ccs/pubs/SACL_faculty.pdf.

Atkins, P. and Jones, L. (2005) *Chemical Principles: The Quest for Insight*, 3rd ed., W.H. Freeman and Co.

Brock, W.H. (1992) *The Norton History of Chemistry*, W. W. Norton & Co.

Brown, T.E., LeMay, H.E, Bursten, B.E., and Burdge, J.R. (2003) *Chemistry: The Central Science*, 9th ed., Prentice Hall.

Council of State Science Supervisors (1984) *School Science Laboratories: A Guide to Some Hazardous Substances,* US Consumer Product Safety Commission. Available at http://www.p2pays.org/ref/26/25699.pdf.

CRC Handbook of Chemistry and Physics (2004), 85th edition, ed. D.R. Lide, CRC Press.

Emsley, J. (1998) *The Elements*, 3rd ed., Clarendon Press.

Florida Department of Education (2005) *Sunshine State Standards*. Available at http://www.firn.edu/doe/curric/prek12/.

Gershey, E.L., Party, E., and Wilkerson, A. (1991) *Laboratory Safety in Practice: A Comprehensive Compliance Program and Safety Manual*, Van Nostrand Reinhold.

IUPAC (1993) *A Guide to IUPAC Nomenclature of Organic Compounds (Recommendations 1993)*, eds. R. Panico, W.H. Powell, J.C. Richer, Blackwell Scientific.

IUPAC (1990) *International Union of Pure and Applied Chemistry Nomenclature of Inorganic Chemistry: Recommendations 1990*, "The Red Book," ed. G.J. Leigh, Blackwell Scientific.

IUPAC (1979) *International Union of Pure and Applied Chemistry Nomenclature of Organic Chemistry: Recommendations 1979*, "The Blue Book," ed. J. Rigaudy, S.P. Klesney, Pergamon Press.

IUPAC (1971) *International Union of Pure and Applied Chemistry Nomenclature of Inorganic Chemistry: 1970*, ed. H.W. Thompson, Butterworths.

Leigh, G.J., Favre, H.A., and Metanomski, W.V. (1998) *Principles of Chemical Nomenclature: A Guide to IUPAC Recommendations*, Blackwell Scientific.

Levere, T.H.. (2001) *Transforming Matter: A History of Chemistry from Alchemy to the Buckyball*, The Johns Hopkins University Press.

Levine, I.N. (2000) *Quantum Chemistry*, 5th ed., Prentice Hall.

Mahn, W.J. (1991) *Academic Laboratory Chemical Hazards Guidebook*, Van Nostrand Reinhold.

McMurray, J. (2004) *Organic Chemistry*, Thomson-Brooks/Cole.

McQuarrie, D.A. and Rock, P.A. (1985) *Descriptive Chemistry*, W.H. Freeman and Co.

Moore, J.W., Stanitski, C.L., and Jurs, P.C. (2005) *Chemistry: The Molecular Science*, 2nd ed., Thomson-Brooks/Cole.

Palleros, D.R. (2000) *Experimental Organic Chemistry*, John Wiley& Sons.

Traynham, J.G. (1996) *Organic Nomenclature: A Programmed Introduction*, 5th ed., Prentice-Hall Inc.

SAMPLE MULTIPLE-CHOICE QUESTIONS

Part I Content Domains for Science Subtest III:Chemistry (121)

1. Potassium crystallizes with two atoms contained in each unit cell. What is the mass of potassium found in a lattice 1.00×10^6 unit cells wide, 2.00×10^6 unit cells high, and 5.00×10^5 unit cells deep?

   A. 85.0 ng
   B. 32.5 μg
   C. 64.9 μg
   D. 130. μg

2. At STP, 20. μL of O_2 contain 5.4×10^{16} molecules. According to Avogadro's hypothesis, how many molecules are in 20. μL of Ne?

   A. 5.4×10^{15}
   B. 1.0×10^{16}
   C. 2.7×10^{16}
   D. 5.4×10^{16}

3. An ideal gas at 50.0 °C and 3.00 atm is in a 300. cm^3 cylinder. The cylinder volume changes by moving a piston until the gas is at 50.0 °C and 1.00 atm. What is the final volume?

   A. 100. cm^3
   B. 450. cm^3
   C. 900. cm^3
   D. 1.20 dm^3

4. Which gas law may be used to solve the previous question?

   A. Charles's law
   B. Boyle's law
   C. Graham's law
   D. Avogadro's law

5. A blimp is filled with 5000. m^3 of helium at 28.0 °C and 99.7 kPa. What is the mass of helium used?

   $$R = 8.3144 \ \frac{J}{mol\text{-}K}$$

   A. 797 kg
   B. 810. kg
   C. 879 kg
   D. 8.57×10^3 kg

6. Which intermolecular attraction explains the following trend in straight-chain alkanes?

Condensed structural formula	Boiling point (°C)
CH_4	-161.5
CH_3CH_3	-88.6
$CH_3CH_2CH_3$	-42.1
$CH_3CH_2CH_2CH_3$	-0.5
$CH_3CH_2CH_2CH_2CH_3$	36.0
$CH_3CH_2CH_2CH_2CH_2CH_3$	68.7

   A. London dispersion forces
   B. Dipole-dipole interactions
   C. Hydrogen bonding
   D. Ion-induced dipole interactions

7. 2.00 L of an unknown gas at 1500. mm Hg and a temperature of 25.0 °C weighs 7.52 g. Assuming the ideal gas equation, what is the molecular mass of the gas?

   760 mm Hg=1 atm
   R=0.08206 L-atm/(mol-K)

   A. 21.6 u
   B. 23.3 u
   C. 46.6 u
   D. 93.2 u

8. Which of the following are true?

   A. Solids have no vapor pressure.
   B. Dissolving a solute in a liquid increases its vapor pressure.
   C. The vapor pressure of a pure substance is characteristic of that substance and its temperature.
   D. All of the above

9. Find the partial pressure of N_2 in a container at 150. kPa holding H_2O and N_2 at 50 °C. The vapor pressure of H_2O at 50 °C is 12 kPa.

   A. 12 kPa
   B. 138 kPa
   C. 162 kPa
   D. The value cannot be determined.

10. The solubility of $CoCl_2$ is 54 g per 100 g of ethanol. Three flasks each contain 100 g of ethanol. Flask #1 also contains 40 g $CoCl_2$ in solution. Flask #2 contains 56 g $CoCl_2$ in solution. Flask #3 contains 5 g of solid $CoCl_2$ in equilibrium with 54 g $CoCl_2$ in solution. Which of the following describe the solutions present in the liquid phase of the flasks?

    A. #1-saturated, #2-supersaturated, #3-unsaturated.
    B. #1-unsaturated, #2-miscible, #3-saturated.
    C. #1-unsaturated, #2-supersaturated, #3-saturated.
    D. #1-unsaturated, #2-not at equilibrium, #3-miscible.

11. Carbonated water is bottled at 25 °C under pure CO_2 at 4.0 atm. Later the bottle is opened at 4 °C under air at 1.0 atm that has a partial pressure of 3×10^{-4} atm CO_2. Why do CO_2 bubbles form when the bottle is opened?

    A. CO_2 falls out of solution due to a drop in solubility at the lower total pressure.
    B. CO_2 falls out of solution due to a drop in solubility at the lower CO_2 pressure.
    C. CO_2 falls out of solution due to a drop in solubility at the lower temperature.
    D. CO_2 is formed by the decomposition of carbonic acid.

12. When KNO_3 dissolves in water, the water grows slightly colder. An increase in temperature will _____ the solubility of KNO_3.

A. increase
B. decrease
C. have no effect on
D. have an unknown effect with the information given on

13. Aluminum sulfate is a strong electrolyte. What is the concentration of all species in a 0.2 M solution of aluminum sulfate?

A. 0.2 M Al^{3+}, 0.2 M SO_4^{2-}
B. 0.4 M Al^{3+}, 0.6 M SO_4^{2-}
C. 0.6 M Al^{3+}, 0.4 M SO_4^{2-}
D. 0.2 M $Al_2(SO_4)_3$

14. 15 g of formaldehyde (CH_2O) are dissolved in 100. g of water. Calculate the weight percentage and mole fraction of formaldehyde in the solution.

A. 13%, 0.090
B. 15%, 0.090
C. 13%, 0.083
D. 15%, 0.083

15. Which of the following would make the best solvent for Br_2?

A. H_2O
B. CS_2
C. NH_3
D. molten NaCl

16. Which of the following is most likely to dissolve in water?

A. H_2
B. CCl_4
C. SF_6
D. CH_3OH

17. Which of the following is not a colligative property?

A. Viscosity lowering
B. Freezing point lowering
C. Boiling point elevation
D. Vapor pressure lowering

18.
$$BaCl_2(aq) + Na_2SO_4(aq) \rightarrow BaSO_4(s) + 2NaCl(aq)$$
is an example of a _____ reaction.

A. acid-base
B. precipitation
C. redox
D. nuclear

19. List the following aqueous solutions in order of increasing boiling point.

I. 0.050 m $AlCl_3$
II. 0.080 m $Ba(NO_3)_2$
III. 0.090 m NaCl
IV. 0.12 m ethylene glycol ($C_2H_6O_2$)

A. I < II < III < IV
B. I < III < IV < II
C. IV < III < I < II
D. IV < III < II < I

20. Osmotic pressure is the pressure required to prevent _____ flowing from low to high _____ concentration across a semipermeable membrane.

   A. solute, solute
   B. solute, solvent
   C. solvent, solute
   D. solvent, solvent

21. A solution of NaCl in water is heated on a mountain in an open container until it boils at 100. °C. The air pressure on the mountain is 0.92 atm. According to Raoult's law, what mole fraction of Na^+ and Cl^- are present in the solution?

   A. 0.04 Na^+, 0.04 Cl^-
   B. 0.08 Na^+, 0.08 Cl^-
   C. 0.46 Na^+, 0.46 Cl^-
   D. 0.92 Na^+, 0.92 Cl^-

22. Write a balanced nuclear equation for the emission of an alpha particle by polonium-209.

   A. $^{209}_{84}Po \rightarrow {}^{205}_{81}Pb + {}^4_2He$
   B. $^{209}_{84}Po \rightarrow {}^{205}_{82}Bi + {}^4_2He$
   C. $^{209}_{84}Po \rightarrow {}^{209}_{85}At + {}^0_{-1}e$
   D. $^{209}_{84}Po \rightarrow {}^{205}_{82}Pb + {}^4_2He$

23. ^3_1H decays with a half-life of 12 years. 3.0 g of pure ^3_1H were placed in a sealed container 24 years ago. How many grams of ^3_1H remain?

   A. 0.38 g
   B. 0.75 g
   C. 1.5 g
   D. 3.0 g

24. Which of the following isotopes can create a chain reaction of nuclear fission?

   A. uranium-235
   B. uranium-238
   C. plutonium-238
   D. all of the above

25. Which of the following is a correct electron arrangement for oxygen?

   A.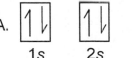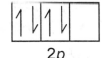
       1s   2s   2p

   B. $1s^2 1p^2 2s^2 2p^2$
   C. 2, 2, 4
   D. none of the above

26. Which of the following statements about radiant energy is <u>not</u> true?

    A. The energy change of an electron transition is directly proportional to the wavelength of the emitted or absorbed photon.

    B. The energy of an electron in a hydrogen atom depends only on the principle quantum number.

    C. The frequency of photons striking a metal determines whether the photoelectric effect will occur.

    D. The frequency of a wave of electromagnetic radiation is inversely proportional to its wavelength

27. Match the orbital diagram for the ground state of carbon with the rule/principle it violates:

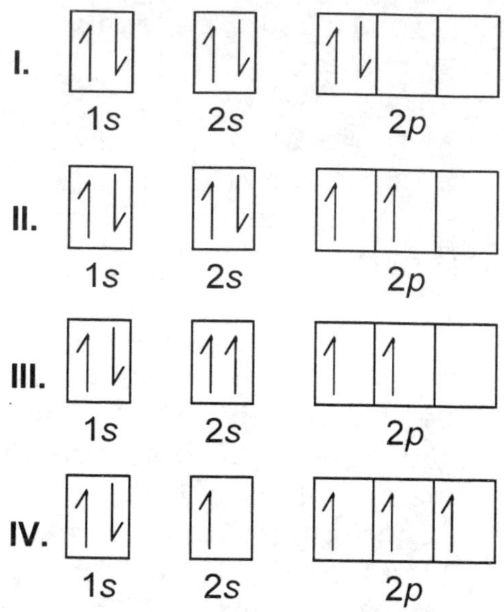

    A. I-Pauli exclusion, II-Aufbau, III-no violation, IV-Hund's

    B. I-Aufbau, II-Pauli exclusion, III-no violation, IV-Hund's

    C. I-Hund's, II-no violation, III-Pauli exclusion, IV-Aufbau

    D. I-Hund's, II-no violation, III-Aufbau, IV-Pauli exclusion

28. Which oxide forms the strongest acid in water?

    A. Al_2O_3
    B. Cl_2O_7
    C. As_2O_5
    D. CO_2

29. Rank the following bonds from least to most polar:

C-H, C-Cl, H-H, C-F

A. C-H < H-H < C-F < C-Cl
B. H-H < C-H < C-F < C-Cl
C. C-F < C-Cl < C-H < H-H
D. H-H < C-H < C-Cl < C-F

30. Which of the following is a proper Lewis dot structure of CHClO?

A.

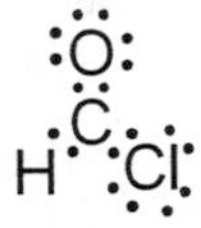

B.

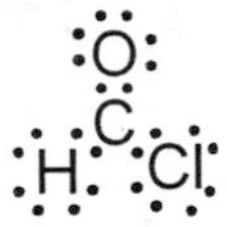

C.

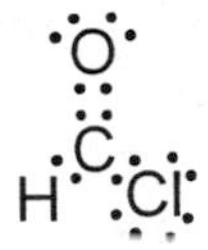

D.

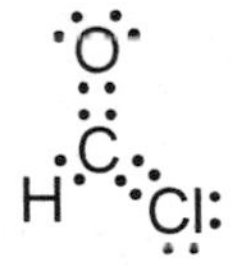

31. Which statement about molecular structures is false?

A. 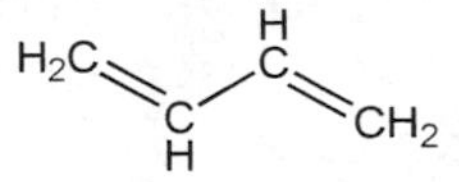 is a conjugated molecule

B. A bonding σ orbital connects two atoms by the straight line between them.

C. A bonding π orbital connects two atoms in a separate region from the straight line between them.

D. The anion with resonance forms

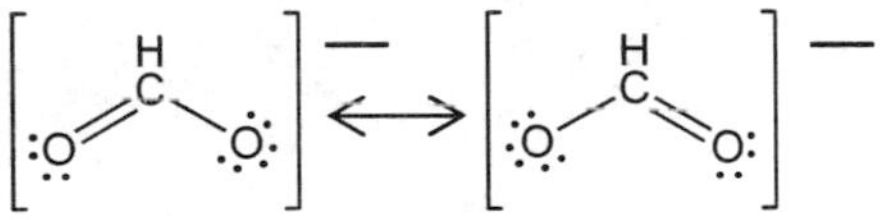

will always exist in one form or the other.

32. What is the shape of the PH_3 molecule? Use the VSEPR model.

A. Trigonal pyramidal
B. Trigonal bipyramidal
C. Trigonal planar
D. Tetrahedral

33. What is the chemical composition of magnesium nitrate?

A. 11.1% Mg, 22.2% N, 66.7% O
B. 16.4% Mg, 18.9% N, 64.7% O
C. 20.9% Mg, 24.1% N, 55.0% O
D. 28.2% Mg, 16.2% N, 55.7% O

34. Balance the equation for the neutralization reaction between phosphoric acid and calcium hydroxide by filling in the blank stoichiometric coefficients.

$$\_H_3PO_4 + \_Ca(OH)_2 \rightarrow$$
$$\_Ca_3(PO_4)_2 + \_H_2O$$

A. 4, 3, 1, 4
B. 2, 3, 1, 8
C. 2, 3, 1, 6
D. 2, 1, 1, 2

35. Find the mass of CO_2 produced by the combustion of 15 kg of isopropyl alcohol in the reaction:

$$2C_3H_7OH + 9O_2 \rightarrow 6CO_2 + 8H_2O$$

A. 33 kg
B. 44 kg
C. 50 kg
D. 60 kg

36. A 100. L vessel of pure O_2 at 500. kPa and 20. °C is used for the combustion of butane:
$$2C_4H_{10} + 13O_2 \rightarrow 8CO_2 + 10H_2O$$

Find the mass of butane to consume all the O_2 in the vessel. Assume O_2 is an ideal gas and use a value of R = 8.314 J/(mol•K).

A. 183 g
B. 467 g
C. 1.83 kg
D. 7.75 kg

37. Three experiments were performed at the same initial temperature and pressure to determine the rate of the reaction
$$2ClO_2(g) + F_2(g) \rightarrow 2ClO_2F(g)$$

Results are shown in the table below. Concentrations are given in millimoles per liter (mM).

Exp.	Initial $[ClO_2]$ (mM)	Initial $[F_2]$ (mM)	Initial rate of $[ClO_2F]$ increase (mM/sec)
1	5.0	5.0	0.63
2	5.0	20	2.5
3	10	10	2.5

What is the rate law for this reaction?

A. $Rate = k\left[F_2\right]$
B. $Rate = k\left[ClO_2\right]\left[F_2\right]$
C. $Rate = k\left[ClO_2\right]^2\left[F_2\right]$
D. $Rate = k\left[ClO_2\right]\left[F_2\right]^2$

38. Write the equilibrium expression K_{eq} for the reaction

$$CO_2(g) + H_2(g) \rightarrow CO(g) + H_2O(l)$$

A. $\dfrac{[CO][H_2O]}{[CO_2][H_2]^2}$

B. $\dfrac{[CO_2][H_2]}{[CO][H_2O]}$

C. $\dfrac{[CO][H_2O]}{[CO_2][H_2]}$

D. $\dfrac{[CO]}{[CO_2][H_2]}$

39. $BaSO_4$ ($K_{sp} = 1 \times 10^{-10}$) is added to pure H_2O. How much is dissolved in 1 L of saturated solution?

A. 2 mg
B. 10 µg
C. 2 µg
D. 100 pg

40. At a certain temperature, T, the equilibrium constant for the reaction

$$2NO(g) \rightarrow N_2(g) + O_2(g)$$

is $K_{eq} = 2 \times 10^3$. If a 1.0 L container at this temperature contains 90 mM N_2, 20 mM O_2, and 5 mM NO, what will occur?

A. The reaction will make more N_2 and O_2.
B. The reaction is at equilibrium.
C. The reaction will make more NO.
D. The temperature, T, is required to solve this problem.

41. Which of the following are listed from weakest to strongest acid?

A. H_2SO_3, H_2SeO_3, H_2TeO_3
B. HBrO, $HBrO_2$, $HBrO_3$, $HBrO_4$
C. HI, HBr, HCl, HF
D. H_3PO_4, $H_2PO_4^-$, HPO_4^{2-}

42. NH₄F is dissolved in water. Which of the following are conjugate acid/base pairs present in the solution?

I. NH_4^+/NH_4OH
II. HF/F^-
III. H_3O^+/H_2O
IV. H_2O/OH^-

A. I, II, and III
B. I, III, and IV
C. II and IV
D. II, III, and IV

43. What are the pH and the pOH of 0.010 M $HNO_3(aq)$?

    A. pH = 1.0, pOH = 9.0
    B. pH = 2.0, pOH = 12.0
    C. pH = 2.0, pOH = 8.0
    D. pH = 8.0, pOH = 6.0

44. What is the pH of a buffer made of 0.128 M sodium formate (HCOONa) and 0.072 M formic acid (HCOOH)? The pK_a of formic acid is 3.75.

    A. 2.0
    B. 3.0
    C. 4.0
    D. 5.0

45. Rank the following from lowest to highest pH. Assume a small volume for the component given in moles:

    I. 0.01 mol HCl added to 1 L H_2O
    II. 0.01 mol HI added to 1 L of an acetic acid/sodium acetate solution at pH 4.0
    III. 0.01 mol NH_3 added to 1 L H_2O
    IV. 0.1 mol HNO_3 added to 1 L of a 0.1 M $Ca(OH)_2$ solution

    A. I < II < III < IV
    B. I < II < IV < III
    C. II < I < III < IV
    D. II < I < IV < III

46. Which reaction is <u>not</u> a redox process?

    A. Combustion of octane:
    $2C_8H_{18} + 25O_2 \rightarrow 16CO_2 + 18H_2O$

    B. Depletion of a lithium battery:
    $Li + MnO_2 \rightarrow LiMnO_2$

    C. Corrosion of aluminum by acid:
    $2Al + 6HCl \rightarrow 2AlCl_3 + 3H_2$

    D. Taking an antacid for heartburn:
    $CaCO_3 + 2HCl \rightarrow CaCl_2 + H_2CO_3$
    $\rightarrow CaCl_2 + CO_2 + H_2O$

47. Molten NaCl is subjected to electrolysis. What reaction takes place at the cathode?

    A. $2Cl^-(l) \rightarrow Cl_2(g) + 2e^-$
    B. $Cl_2(g) + 2e^- \rightarrow 2Cl^-(l)$
    C. $Na^+(l) + e^- \rightarrow Na(l)$
    D. $Na^+(l) \rightarrow Na(l) + e^-$

48. What is the purpose of the salt bridge in an electrochemical cell?
    A. To receive electrons from the oxidation half-reaction
    B. To relieve the buildup of positive charge in the anode half-cell
    C. To conduct electron flow
    D. To permit positive ions to flow from the cathode half-cell to the anode half-cell.

49. What is the oxidant in the reaction:
$2H_2S + SO_2 \rightarrow 3S + 2H_2O$?

A. H_2S
B. SO_2
C. S
D. H_2O

50. Given:

$E°=-2.37V$ for $Mg^{2+}(aq)+2e^- \rightarrow Mg(s)$

and

$E°=0.80$ V for $Ag^{+}(aq)+e^- \rightarrow Ag(s)$,

what is the standard potential of a voltaic cell composed of a piece of magnesium dipped in a 1 M Ag^+ solution and a piece of silver dipped in 1 M Mg^{2+}?

A. 0.77 V
B. 1.57 V
C. 3.17 V
D. 3.97 V

<u>Part I Content Domains for Science Subtest II:General Science (119) and Science Subtest IV:Chemistry (125)</u>

51. In the following phase diagram, _______ occurs as P is decreased from A to B at constant T and _______ occurs as T is increased from C to D at constant P.

A. deposition, melting
B. sublimation, melting
C. deposition, vaporization
D. sublimation, vaporization

Pressure (P)

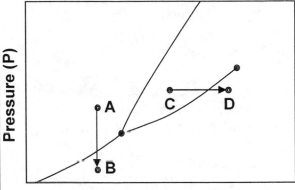

Temperature (T)

52. Heat is added to a pure solid at its melting point until it all becomes liquid at its freezing point. Which of the following occur?

A. Intermolecular attractions are weakened.
B. The kinetic energy of the molecules does not change.
C. The freedom of the molecules to move about increases.
D. All of the above.

53. Why does $CaCl_2$ have a higher normal melting point than NH_3?

A. Covalent bonds are stronger than London dispersion forces.
B. Covalent bonds are stronger than hydrogen bonds.
C. Ionic bonds are stronger than London dispersion forces.
D. Ionic bonds are stronger than hydrogen bonds.

54. The temperature of a liquid is raised at atmospheric pressure. Which liquid property increases?

A. critical pressure
B. vapor pressure
C. surface tension
D. viscosity

55. Which of the following are able to flow from one place to another?

II. Gases
III. Liquids
IV. Solids
V. Supercritical fluids

A. I and II
B. II only
C. I, II, and IV
D. I, II, III, and IV

56. List the substances NH_3, PH_3, $MgCl_2$, Ne, and N_2 in order of increasing melting point.

A. $N_2 < Ne < PH_3 < NH_3 < MgCl_2$
B. $N_2 < NH_3 < Ne < MgCl_2 < PH_3$
C. $Ne < N_2 < NH_3 < PH_3 < MgCl_2$
D. $Ne < N_2 < PH_3 < NH_3 < MgCl_2$

57. 1-butanol, ethanol, methanol, and 1-propanol are all liquids at room temperature. Rank them in order of increasing viscosity.

A. 1-butanol < 1-propanol < ethanol < methanol
B. methanol < ethanol < 1-propanol < 1-butanol
C. methanol < ethanol < 1-butanol < 1-propanol
D. 1-propanol < 1-butanol < ethanol < methanol

58. Which phase may be present at the triple point of a substance?

VI. Gas
VII. Liquid
VIII. Solid
IX. Supercritical fluid

A. I, II, and III
B. I, II, and IV
C. II, III, and IV
D. I, II, III, and IV

59. Which substance is most likely to be a gas at room temperature?

A. SeO_2
B. F_2
C. $CaCl_2$
D. I_2

60. How many neutrons are in $^{60}_{27}Co$?

A. 27
B. 33
C. 60
D. 87

61. The terrestrial composition of an element is: 50.7% as an isotope with an atomic mass of 78.9 u and 49.3% as an isotope with an atomic mass of 80.9 u. Both isotopes are stable. Calculate the atomic mass of the element.

    A. 79.0 u
    B. 79.8 u
    C. 79.9 u
    D. 80.8 u

62. Select the list of atoms that are arranged in order of increasing size.

    A. Mg, Na, Si, Cl
    B. Si, Cl, Mg, Na
    C. Cl, Si, Mg, Na
    D. Na, Mg, Si, Cl

63. Based on trends in the periodic table, which of the following properties would you expect to be greater for Rb than for K?

    X. Density
    XI. Melting point
    XII. Ionization energy
    XIII. Oxidation number in a compound with chlorine

    A. I only
    B. I, II, and III
    C. II and III
    D. I, II, III, and IV

64. At room temperature, $CaBr_2$ is expected to be:
    A. a ductile solid
    B. a brittle solid
    C. a soft solid
    D. a gas

65. Which name or formula is **not** represented properly?

    A. Cl_4S
    B. $KClO_3$
    C. Calcium dihydrogen phosphate
    D. Sulfurous acid

66. The curve below resulted from the titration of a _____ _____ with a _____ _____ titrant.

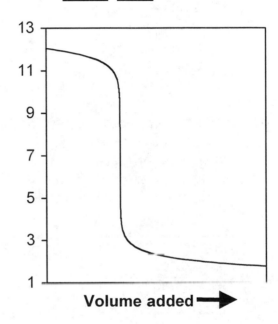

Volume added ➔

    A. weak acid, strong base
    B. weak base, strong acid
    C. strong acid, strong base
    D. strong base, strong acid

67. **Which statement about thermochemistry is true?**

  A. Particles in a system move about less freely at high entropy
  B. Water at 100 °C has the same internal energy as water vapor at 100°C
  C. A decrease in the order of a system corresponds to an increase in entropy.
  D. At its sublimation temperature, dry ice has a higher entropy than gaseous CO_2

68. **What is the heat change of 36.0 g H_2O at atmospheric pressure when its temperature is reduced from 125 °C to 40. °C? Use the following data:**

Values for water

Heat capacity of solid	37.6 J/mol•°C
Heat capacity of liquid	75.3 J/mol•°C
Heat capacity of gas	33.1 J/mol•°C
Heat of fusion	6.02 kJ/mol
Heat of vaporization	40.67 kJ/mol

  A. −92.0 kJ
  B. −10.8 kJ
  C. 10.8 kJ
  D. 92.0 kJ

69. **What is the standard heat of combustion of $CH_4(g)$? Use the following data:**

Standard heats of formation

$CH_4(g)$	−74.8 kJ/mol
$CO_2(g)$	−393.5 kJ/mol
$H_2O(l)$	−285.8 kJ/mol

  A. −890.3 kJ/mol
  B. −604.6 kJ/mol
  C. −252.9 kJ/mol
  D. −182.5 kJ/mol

70. **Which reaction creates products at a lower total entropy than the reactants?**

  A. Dissolution of table salt:
    $NaCl(s) \rightarrow Na^+(aq) + Cl^\text{š}(aq)$
  B. Oxidation of iron:
    $4Fe(s) + 3O_2(g) \rightarrow 2Fe_2O_3(s)$
  C. Dissociation of ozone:
    $O_3(g) \rightarrow O_2(g) + O(g)$
  D. Vaporization of butane:
    $C_4H_{10}(l) \rightarrow C_4H_{10}(g)$

71. Which statement about reactions is true?

   A. All spontaneous reactions are both exothermic and cause an increase in entropy.
   B. An endothermic reaction that increases the order of the system cannot be spontaneous.
   C. A reaction can be non-spontaneous in one direction and also non-spontaneous in the opposite direction.
   D. Melting snow is an exothermic process.

72. 10. kJ of heat are added to one kilogram of Iron at 10. °C. What is its final temperature? The specific heat of iron is 0.45 J/g•°C.

   A. 22 °C
   B. 27 °C
   C. 32 °C
   D. 37 °C

73. A proper name for this hydrocarbon is:

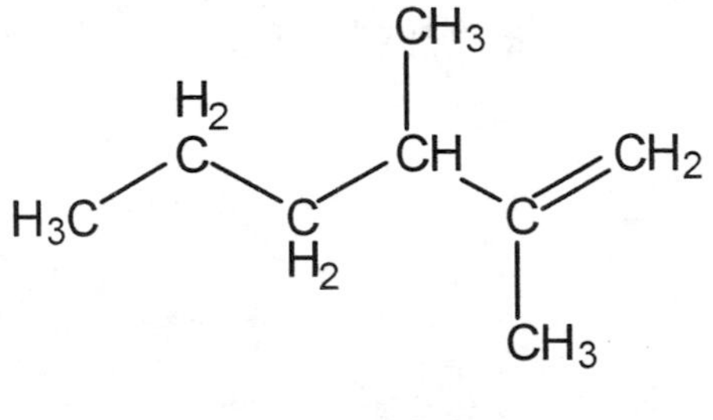

   A. 4,5-dimethyl-6-hexene
   B. 2,3-dimethyl-1-hexene
   C. 4,5-dimethyl-6-hexyne
   D. 2-methyl-3-propyl-1-butene

74. Given the following heats of reaction:

$$\Delta H = -0.3 \text{ kJ / mol for}$$
$$Fe(s) + CO_2(g) \rightarrow FeO(s) + CO(g)$$
$$\Delta H = 5.7 \text{ kJ / mol for}$$
$$2Fe(s) + 3CO_2(g) \rightarrow Fe_2O_3(s) + 3CO(g)$$
$$\text{and } \Delta H = 4.5 \text{ kJ / mol for}$$
$$3FeO(s) + CO_2(g) \rightarrow Fe_3O_4(s) + CO(g)$$

   use Hess's Law to determine the heat of reaction for:
$$3Fe_2O_3(s) + CO(g) \rightarrow 2Fe_3O_4(s) + CO_2(g)$$

   A. −10.8 kJ/mol
   B. −9.9 kJ/mol
   C. −9.0 kJ/mol
   D. −8.1 kJ/mol

75. Classify these biochemicals.

I.

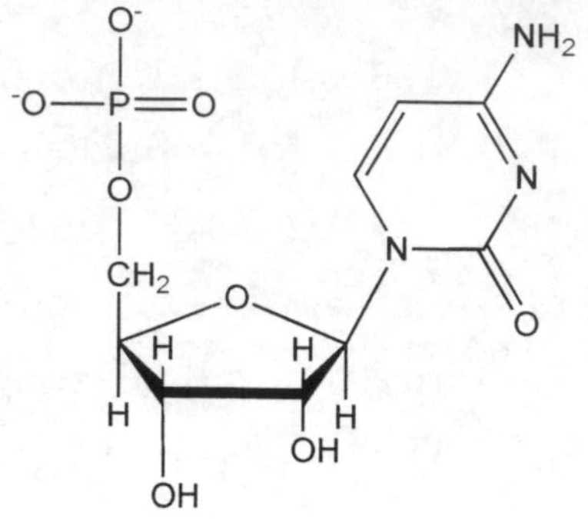

II.

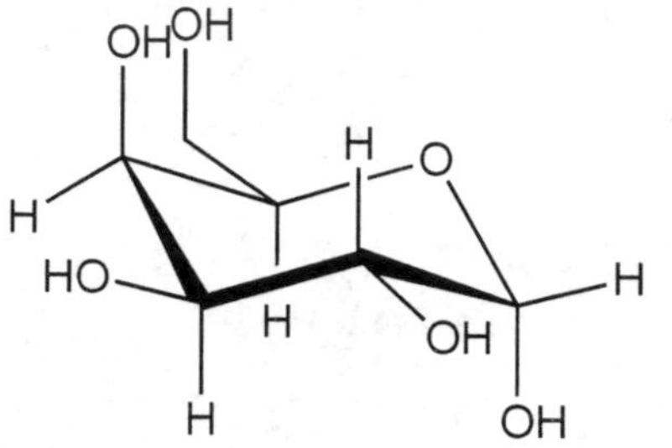

III.

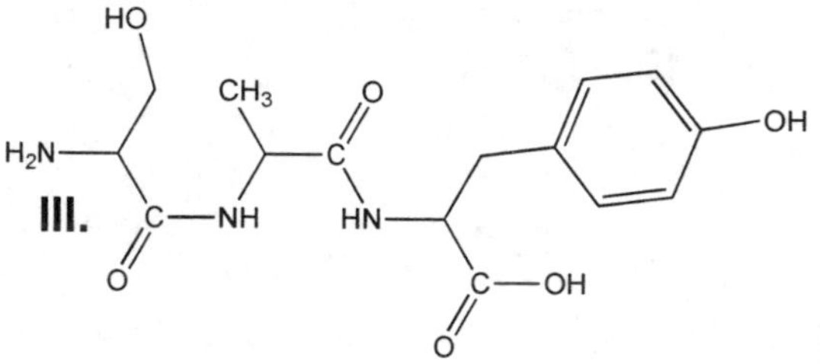

IV.

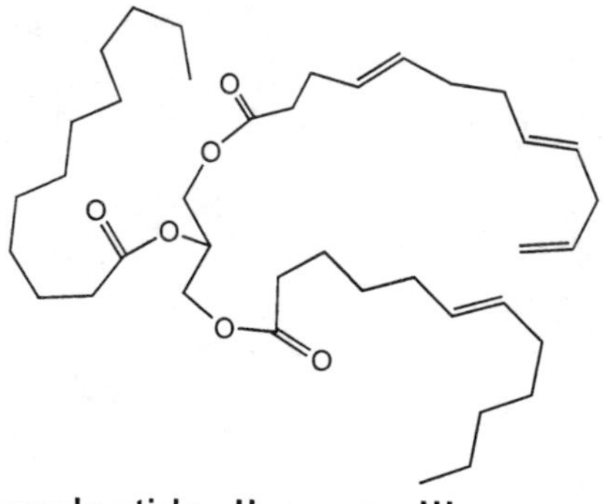

A. I-nucleotide, II-sugar, III-peptide, IV-fat
B. I-disaccharide, II-sugar, III-fatty acid, IV-polypeptide
C. I-disaccharide, II-amino acid, III-fatty acid, IV-polysaccharide
D. I I-nucleotide, II-sugar, III-triacylglyceride, and IV-DNA

76. Four nearly identical gems from the same mineral are weighed using different balances.

Their masses are:
3.4533 g, 3.459 g, 3.4656 g, 3.464 g

The four gems are then collected and added to a volumetric cylinder containing 10.00 ml of liquid, and a new volume of 14.97 ml is read. What is the average mass of the four stones and what is the density of the mineral?

A. 3.460 g, and 2.78 g/ml
B. 3.460 g and 2.79 g/ml
C. 3.4605 g and 2.78 g/ml
D. 3.461 g and 2.79 g/ml

77. Which of the following pairs are isomers?

I.

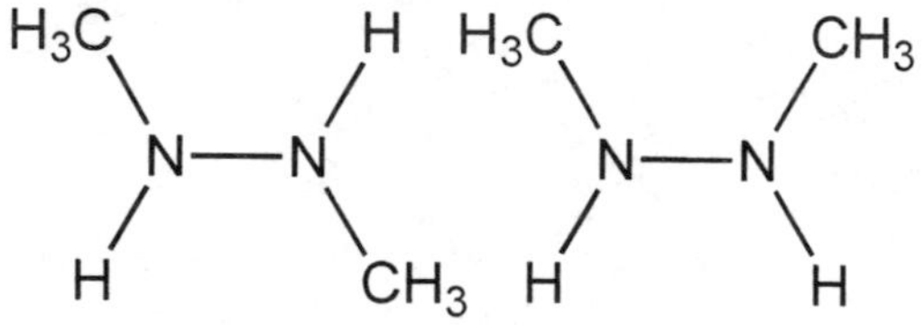

II.   pentanal   2-pentanone

III.

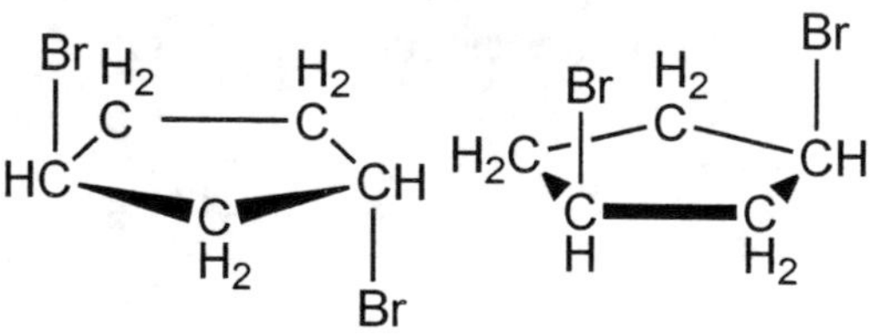

IV.

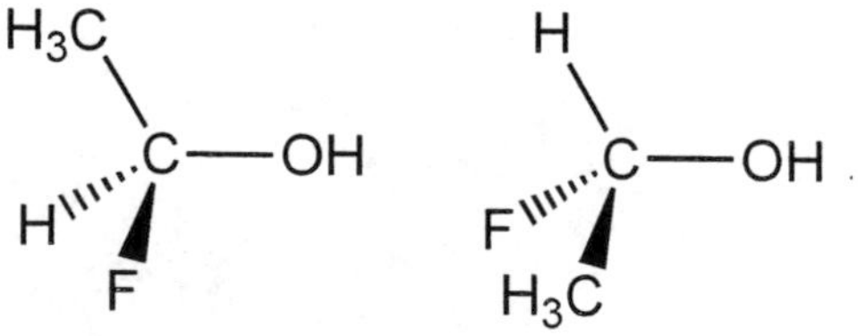

A. I and IV
B. II and III
C. I, II, and III
D. I, II, III, and IV

78. The following procedure was developed to find the specific heat capacity of metals:

1. **Place pieces of the metals in an ice-water bath so their initial temperature is 0 °C.**
2. **Weigh a styrofoam cup.**
3. **Add water at room temperature to the cup and weigh it again**
4. **Add a cold metal from the bath to the cup and weigh the cup a third time.**
5. **Monitor the temperature drop of the water until a final temperature at thermal equilibrium is found.**

_____ is also required as additional information in order to obtain heat capacities for the metals. The best control would be to follow the same protocol except to use _____ in step 4 instead of a cold metal.

A. The heat capacity of water / a metal at 100 °C
B. The heat of formation of water / ice from the 0 °C bath
C. The heat of capacity of ice / glass at 0 °C
D. The heat capacity of water / water from the 0 °C bath

79. What could cause this change in the energy diagram of a reaction?

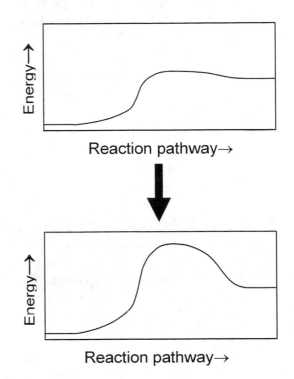

A. Adding catalyst to an endothermic reaction
B. Removing catalyst from an endothermic reaction
C. Adding catalyst to an exothermic reaction
D. Removing catalyst from an exothermic reaction

80. Some scientists have hypothesized that life on other planets may not be carbon-based, but instead, rely on another element as the primary "building block" for organic compounds. Which of the following is most likely able to fill this role?

A. Silicon
B. Oxygen
C. Calcium
D. Chromium

81. An approximately cylindrical piece of wood is found to have a mass of 180 grams. If the diameter of the wood is 5 cm and it is 20 cm long, what is the density of the wood and will it float in water?

A. 0.11 g/cm^3; will not float
B. 0.11 g/cm^3; will float
C. 0.46 g/cm^3; will not float
D. 0.46 g/cm^3; will float

82. Which biomolecule is the primary component in the cellular membrane?

A. Nucleic acids
B. Lipids
C. Carbohydrates
D. Amino acids

83. Place the following elements in order from least to most metallic: Carbon, Francium, Chlorine, Manganese

A. Chlorine< Carbon< Manganese <Francium
B. Francium<Carbon<Manganese <Chlorine
C. Chlorine<Manganese<Carbon< Francium
D. Francium<Manganese<Carbon <Chlorine

84. Which of the following is the best predictor of an element's chemical reactivity?

A. Its atomic number
B. Its group
C. Its period
D. The phase at which it exists at STP

85. Which combination of characteristics would indicate that an unknown substance is an acid?
   I.   Feels slippery
   II. Dissolves metals
   III. Turns litmus paper red
   IV. Turns litmus paper blue
   V.   Is neutralized by KOH
   VI. Is neutralized by HCl

   A.   II, III, and V
   B.   I, II, III, and V
   C.   I, IV, and VI
   D.   II, III, and VI

86. A person holds a paper cup of hot chocolate and her hands are warmed. What type of heat transfer is occurring?

    A. Radiation
    B. Conduction
    C. Convection
    D. Both B and C

87. Which of the following is not a real world example of a phase change?

    A. Dry ice used to produce "fog" during a play
    B. A log in a campfire turning to ash
    C. An abandoned popsicle creating a sticky puddle
    D. The formation of beads of "sweat" on a cold glass

88. A test tube containing 5ml of liquid A is placed in a beaker holding 50 ml of liquid B. Some time later, the temperatures of the liquid A and liquid B are both measured to be 45°C. Assuming the two liquids have the same specific heat capacity, which of the following are true?
I. The liquids A and B are in thermal equilibrium.
II. The liquids contain the same amount of thermal energy.
III. The average kinetic energy of a molecule of liquid A is the same as a molecule of liquid B.

    A. All of the above
    B. None of the above
    C. I and III only
    D. I and II only

89. In humans, energy stored in adenosine triphosphate (ATP) is released when a phosphate group is removed to create adenosine diphosphate (ADP). The energy is used to cause muscle contractions. What type of energy transformation does this represent?

    A. Chemical to mechanical
    B. Chemical to thermal
    C. Thermal to mechanical
    D. Electrical to mechanical

90. Alkali metals are most likely to form ionic compounds with which other group of elements?

    A. Any of the transition metals (Groups 3-12)
    B. Halogens (Group 17)
    C. Other alkali metals (Group 1)
    D. Alkaline earth meals (Group 2)

Part II Content Domains: Subject
Matter Skills and Abilities
Applicable to the Content
Domains in Science
(all CSET science exams)

91. A student designed a
science project testing
the effects of light and
water on plant growth.
You would recommend
that she

A. manipulate the temperature
as well.
B. also alter the pH of the water
as another variable.
C. omit either water or light as a
variable.
D. also alter the light
concentration as another
variable.

92. Identify the control in the
following experiment. A student
had four plants grown under the
following conditions and was
measuring photosynthetic rate by
measuring mass. 2 plants in 50%
light and 2 plants in 100% light.

A. plants grown with no added
nutrients
B. plants grown in the dark
C plants in 100% light
D. plants in 50% light

93. A scientific theory

A. proves scientific accuracy.
B. is never rejected.
C. results in a medical
breakthrough.
D. may be altered at a later time.

94. Which is the correct order of
methodology? 1) testing revised
explanation, 2) setting up a
controlled experiment to test
explanation, 3) drawing a
conclusion, 4) suggesting an
explanation for observations, and
5) compare observed results to
hypothesized results

A. 4, 2, 3, 1, 5
B. 3, 1, 4, 2, 5
C. 4, 2, 5, 1, 3
D. 2, 5, 4, 1, 3

95. Which of the following is not a
legitimate source of unavoidable
error?

A. Contamination of sample
B. Randomness of population
sampling
C. Timing of population sampling
D. Use of measuring devices

96. Which of the following is not
true of the extrapolation of
graphical data points?

A. When exprapolating data of a
linear relationship, we extend
the line of best fit beyond the
known values.
B. Extrapolation is the process of
estimating data points outside
a known set of data points.
C. Extrapolating data will yield
appropriate results as long as
it is done in a strictly linear
fashion.
D. Extrapolating data is only
appropriate if one is relatively
certain that the relationship
between x and y is linear.

97. Given the choice of lab activities, which would you omit?

   A. a genetics experiment tracking the fur color of mice
   B. dissecting a preserved fetal pig
   C. a lab relating temperature to respiration rate using live goldfish.
   D. pithing a frog to see the action of circulation

98. Who should be notified in the case of a serious chemical spill?

   I. the custodian
   II. The fire department
   III. the chemistry teacher
   IV. the administration

   A. I
   B. II
   C. II and III
   D. II and IV

99. In which situation would a science teacher be liable?

   A. a teacher leaves to receive an emergency phone call and a student slips and falls.
   B. a student removes their goggles and gets dissection fluid in their eye.
   C. a faulty gas line results in a fire.
   D. a student cuts themselves with a scalpel.

100. Which statement best defines negligence?

   A. failure to give oral instructions for those with reading disabilities
   B. failure to exercise ordinary care
   C. inability to supervise a large group of students.
   D. reasonable anticipation that an event may occur

MULTIPLE-CHOICE QUESTIONS ANSWER KEY

1. D	35. A	69. A
2. D	36. A	70. B
3. C	37. B	71. B
4. B	38. D	72. C
5. A	39. A	73. B
6. A	40. A	74. B
7. C	41. B	75. A
8. C	42. D	76. B
9. B	43. B	77. B
10. C	44. C	78. D
11. B	45. A	79. B
12. A	46. D	80. A
13. B	47. C	81. D
14. C	48. D	82. B
15. B	49. B	83. A
16. D	50. C	84. A
17. A	51. D	85. A
18. B	52. D	86. D
19. C	53. D	87. B
20. C	54. B	88. C
21. A	55. C	89. A
22. D	56. D	90. B
23. B	57. B	91. C
24. A	58. A	92. B
25. D	59. B	93. D
26. A	60. B	94. C
27. C	61. C	95. A
28. B	62. C	96. C
29. D	63. A	97. D
30. C	64. B	98. D
31. D	65. A	99. A
32. A	66. D	100. B
33. B	67. C	
34. C	68. A	

MULTIPLE-CHOICE ANSWERS WITH SOLUTIONS

Note: The first insignificant digit should be carried through intermediate calculations. This digit is shown using **italics** in the solutions below.

1. **Potassium crystallizes with two atoms contained in each unit cell. What is the mass of potassium found in a lattice 1.00×10^6 unit cells wide, 2.00×10^6 unit cells high, and 5.00×10^5 unit cells deep?**

   A. 85.0 ng
   B. 32.5 μg
   C. 64.9 μg
   D. 130. μg

   D. First we find the number of unit cells in the lattice by multiplying the number in each row, stack, and column:

   1.00×10^6 unit cell lengths $\times 2.00 \times 10^6$ unit cell lengths $\times 5.00 \times 10^5$ unit cell lengths

   $= 1.00 \times 10^{18}$ unit cells

   Avogadro's number and the molecular weight of potassium (K) are used in the solution:

   $$1.00 \times 10^{18} \text{ unit cells} \times \frac{2 \text{ atoms of K}}{\text{unit cell}} \times \frac{1 \text{ mole of K}}{6.02 \times 10^{23} \text{ atoms of K}} \times \frac{39.098 \text{ g K}}{1 \text{ mole of K}}$$
   $$= 1.30 \times 10^{-4} \text{ g}$$
   $$= 130. \mu g$$

2. **At STP, 20. μL of O_2 contain 5.4×10^{16} molecules. According to Avogadro's hypothesis, how many molecules are in 20. μL of Ne at STP?**

   A. 5.4×10^{15}
   B. 1.0×10^{16}
   C. 2.7×10^{16}
   D. 5.4×10^{16}

   D. Avogadro's hypothesis states that equal volumes of different gases at the same temperature and pressure contain equal numbers of molecules.

3. An ideal gas at 50.0 °C and 3.00 atm is in a 300. cm^3 cylinder. The cylinder volume changes by moving a piston until the gas is at 50.0 °C and 1.00 atm. What is the final volume?

    A. 100. cm^3
    B. 450. cm^3
    C. 900. cm^3
    D. 1.20 dm^3

C. A three-fold decrease in pressure of a constant quantity of gas at constant temperature will cause a three-fold increase in gas volume.

4. Which gas law may be used to solve the previous question?

    A. Charles's law
    B. Boyle's law
    C. Graham's law
    D. Avogadro's law

B. The inverse relationship between volume and pressure is Boyle's law.

5. **A blimp is filled with 5000. m³ of helium at 28.0 °C and 99.7 kPa. What is the mass of helium used?**

$$R = 8.3144 \frac{J}{mol\text{-}K}$$

A. 797 kg
B. 810. kg
C. 1.99×10^3 kg
D. 8.57×10^3 kg

A. First the ideal gas law is manipulated to solve for moles.

$$PV = nRT \implies n = \frac{PV}{RT}$$

Temperature must be expressed in Kelvin: $T = (28.0 + 273.15)\, K = 301.15\, K$. The ideal gas law is then used with the knowledge that joules are equivalent to Pa-m³:

$$n = \frac{PV}{RT} = \frac{(99.7 \times 10^3\ Pa)(5000.\ m^3)}{\left(8.3144 \frac{m^3\text{-}Pa}{mol\text{-}K}\right)(301.15\ K)} = 1.991 \times 10^3\ mol\ He .$$

Moles are then converted to grams using the molecular weight of helium:

$$1.991 \times 10^3\ mol\ He \times \frac{4.0026\ g\ He}{1\ mol\ He} = 797 \times 10^3\ g\ He = 797\ kg\ He .$$

6. **Which intermolecular attraction explains the following trend in straight-chain alkanes?**

Condensed structural formula	Boiling point (°C)
CH_4	-161.5
CH_3CH_3	-88.6
$CH_3CH_2CH_3$	-42.1
$CH_3CH_2CH_2CH_3$	-0.5
$CH_3CH_2CH_2CH_2CH_3$	36.0
$CH_3CH_2CH_2CH_2CH_2CH_3$	68.7

A. London dispersion forces
B. Dipole-dipole interactions
C. Hydrogen bonding
D. Ion-induced dipole interactions

A. Alkanes are composed entirely of non-polar C-C and C-H bonds, resulting in no dipole interactions or hydrogen bonding. London dispersion forces increase with the size of the molecule, resulting in a higher temperature requirement to break these bonds and a higher boiling point.

7. **2.00 L of an unknown gas at 1500. mm Hg and a temperature of 25.0 °C weighs 7.52 g. Assuming the ideal gas equation, what is the molecular weight of the gas?**

$$760 \text{ mm Hg}=1 \text{ atm}$$
$$R=0.08206 \text{ L-atm/(mol-K)}$$

    A. 21.6 u
    B. 23.3 u
    C. 46.6 u
    D. 93.2 u

C. Pressure and temperature must be expressed in the proper units. Next the ideal gas law is used to find the number of moles of gas.

$$P = 1500 \text{ mm Hg} \times \frac{1 \text{ atm}}{760 \text{ mm Hg}} = 1.974 \text{ atm and } T = 25.0 + 273.15 = 298.15 \text{ K}$$

$$PV = nRT \implies n = \frac{PV}{RT}$$

$$n = \frac{(1.974 \text{ atm})(2.00 \text{ L})}{\left(0.08206 \dfrac{\text{L-atm}}{\text{mol-K}}\right)(298.15 \text{ K})} = 0.1613 \text{ mol.}$$

The molecular mass may be found from the mass of one mole.

$$\frac{7.52 \text{ g}}{0.1613 \text{ mol}} = 46.6 \frac{\text{g}}{\text{mol}} \implies 46.6 \text{ u}$$

8. **Which of the following statements are true of vapor pressure at equilibrium?**

    A. Solids have no vapor pressure.
    B. Dissolving a solute in a liquid increases its vapor pressure.
    C. The vapor pressure of a pure substance is characteristic of that substance and its temperature.
    D. All of the above

C. Only temperature and the identity of the substance determine vapor pressure. Solids have a vapor pressure, and solutes decrease vapor pressure.

9. Find the partial pressure of N_2 in a container holding H_2O and N_2 at 150. kPa and 50 °C. The vapor pressure of H_2O at 50 °C is 12 kPa.

    A. 12 kPa
    B. 138 kPa
    C. 162 kPa
    D. The value cannot be determined.

B. The partial pressure of H_2O vapor in the container is its vapor pressure. The partial pressure of N_2 may be found by manipulating Dalton's law:

$$P_{total} = P_{H_2O} + P_{N_2} \Rightarrow P_{N_2} = P_{total} - P_{H_2O}$$
$$P_{N_2} = P_{total} - P_{H_2O} = 150.\ kPa - 12\ kPa = 138\ kPa$$

10. The solubility of $CoCl_2$ is 54 g per 100 g of ethanol. Three flasks each contain 100 g of ethanol. Flask #1 also contains 40 g $CoCl_2$ in solution. Flask #2 contains 56 g $CoCl_2$ in solution. Flask #3 contains 5 g of solid $CoCl_2$ in equilibrium with 54 g $CoCl_2$ in solution. Which of the following describe the solutions present in the liquid phase of the flasks?

    A. #1-saturated, #2-supersaturated, #3-unsaturated.
    B. #1-unsaturated, #2-miscible, #3-saturated.
    C. #1-unsaturated, #2-supersaturated, #3-saturated.
    D. #1-unsaturated, #2-not at equilibrium, #3-miscible.

C. Flask #1 contains less solute than the solubility limit, and is unsaturated. Flask #2 contains more solute than the solubility limit, and is supersaturated and also not at equilibrium. Flask #3 contains the solubility limit and is a saturated solution. The term "miscible" applies only to liquids that mix together in all proportions.

11. Carbonated water is bottled at 25 °C under pure CO_2 at 4.0 atm. Later the bottle is opened at 4 °C under air at 1.0 atm that has a partial pressure of 3×10^{-4} atm CO_2. Why do CO_2 bubbles form when the bottle is opened?

    A. CO_2 leaves the solution due to a drop in solubility at the lower total pressure.
    B. CO_2 leaves the solution due to a drop in solubility at the lower CO_2 pressure.
    C. CO_2 leaves the solution due to a drop in solubility at the lower temperature.
    D. CO_2 is formed by the decomposition of carbonic acid.

B. A is incorrect because if the water were bottled under a different gas at a high pressure, it would not be carbonated. CO_2 partial pressure is the important factor in solubility. C is incorrect because a decrease in temperature will increase solubility, and the chance from 298 K to 277 K is relatively small. D may occur, but this represents a small fraction of the gas released.

12. When KNO_3 dissolves in water, the water grows slightly colder. An increase in temperature will _____ the solubility of KNO_3.

    A. increase
    B. decrease
    C. have no effect on
    D. have an unknown effect with the information given on

A. The decline in water temperature indicates that the net solution process is endothermic (requiring heat). A temperature increase supplying more heat will favor the solution and increase solubility according to Le Chatelier's principle.

13. Aluminum sulfate is a strong electrolyte. What is the concentration of all species in a 0.2 M solution of aluminum sulfate?

    A. 0.2 M Al^{3+}, 0.2 M SO_4^{2-}
    B. 0.4 M Al^{3+}, 0.6 M SO_4^{2-}
    C. 0.6 M Al^{3+}, 0.4 M SO_4^{2-}
    D. 0.2 M $Al_2(SO_4)_3$

B. A strong electrolyte will completely ionize into its cation and anion. Aluminum sulfate is $Al_2(SO_4)_3$. Each mole of aluminum sulfate ionizes into 2 moles of Al^{3+} and 3 moles of SO_4^{2-}:

$$0.2\frac{mol\ Al_2(SO_4)_3}{L} \times \frac{2\ mol\ Al^{3+}}{mol\ Al_2(SO_4)_3} = 0.4\frac{mol\ Al^{3+}}{L}\ and$$

$$0.2\frac{mol\ Al_2(SO_4)_3}{L} \times \frac{3\ mol\ SO_4^{2-}}{mol\ Al_2(SO_4)_3} = 0.6\frac{mol\ SO_4^{2-}}{L}.$$

14. 15 g of formaldehyde (CH_2O) are dissolved in 100. g of water. Calculate the weight percentage and mole fraction of formaldehyde in the solution.

    A. 13%, 0.090
    B. 15%, 0.090
    C. 13%, 0.083
    D. 15%, 0.083

C. Remember to use the total amounts in the denominator.

For weight percentage: $\dfrac{15\ g\ CH_2O}{(15+100)\ g\ total} = 0.13 = 13\%$.

For mole fraction, first convert grams of each substance to moles:

$$15\ g\ CH_2O \times \frac{mol\ CH_2O}{(12.011+2\times 1.0079+15.999)\ g\ CH_2O} = 0.4996\ mol\ CH_2O$$

$$100\ g\ H_2O \times \frac{mol\ H_2O}{(2\times 1.0079+15.999)\ g\ H_2O} = 5.551\ mol\ H_2O.$$

Again use the total amount in the denominator $\dfrac{0.4996\ mol\ CH_2O}{(0.4996+5.551)\ mol\ total} = 0.083$.

15. Which of the following would make the best solvent for Br_2?

    A. H_2O
    B. CS_2
    C. NH_3
    D. molten NaCl

B. The best solvents for a solute have intermolecular bonds of similar strength to the solute ("like dissolves like"). Bromine is a non-polar molecule with intermolecular attractions due to weak London dispersion forces. The relatively strong hydrogen bonding in H_2O and NH_3 and the very strong electrostatic attractions in molten NaCl would make each of them a poor solvent for Br_2 because these molecules would prefer to remain attracted to one another. CS_2 is a fairly small non-polar molecule.

16. Which of the following is most likely to dissolve in water?

    A. H_2
    B. CCl_4
    C. $(SiO_2)_n$
    D. CH_3OH

D. The best solutes for a solvent have intermolecular bonds of similar strength to the solvent. H_2O molecules are connected by fairly strong hydrogen bonds. H_2 and CCl_4 are molecules with intermolecular attractions due to weak London dispersion forces. $(SiO_2)_n$ is a covalent network solid and is essentially one large molecule with bonds that much stronger than hydrogen bonds. CH_3OH (methanol) is miscible with water because it contains hydrogen bonds between molecules.

17. Which of the following is <u>not</u> a colligative property?

    A. Viscosity lowering
    B. Freezing point lowering
    C. Boiling point elevation
    D. Vapor pressure lowering

A. Vapor pressure lowering, boiling point elevation, and freezing point lowering may all be visualized as a result of solute particles interfering with the interface between phases in a consistent way. This is not the case for viscosity.

18. $BaCl_2(aq) + Na_2SO_4(aq) \rightarrow BaSO_4(s) + 2NaCl(aq)$ is an example of a _____ reaction.

    A. acid-base
    B. precipitation
    C. redox
    D. nuclear

B. $BaSO_4$ falls out of the solution as a precipitate, but the charges on Ba^{2+} and SO_4^{2-} remain unchanged, so this is not a redox reaction. Neither $BaCl_2$ nor Na_2SO_4 are acids or bases, and the nuclei involved also remain unaltered

19. **List the following aqueous solutions in order of increasing boiling point.**

    I.   0.050 *m* $AlCl_3$
    II. 0.080 *m* $Ba(NO_3)_2$
    III. 0.090 *m* NaCl
    IV. 0.12 *m* ethylene glycol ($C_2H_6O_2$)

    A. I < II < III < IV
    B. I < III < IV < II
    C. IV < III < I < II
    D. IV < III < II < I

C. Particles in solution determine colligative properties. The first three materials are strong electrolyte salts, and $C_2H_6O_2$ is a non-electrolyte.

$AlCl_3(aq)$ is Al^{3+} +3 Cl^-. So $0.050 \dfrac{\text{mol } AlCl_3}{\text{kg } H_2O} \times \dfrac{4 \text{ mol particles}}{\text{mol } AlCl_3} = 0.200$ *m* particles

$Ba(NO_3)_2(aq)$ is Ba^{2+} +2 NO_3^-. So $0.080 \dfrac{\text{mol } Ba(NO_3)_2}{\text{kg } H_2O} \times \dfrac{3 \text{ mol particles}}{\text{mol } Ba(NO_3)_2} = 0.240$ *m* particles

$NaCl(aq)$ is Na^+ +Cl^-. So $0.090 \dfrac{\text{mol } NaCl}{\text{kg } H_2O} \times \dfrac{2 \text{ mol particles}}{\text{mol } NaCl} = 0.180$ *m* particles

$C_2H_6O_2(aq)$ is not an electrolyte. So $0.12 \dfrac{\text{mol } C_2H_6O_2}{\text{kg } H_2O} \times \dfrac{1 \text{ mol particles}}{\text{mol } C_2H_6O_2} = 0.12$ *m* particles

The greater the number of dissolved particles, the greater the boiling point elevation.

20. Osmotic pressure is the pressure required to prevent _____ flowing from low to high _____ concentration across a semipermeable membrane.

    A. solute, solute
    B. solute, solvent
    C. solvent, solute
    D. solvent, solvent

C. Osmotic pressure is the pressure required to prevent osmosis, which is the flow of solvent across the membrane from low to high solute concentration. This is also the direction from high to low solvent concentration.

21. A solution of NaCl in water is heated on a mountain in an open container until it boils at 100. °C. The air pressure on the mountain is 0.92 atm. According to Raoult's law, what mole fraction of Na^+ and Cl^- are present in the solution?

    A. 0.04 Na^+, 0.04 Cl^-
    B. 0.08 Na^+, 0.08 Cl^-
    C. 0.46 Na^+, 0.46 Cl^-
    D. 0.92 Na^+, 0.92 Cl^-

A. The vapor pressure of H_2O at 100. °C is exactly 1 atm. Boiling point decreases with external pressure, so the boiling point of pure H_2O at 0.9 atm will be less than 100. °C. Adding salt raises the boiling point at 0.92 atm to 100. °C by decreasing vapor pressure to 0.92 atm. According to Raoult's law:

$$P^{vapor}_{solution} = P^{vapor}_{pure\ solvent}\left(mole\ fraction\right)_{solvent} \Rightarrow \left(mole\ fraction\right)_{solvent} = \frac{P^{vapor}_{solution}}{P^{vapor}_{pure\ solvent}}.$$

$$\text{Therefore, } \left(mole\ fraction\right)_{H_2O} = \frac{0.92\ atm\ at\ 100.\ °C}{1.0\ atm\ at\ 100.\ °C} = 0.92\ \frac{mol\ H_2O}{mol\ total}.$$

The remaining 0.08 mole fraction of solute is evenly divided between the two ions:

$$\left(mole\ fraction\right)_{solute} = 1 - \left(mole\ fraction\right)_{H_2O} = 1 - 0.92 = 0.08\ \frac{mol\ solute\ particles}{mol\ total}$$

$$\left(mole\ fraction\right)_{Na^+} = 0.08\ \frac{mol\ solute\ particles}{mol\ total} \times \frac{1\ mol\ Na^+}{2\ mol\ solute\ particles} = 0.04\ \frac{mol\ Na^+}{mol\ total}$$

$$\left(mole\ fraction\right)_{Cl^-} = 0.08\ \frac{mol\ solute\ particles}{mol\ total} \times \frac{1\ mol\ Cl^-}{2\ mol\ solute\ particles} = 0.04\ \frac{mol\ Cl^-}{mol\ total}.$$

22. Write a balanced nuclear equation for the emission of an alpha particle by polonium-209.

    A. $^{209}_{84}Po \rightarrow \; ^{205}_{81}Pb + ^{4}_{2}He$

    B. $^{209}_{84}Po \rightarrow \; ^{205}_{82}Bi + ^{4}_{2}He$

    C. $^{209}_{84}Po \rightarrow \; ^{209}_{85}At + ^{0}_{-1}e$

    D. $^{209}_{84}Po \rightarrow \; ^{205}_{82}Pb + ^{4}_{2}He$

D. The periodic table before skill 1.1 shows that polonium has an atomic number of 84. The emission of an alpha particle, $^{4}_{2}He$ (eliminating choice C), will leave an atom with an atomic number of 82 and a mass number of 205 (eliminating choice A). The periodic table identifies this element as lead, $^{205}_{82}Pb$, not bismuth (eliminating choice B).

23. $^{3}_{1}H$ decays with a half-life of 12 years. 3.0 g of pure $^{3}_{1}H$ were placed in a sealed container 24 years ago. How many grams of $^{3}_{1}H$ remain?

    A. 0.38 g
    B. 0.75 g
    C. 1.5 g
    D. 3.0 g

B. Every 12 years, the amount remaining is cut in half. After 12 years, 1.5 g will remain. After another 12 years, 0.75 g will remain.

24. Which of the following isotopes can create a chain reaction of nuclear fission?

    A. uranium-235
    B. uranium-238
    C. plutonium-238
    D. all of the above

A. Uranium-235 and plutonium-239 are the two fissile isotopes used for nuclear power. ^{238}U is the most common uranium isotope. ^{238}Pu is used as a heat source for energy in space probes and some pacemakers.

25. Which of the following is a correct electron arrangement for oxygen?

A.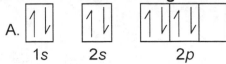

   1s   2s   2p

B. $1s^21p^22s^22p^2$
C. 2, 2, 4
D. none of the above

D. Choice A violates Hund's rule. The two electrons on the far right should occupy the final two orbitals. B should be $1s^22s^22p^4$. There is no $1p$ subshell. C should be 2, 6. Number lists indicate electrons in shells.

26. Which of the following statements about radiant energy is **not** true?

   A. The energy change of an electron transition is directly proportional to the wavelength of the emitted or absorbed photon.
   B. The energy of an electron in a hydrogen atom depends only on the principle quantum number.
   C. The frequency of photons striking a metal determines whether the photoelectric effect will occur.
   D. The frequency of a wave of electromagnetic radiation is inversely proportional to its wavelength.

A. The energy change (ΔE) is <u>inversely</u> proportional to the wavelength (λ) of the photon according the equations:

$$\Delta E = \frac{hc}{\lambda}.$$

where h is Planck's constant and c is the speed of light.

Choice B is true for hydrogen. Atoms with more than one electron are more complex. The frequency of individual photons, not the number of photons determines whether the photoelectric effect occurs, so choice C is true. Choice D is true. The proportionality constant is the speed of light according to the equation:

$$\nu = \frac{c}{\lambda}.$$

27. Match the orbital diagram for the ground state of carbon with the rule/principle it violates:

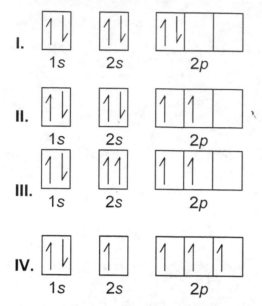

I.   1s   2s   2p

II.   1s   2s   2p

III. 1s   2s   2p

IV.   1s   2s   2p

    A. I-Pauli exclusion, II-Aufbau, III-no violation, IV-Hund's
    B. I-Aufbau, II-Pauli exclusion, III-no violation, IV-Hund's
    C. I-Hund's, II-no violation, III-Pauli exclusion, IV-Aufbau
    D. I-Hund's, II-no violation, III-Aufbau, IV-Pauli exclusion

C. Diagram I violates Hund's rule because a second electron is added to a degenerate orbital before all orbitals in the subshell have one electron. Diagram III violates the Pauli exclusion principle because both electrons in the $2s$ orbital have the same spin. They would have the same 4 quantum numbers. Diagram IV violates the Aufbau principle because an electron occupies the higher energy $2p$ orbital before $2s$ orbital has been filled; this configuration is not at the ground state.

28. Which oxide forms the strongest acid in water?

    A. Al_2O_3
    B. Cl_2O_7
    C. As_2O_5
    D. CO_2

B. The strength of acids formed from oxides increases with electronegativity and with oxidation state. We know Cl has a greater electronegativity than Al, As, and C because it is closer to the top right of the periodic table. The oxidation numbers of our choices are +3 for Al, +7 for Cl, +5 for As, and +4 for C. Both its electronegativity and its oxidation state indicate Cl_2O_7 will form the strongest acid.

29. Rank the following bonds from least to most polar:

C-H, C-Cl, H-H, C-F

  A. C-H < H-H < C-F < C-Cl
  B. H-H < C-H < C-F < C-Cl
  C. C-F < C-Cl < C-H < H-H
  D. H-H < C-H < C-Cl < C-F

D. Bonds between atoms of the same element are completely non-polar, so H-H is the least polar bond in the list, eliminating choices A and C. The C-H bond is considered to be non-polar even though the electrons of the bond are slightly unequally shared. C-Cl and C-F are both polar covalent bonds, but C-F is more strongly polar because F has a greater electronegativity.

30. Which of the following is a proper Lewis dot structure of CHClO?

  A. 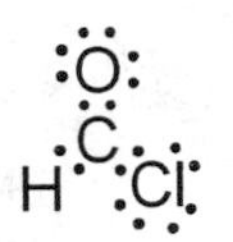 B. 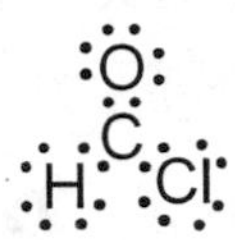 C. 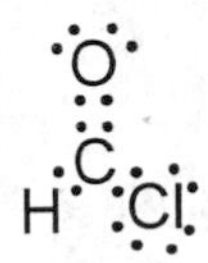 D.

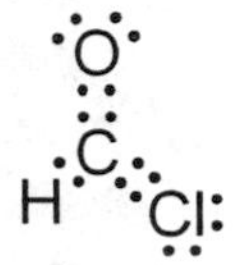

C. C has 4 valence shell electrons, H has 1, Cl has 7, and O has 6. The molecule has a total of 18 valence shell electrons. This eliminates choice B which has 24. Choice B is also incorrect because has an octet around a hydrogen atom instead of 2 electrons and because there are only six electrons surrounding the central carbon. A single bond connecting all atoms would give choice A. This is incorrect because there are only 6 electrons surrounding the central carbon. A double bond between C and O gives the correct answer, C. A double bond between C and O and also between C and Cl would give choice D. This is incorrect because there are 10 electrons surrounding the central carbon.

31. Which statement about molecular structures is false?

A. 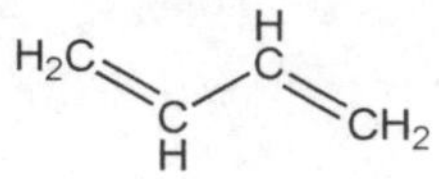 is a conjugated molecule.

B. A bonding σ orbital connects two atoms by the straight line between them.

C. A bonding π orbital connects two atoms in a separate region from the straight line between them.

D. The anion with resonance forms will always exist in one form or the other.

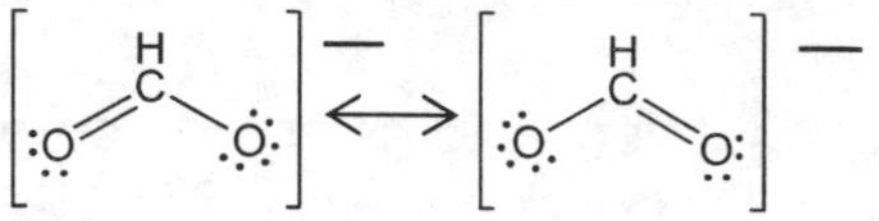

D. A conjugated molecule is a molecule with double bonds on adjacent atoms such as the molecule shown in A. Choice B and C give the definition of sigma and pi molecular orbitals. D is false because a resonance form is one of multiple equivalent Lewis structures, but these structures do not describe the actual state of the molecule. The anion will exist in a state between the two forms.

32. What is the shape of the PH_3 molecule? Use the VSEPR model.

A. Trigonal pyramidal
B. Trigonal bipyramidal
C. Trigonal planar
D. Tetrahedral

A. The Lewis structure for PH_3 is given to the right. This structure contains 4 electron pairs around the central atom, so the geometral arrangement is tetrahedral. However, the shape of a molecule is given by its atom locations, and there are only three atoms so choice D is not correct. Four electrons pairs with one unshared pair (3 bonds and one lone pair) give a trigonal pyramidal shape as shown to the left.

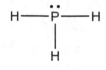

33. What is the chemical composition of magnesium nitrate?

A. 11.1% Mg, 22.2% N, 66.7% O
B. 16.4% Mg, 18.9% N, 64.7% O
C. 20.9% Mg, 24.1% N, 55.0% O
D. 28.2% Mg, 16.2% N, 55.7% O

B. First find the formula for magnesium nitrate. Mg is an alkali earth metal and will always have a 2+ charge. The nitrate ion is NO_3^-. Two nitrate ions are required for each Mg^{2+} ion. Therefore the formula is $Mg(NO_3)_2$

Skill 5.1 describes determination chemical composition.
  1) Determine the number of atoms for elemen in $Mg(NO_3)_2$: 1 Mg, 2 N, 6 O.
  2) Multiply by the molecular weight of the elements to determine the grams of each in one mole of the formula.

$$\frac{1 \text{ mol Mg}}{\text{mol } Mg(NO_3)_2} \times \frac{24.3 \text{ g Mg}}{\text{mol Mg}} = 24.3 \text{ g Mg/mol } Mg(NO_3)_2$$

$$2(14.0) = 28.0 \text{ g N/mol } Mg(NO_3)_2$$

$$6(16.0) = 96.0 \text{ g O/mol } Mg(NO_3)_2$$

  3) Determine formula mass $\qquad$ 148.3 g $Mg(NO_3)_2$/mol $Mg(NO_3)_2$
  4) Divide to determine % composition

$$\%Mg = \frac{24.3 \text{ g Mg/mol } Mg(NO_3)_2}{148.3 \text{ g } Mg(NO_3)_2/\text{mol } Mg(NO_3)_2} = 0.164 \text{ g Mg/g } Mg(NO_3)_2 \times 100\% = 16.4\%$$

$$\%N = \frac{28.0}{148.3} \times 100\% = 18.9\% \qquad \%O = \frac{96.0}{148.3} \times 100\% = 64.7\%$$

Answer A is the fractional representation of the presence of each atom in the formula. Composition is based on mass percentage. Answer C is the chemical composition of $Mg(NO_2)_2$, magnesium nitrite. Answer D is the chemical composition of "$MgNO_3$", a formula that results from not balancing charges.

34. Balance the equation for the neutralization reaction between phosphoric acid and calcium hydroxide by filling in the blank stoichiometric coefficients.

$$\_\_H_3PO_4 + \_\_Ca(OH)_2 \rightarrow \_\_Ca_3(PO_4)_2 + \_\_H_2O$$

A. 4, 3, 1, 4
B. 2, 3, 1, 8
C. 2, 3, 1, 6
D. 2, 1, 1, 2

C. We are given the unbalanced equation (**step 1**).

Next we determine the number of atoms on each side (**step 2**). For reactants (left of the arrow): 5H, 1P, 6O, and 1Ca. For products: 2H, 2P, 9O, and 3Ca.

We assume that the molecule with the most atoms—i.e. $Ca_3(PO_4)_2$—has a coefficient of one, and find the other coefficients required to have the same number of atoms on each side of the equation (**step 3**). Assuming $Ca_3(PO_4)_2$ has a coefficient of one means that there will be 3 Ca and 2 P on the right because H_2O has no Ca or P. A balanced equation would also have 3 Ca and 2 P on the left. This is achieved with a coefficient of 2 for H_3PO_4 and 3 for $Ca(OH)_2$. Now we have:

$$2H_3PO_4 + 3Ca(OH)_2 \rightarrow Ca_3(PO_4)_2 + ?H_2O$$

The coefficient for H_2O is found by a balance on H or on O. Whichever one is chosen, the other atom should be checked to confirm that a balance actually occurs. For H, there are 6 H from $2H_3PO_4$ and 6 from $3Ca(OH)_2$ for a total of 12 H on the left. There must be 12 H on the right for balance. None are accounted for by $Ca_3(PO_4)_2$, so all 12 H must occur on H_2O. It has a coefficient of 6.

$$2H_3PO_4 + 3Ca(OH)_2 \rightarrow Ca_3(PO_4)_2 + 6H_2O$$

This is choice C, but if time is available, it is best to check that the remaining atom is balanced. There are 8 O from $2H_3PO_4$ and 6 from $3Ca(OH)_2$ for a total of 14 on the left, and 8 O from $Ca_3(PO_4)_2$ and 6 from $6H_2O$ for a total of 14 on the right. The equation is balanced.

Mulitplication by a whole number (**step 4**) is not required because the stoichiometric coefficients from step 3 already are whole numbers.

An alternative method would be to try the coefficients given for answer A, answer B, etc. until we recognize a properly balanced equation.

35. Find the mass of CO_2 produced by the combustion of 15 kg of isopropyl alcohol in the reaction:

$$2C_3H_7OH + 9O_2 \rightarrow 6CO_2 + 8H_2O$$

A. 33 kg
B. 44 kg
C. 50 kg
D. 60 kg

A Remember "grams to moles to moles to grams." Step 1 converts mass to moles for the known value. In this case, kg and kmol are used. Step 2 relates moles of the known value to moles of the unknown value by their stoichiometry coefficients. Step 3 converts moles off the unknown value to a mass.

$$15 \times 10^3 \text{ g } C_4H_8O \times \underset{\text{step 1}}{\frac{1 \text{ mol } C_4H_8O}{60 \text{ g } C_4H_8O}} \times \underset{\text{step 2}}{\frac{6 \text{ mol } CO_2}{2 \text{ mol } C_4H_8O}} \times \underset{\text{step 3}}{\frac{44 \text{ g } CO_2}{1 \text{ mol } CO_2}} = 33 \times 10^3 \text{ g } CO_2$$

$$= 33 \text{ kg } CO_2$$

36. A 100. L vessel of pure O_2 at 500. kPa and 20. °C is used for the combustion of butane:

$$2C_4H_{10} + 13O_2 \rightarrow 8CO_2 + 10H_2O.$$

Find the mass of butane to consume all the O_2 in the vessel. Assume O_2 is an ideal gas and use a value of $R = 8.314$ J/(mol•K).

A. 183 g
B. 467 g
C. 1.83 kg
D. 7.75 kg

A We are given a volume and asked for a mass. The steps will be "volume to moles to moles to mass."

"Volume to moles..." requires the ideal gas law, but first several units must be altered.

Units of joules are identical to m^3•Pa.
500 kPa is 500×10^3 Pa.
100 L is 0.100 m^3.
20 °C is 293.15 K.
$PV = nRT$ is rearranged to give:

$$n = \frac{PV}{RT} = \frac{(500 \times 10^3 \text{ Pa})(0.100 \text{ m}^3 \text{ O}_2)}{\left(8.314 \frac{\text{m}^3 \text{Pa}}{\text{mol·K}}\right)(293.15 \text{ K})} = 20.51 \text{ mol O}_2$$

"...to moles to mass" utilizes stoichiometry. The molecular weight of butane is 58.1 u.

$$20.51 \text{ mol O}_2 \times \frac{2 \text{ mol C}_4\text{H}_{10}}{13 \text{ mol O}_2} \times \frac{58.1 \text{ g C}_4\text{H}_{10}}{1 \text{ mol C}_4\text{H}_{10}} = 183 \text{ g C}_4\text{H}_{10}$$

37. Three experiments were performed at the same initial temperature and pressure to determine the rate of the reaction

$$2ClO_2(g) + F_2(g) \rightarrow 2ClO_2F(g).$$

Results are shown in the table below. Concentrations are given in millimoles per liter (mM).

Exp.	Initial $[ClO_2]$ (mM)	Initial $[F_2]$ (mM)	Initial rate of $[ClO_2F]$ increase (mM/sec)
1	5.0	5.0	0.63
2	5.0	20	2.5
3	10	10	2.5

What is the rate law for this reaction?

A. Rate $= k\left[F_2\right]$

B. Rate $= k\left[ClO_2\right]\left[F_2\right]$

C. Rate $= k\left[ClO_2\right]^2\left[F_2\right]$

D. Rate $= k\left[ClO_2\right]\left[F_2\right]^2$

B A four-fold increase in $[F_2]$ at constant $[ClO_2]$ between experiment one and two caused a four-fold increase in rate. Rate is therefore proportional to $[F_2]$ at constant $[ClO_2]$, eliminating choice D (Choice D predicts rate to increase by a factor of 16).

Between experiment 1 and 3, $[F_2]$ and $[ClO_2]$ both double in value. Once again, there is a four-fold increase in rate. If rate were only dependent on $[F_2]$ (choice A), there would be a two-fold increase. The correct answer, B, attributes a two-fold increase in rate to the doubling of $[F_2]$ and a two-fold increase to the doubling of $[ClO_2]$, resulting in a net four-fold increase. Choice C predicts a rate increase by a factor of 8.

If this were an elementary reaction describing a collision event between three molecules, choice C would be expected, but stoichiometry cannot be used to predict a rate law.

38. Write the equilibrium expression K_{eq} for the reaction

$$CO_2(g) + H_2(g) \rightarrow CO(g) + H_2O(l)$$

A. $\dfrac{[CO][H_2O]}{[CO_2][H_2]^2}$

B. $\dfrac{[CO_2][H_2]}{[CO][H_2O]}$

C. $\dfrac{[CO][H_2O]}{[CO_2][H_2]}$

D. $\dfrac{[CO]}{[CO_2][H_2]}$

D Product concentrations are multiplied together in the numerator and reactant concentrations in the denominator, eliminating choice B. The stoichiometric coefficient of H_2 is one, eliminating choice A. For heterogeneous reactions, concentrations of pure liquids or solids are absent from the expression because they are constant, eliminating choice C. D is correct.

39. $BaSO_4$ (K_{sp} = 1X10^{-10}) is added to pure H_2O. How much is dissolved in 1 L of saturated solution?

A. 2 mg
B. 10 μg
C. 2 μg
D. 100 pg

A $BaSO_4(s) \rightleftharpoons Ba^{2+}(aq) + SO_4^{2-}(aq)$, therefore: $K_{sp} = \left[Ba^{2+}\right]\left[SO_4^{2-}\right]$.

In a saturated solution: $\left[Ba^{2+}\right] = \left[SO_4^{2-}\right] = \sqrt{1 \times 10^{-10}} = 1 \times 10^{-5}$ M.

The mass in one liter is found from the molarity:

$$1 \times 10^{-5} \frac{\text{mol } Ba^{2+} \text{ or } SO_4^{2-}}{L} \times \frac{1 \text{ mol dissolved } BaSO_4}{1 \text{ mol } Ba^{2+} \text{ or } SO_4^{2-}} \times \frac{(137+32+4 \times 16)\text{g } BaSO_4}{1 \text{ mol } BaSO_4}$$

$$= 0.002 \frac{g}{L} BaSO_4 \times 1 \text{ L solution} \times \frac{1000 \text{ mg}}{g} = 2 \text{ mg } BaSO_4$$

40. At a certain temperature, T, the equilibrium constant for the reaction

$$2NO(g) \rightarrow N_2(g) + O_2(g)$$

is $K_{eq} = 2 \times 10^3$. If a 1.0 L container at this temperature contains 90 mM N_2, 20 mM O_2, and 5 mM NO, what will occur?

    A. The reaction will make more N_2 and O_2.
    B. The reaction is at equilibrium.
    C. The reaction will make more NO.
    D. The temperature, T, is required to solve this problem.

A Calculate the reaction quotient at the actual conditions:

$$Q = \frac{[N_2][O_2]}{[NO]^2} = \frac{(0.090 \text{ M})(0.020 \text{ M})}{(0.005 \text{ M})^2} = 72$$

This value is less than K_{eq}: $72 < 2 \times 10^3$, therefore $Q < K_{eq}$. To achieve equilibrium, the numerator of Q must be larger relative to the denominator. This occurs when products turn into reactants. Therefore NO will react to make more N_2 and O_2.

41. Which of the following are listed from weakest to strongest acid?

    A. H_2SO_3, H_2SeO_3, H_2TeO_3
    B. HBrO, $HBrO_2$, $HBrO_3$, $HBrO_4$
    C. HI, HBr, HCl, HF
    D. H_3PO_4, $H_2PO_4^-$, HPO_4^{2-}

B The electronegativity of the central atom decreases from S to Se to Te as period number increases in the same periodic table group. The acidity of the oxide also decreases. Choice B is correct because acid strength increases with the oxidation state of the central atom. C is wrong because HI, HBr, and HCl are all strong acids but HF is a weak acid. D is wrong because acid strength is greater for polyprotic acids.

42. NH$_4$F is dissolved in water. Which of the following are conjugate acid/base pairs present in the solution?

   I.   NH$_4^+$/NH$_4$OH
   II. HF/F$^-$
   III. H$_3$O$^+$/H$_2$O
   IV. H$_2$O/OH$^-$

   A. I, II, and III
   B. I, III, and IV
   C. II and IV
   D. II, III, and IV

D NH$_4$F is soluble in water and completely dissociates to NH$_4^+$ and F$^-$. F$^-$ is a weak base with HF as its conjugate acid (**II**). NH$_4^+$ is a weak acid with NH$_3$ as its conjugate base. A conjugate acid/base pair must have the form HX/X (where X is one lower charge than HX). NH$_4^+$/NH$_4$OH (**I**) is <u>not</u> a conjugate acid/base pair, eliminating choice A and B. H$_3$O$^+$/H$_2$O and H$_2$O/OH$^-$ (**III** and **IV**) are always present in water and in all aqueous solutions as conjugate acid/base pairs. All of the following equilibrium reactions occur in NH$_4$F(aq):

$$NH_4^+(aq) + OH^-(aq) \rightleftharpoons NH_3(aq) + H_2O(l)$$
$$F^-(aq) + H_3O^+(aq) \rightleftharpoons HF(aq) + H_2O(l)$$
$$2H_2O(l) \rightleftharpoons H_3O^+(aq) + OH^-(aq)$$

43. What are the pH and the pOH of 0.010 M HNO$_3$(aq)?

   A. pH = 1.0, pOH = 9.0
   B. pH = 2.0, pOH = 12.0
   C. pH = 2.0, pOH = 8.0
   D. pH = 8.0, pOH = 6.0

B HNO$_3$ is a strong acid, so it completely dissociates:

$$\left[H^+\right] = 0.010 \text{ M} = 1.0 \times 10^{-2} \text{ M}.$$
$$pH = -\log_{10}\left[H^+\right] = -\log_{10}\left(1.0 \times 10^{-2}\right) = 2.0 \text{ (choices B or C)}.$$
$$\text{From pH} + pOH = 14: \quad pOH = 12.0 \text{ (choice B)}.$$

44. What is the pH of a buffer made of 0.128 M sodium formate (HCOONa) and 0.072 M formic acid (HCOOH)? The pK_a of formic acid is 3.75.

A. 2.0
B. 3.0
C. 4.0
D. 5.0

C From the pK_a, we may find the K_a of formic acid:

$$K_a = 10^{-pK_a} = 10^{-3.75} = 1.78 \times 10^{-4}$$

This is the equilibrium constant:

$$K_a = \frac{[H^+][HCOO^-]}{[HCOOH]} = 1.78 \times 10^{-4} \text{ for the dissociation: } HCOOH \rightleftharpoons H^+ + HCOO^-.$$

The pH is found by solving for the H^+ concentration:

$$[H^+] = K_a \frac{[HCOOH]}{[HCOO^-]} = (1.78 \times 10^{-4}) \frac{0.072}{0.128} = 1.0 \times 10^{-4} \text{ M}$$

$$pH = -\log_{10}[H^+] = -\log_{10}(1.0 \times 10^{-4}) = 4.0 \text{ (choice C)}$$

45. Rank the following from lowest to highest pH. Assume a small volume for the added component:

I. 0.01 mol HCl added to 1 L H_2O
II. 0.01 mol HI added to 1 L of an acetic acid/sodium acetate solution at pH 4.0
III. 0.01 mol NH_3 added to 1 L H_2O
IV. 0.1 mol HNO_3 added to 1 L of a 0.1 M $Ca(OH)_2$ solution

A. I < II < III < IV
B. I < II < IV < III
C. II < I < III < IV
D. II < I < IV < III

A HCl is a strong acid. Therefore solution I has a <u>pH of 2</u> because
$$pH = -\log_{10}\left[H^+\right] = -\log_{10}(0.01) = 2.$$

HI is also a strong acid and would have a pH of 2 at this concentration in water, but the buffer will prevent pH from dropping this low. Solution II will have a pH <u>above 2</u> and below 4, eliminating choices C and D.

If a strong base were in solution III, its pOH would be 2. Using the equation pH + pOH = 14, its pH would be 12. Because NH_3 is a weak base, the pH of solution III will be greater than 7 and <u>less than 12</u>.

A neutralization reaction occurs in solution IV between 0.1 mol of H^+ from the strong acid HNO_3 and <u>0.2 mol of OH^-</u> from the strong base $Ca(OH)_2$. Each mole of $Ca(OH)_2$ contributes two base equivalents for the neutralization reaction. The base is the excess reagent, and 0.1 mol of OH^- remain after the reaction. This resulting solution will have a pOH of 1 and a <u>pH of 13</u>.

A is correct because: 2 < between 2 and 4 < betweeen 7 and 12 < 13

46. Which reaction is <u>not</u> a redox process?

    A. Combustion of octane: $2C_8H_{18} + 25O_2 \rightarrow 16CO_2 + 18H_2O$

    B. Depletion of a lithium battery: $Li + MnO_2 \rightarrow LiMnO_2$

    C. Corrosion of aluminum by acid: $2Al + 6HCl \rightarrow 2AlCl_3 + 3H_2$

    D. Taking an antacid for heartburn:
        $CaCO_3 + 2HCl \rightarrow CaCl_2 + H_2CO_3 \rightarrow CaCl_2 + CO_2 + H_2O$

D The oxidation state of atoms is altered in a redox process. During combustion (choice A), the carbon atoms are oxidized from an oxidation number of –4 to +4. Oxygen atoms are reduced from an oxidation number of 0 to –2. All batteries (choice B) generate electricity by forcing electrons from a redox process through a circuit. Li is oxidized from 0 in the metal to +1 in the $LiMnO_2$salt. Mn is reduced from +4 in manganese(IV) oxide to +3 in lithium manganese(III) oxide salt. Corrosion (choice C) is due to oxidation. Al is oxidized from 0 to +3. H is reduced from +1 to 0. Acid-base neutralization (choice D) transfers a proton (an H atom with an oxidation state of +1) from an acid to a base. The oxidation state of all atoms remains unchanged (Ca at +2, C at +4, O at –2, H at +1, and Cl at –1), so D is correct. Note that choices C and D both involve an acid. The availability of electrons in aluminum metal favors electron transfer but the availability of CO_3^{2-} as a proton acceptor favors proton transfer.

47. Molten NaCl is subjected to electrolysis. What reaction takes place at the cathode?

    A. $2Cl^-(l) \rightarrow Cl_2(g) + 2e^-$

    B. $Cl_2(g) + 2e^- \rightarrow 2Cl^-(l)$

    C. $Na^+(l) + e^- \rightarrow Na(l)$

    D. $Na^+(l) \rightarrow Na(l) + e^-$

C Reduction (choices B and C) always occurs at the cathode. Molten NaCl is composed of ions in liquid form before electrolysis (answer C). A and D are oxidation reactions, and D is also not properly balanced because a +1 charge is on the left and a –1 charge is on the right. The two half-reactions are:

$$Na^+(l) + e^- \xrightarrow{\text{reduction at cathode}} Na(l)$$

$$2Cl^-(l) \xrightarrow{\text{oxidation at anode}} Cl_2(g) + 2e^-$$

The net reaction is:

$$2NaCl(l) \rightarrow 2Na(l) + Cl_2(g)$$

48. What is the purpose of the salt bridge in a voltaic cell?

   A. To receive electrons from the oxidation half-reaction
   B. To relieve the buildup of positive charge in the anode half-cell
   C. To conduct electron flow
   D. To permit positive ions to flow from the cathode half-cell to the anode half-cell

D The anode receives electrons from the oxidation half-reaction (choice A) and the circuit conducts electron flow (choice C) to the cathode which supplies electrons for the reduction half-reaction. This flow of electrons from the anode to the cathode is relieved by a flow of ions through the salt bridge from the cathode to the anode (answer D). The salt bridge relieves the buildup of positive charge in the cathode half-cell (choice B is incorrect).

49. What is the oxidant in the reaction: $2H_2S + SO_2 \rightarrow 3S + 2H_2O$?

   A. H_2S
   B. SO_2
   C. S
   D. H_2O

B The S atom in H_2S has an oxidation number of –2 and is oxidized by SO_2 (the oxidant, choice B) to elemental sulfer (oxidation number = 0). The S atom in SO_2 has an oxidation number of +4 and is reduced. The two half-reactions are:

$$SO_2 + 4e^- + 4H^+ \xrightarrow{\text{reduction}} S + 2H_2O$$

$$2H_2S \xrightarrow{\text{oxidation}} 2S + 4e^- + 4H^+$$

50. Given $E°=-2.37$ V for $Mg^{2+}(aq)+2e^-\rightarrow Mg(s)$ and $E°=0.80$ V for $Ag^+(aq)+e^-\rightarrow Ag(s)$, what is the standard potential of a voltaic cell composed of a piece of magnesium dipped in a 1 M Ag^+ solution and a piece of silver dipped in 1 M Mg^{2+}?

    A. 0.77 V
    B. 1.57 V
    C. 3.17 V
    D. 3.97 V

C $Ag^+(aq)+e^-\rightarrow Ag(s)$ has a larger value for $E°$ (reduction potential) than $Mg^{2+}(aq)+2e^-$ $\rightarrow Mg(s)$. Therefore, in the cell described, reduction will occur at the Ag electrode and it will be the cathode. Using the equation:

$$E^O_{cell} = E^O(cathode) - E^O(anode), \text{ we obtain:}$$

$$E^O_{cell} = 0.80 \text{ V} - (-2.37 \text{ V}) = 3.17 \text{ V (Answer C)}.$$

Choice D results from the incorrect assumption that electrode potentials depend on the amount of material present. The balanced net reaction for the cell is:

$$Mg(s) \rightarrow Mg^{2+}(aq) + 2e^- \qquad\qquad E°_{ox} = 2.37 \text{ V}$$

$$\underline{2Ag^+(aq) + 2e^- \rightarrow 2Ag(s) \qquad\qquad E°_{red} = 0.80 \text{ V (not 1.60 V)}}$$

$$Mg(s) + 2Ag^+(aq) \rightarrow 2Ag(s) + Mg^{2+}(aq) \quad E°_{cell} = 3.17 \text{ V (not 3.97 V)}$$

51. In the following phase diagram, _____ occurs as P is decreased from A to B at constant T and _____ occurs as T is increased from C to D at constant P.

    A. deposition, melting
    B. sublimation, melting
    C. deposition, vaporization
    D. sublimation, vaporization

D. Point A is located in the solid phase, point C is located in the liquid phase. Points B and D are located in the gas phase. The transition from solid to gas is sublimation and the transition from liquid to gas is vaporization.

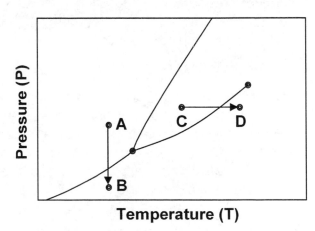

52. Heat is added to a pure solid at its melting point until it all becomes liquid at its freezing point. Which of the following occur?

A. Intermolecular attractions are weakened.
B. The kinetic energy of the molecules does not change.
C. The freedom of the molecules to move about increases.
D. All of the above

D. Intermolecular attractions are lessened during melting. This permits molecules to move about more freely, but there is no change in the kinetic energy of the molecules because the temperature has remained the same.

53. Why does $CaCl_2$ have a higher normal melting point than NH_3?

A. London dispersion forces in $CaCl_2$ are stronger than covalent bonds in NH_3.
B. Covalent bonds in NH_3 are stronger than dipole-dipole bonds in $CaCl_2$.
C. Ionic bonds in $CaCl_2$ are stronger than London dispersion forces in NH_3.
D. Ionic bonds in $CaCl_2$ are stronger than hydrogen bonds in NH_3.

D. London dispersion forces are weaker than covalent bonds, eliminating choice A. A higher melting point will result from stronger intermolecular bonds, eliminating choice B. $CaCl_2$ is an ionic solid resulting from a cation on the left and an anion on the right of the periodic table. The dominant attractive forces between NH_3 molecules are hydrogen bonds.

54. The temperature of a liquid is raised at atmospheric pressure. Which liquid property increases?

A. critical pressure
B. vapor pressure
C. surface tension
D. viscosity

B. The critical pressure of a liquid is its vapor pressure at the critical temperature and is always a constant value. A rising temperature increases the kinetic energy of molecules and decreases the importance of intermolecular attraction. More molecules will be free to escape to the vapor phase (vapor pressure increases), but the effect of attractions at the liquid-gas interface will fall (surface tension decreases) and molecules will flow against each other more easily (viscosity decreases).

55. Which of the following are able to flow from one place to another?

I. Gases
II. Liquids
III. Solids
IV. Supercritical fluids

A. I and II
B. II only
C. I, II, and IV
D. I, II, III, and IV

C. Gases and liquids both flow. Supercritical fluids have some traits in common with gases and some in common with liquids, and so they flow also. Solids have a fixed volume and shape.

56. List NH_3, PH_3, $MgCl_2$, Ne, and N_2 in order of increasing melting point.

A. $N_2 < Ne < PH_3 < NH_3 < MgCl_2$
B. $N_2 < NH_3 < Ne < MgCl_2 < PH_3$
C. $Ne < N_2 < NH_3 < PH_3 < MgCl_2$
D. $Ne < N_2 < PH_3 < NH_3 < MgCl_2$

D. Higher melting points result from stronger intermolecular forces. $MgCl_2$ is the only material listed with ionic bonds and will have the highest melting point. Dipole-dipole interactions are present in NH_3 and PH_3 but not in Ne and N_2. Ne and N_2 are also small molecules expected to have very weak London dispersion forces and so will have lower melting points than NH_3 and PH_3. NH_3 will have stronger intermolecular attractions and a higher melting point than PH_3 because hydrogen bonding occurs in NH_3. Ne has a molecular weight of 20 and a spherical shape and N_2 has a molecular weight of 28 and is not spherical. Both of these factors predict stronger London dispersion forces and a higher melting point for N_2. Actual melting points are: Ne (25 K) < N_2 (63 K) < PH_3 (140 K) < NH_3 (195 K) < $MgCl_2$ (987 K).

57. 1-butanol, ethanol, methanol, and 1-propanol are all liquids at room temperature. Rank them in order of increasing viscosity.

    A. 1-butanol < 1-propanol < ethanol < methanol
    B. methanol < ethanol < 1-propanol < 1-butanol
    C. methanol < ethanol < 1-butanol < 1-propanol
    D. 1-propanol < 1-butanol < ethanol < methanol

B. Higher viscosities result from stronger intermolecular attractive forces. The molecules listed are all alcohols with the -OH functional group attached to the end of a straight-chain alkane. In other words, they all have the formula $CH_3(CH_2)_{n-1}OH$. The only difference between the molecules is the length of the alkane corresponding to the value of n. With all else identical, larger molecules have greater intermolecular attractive forces due to a greater molecular surface for the attractions. Therefore the viscosities are ranked: methanol (CH_3OH) < ethanol (CH_3CH_2OH) < 1-propanol ($CH_3CH_2CH_2OH$) < 1-butanol ($CH_3CH_2CH_2CH_2OH$).

58. Which phase may be present at the triple point of a substance?

    I. Gas
    II. Liquid
    III. Solid
    IV. Supercritical fluid

    A. I, II, and III
    B. I, II, and IV
    C. II, III, and IV
    D. I, II, III, and IV

A. Gas, liquid and solid may exist together at the triple point.

59. Which substance is most likely to be a gas at STP?

    A. SeO_2
    B. F_2
    C. $CaCl_2$
    D. I_2

B. A gas at STP has a normal boiling point under 0 °C. The substance with the lowest boiling point will have the weakest intermolecular attractive forces and will be the most likely gas at STP. F_2 has the lowest molecular weight, is not a salt, metal, or covalent network solid, and is non-polar, indicating the weakest intermolecular attractive forces of the four choices. F_2 actually is a gas at STP, and the other three are solids.

60. How many neutrons are in $^{60}_{27}Co$?

    A. 27
    B. 33
    C. 60
    D. 87

B. The number of neutrons is found by subtracting the atomic number (27) from the mass number (60).

61. The terrestrial composition of an element is: 50.7% as an isotope with an atomic mass of 78.9 u and 49.3% as an isotope with an atomic mass of 80.9 u. Both isotopes are stable. Calculate the atomic mass of the element.

    A. 79.0 u
    B. 79.8 u
    C. 79.9 u
    D. 80.8 u

C.

Atomic mass of element = (Fraction as 1st isotope) (Atomic mass of 1st isotope)

+

(Fraction as 2nd isotope) (Atomic mass of 2nd isotope)

$$= (0.507)(78.9\ u) + (0.493)(80.9\ u) = 79.89\ u = 79.9\ u$$

62. Select the list of atoms that are arranged in order of increasing size.

    A. Mg, Na, Si, Cl
    B. Si, Cl, Mg, Na
    C. Cl, Si, Mg, Na
    D. Na, Mg, Si, Cl

C. These atoms are all in the same row of the periodic table. Size increases further to the left for atoms in the same row.

63. Based on trends in the periodic table, which of the following properties would you expect to be greater for Rb than for K?

    I.   Density
    II. Melting point
    III. Ionization energy
    IV. Oxidation number in a compound with chlorine

    A. I only
    B. I, II, and III
    C. II and III
    D. I, II, III, and IV

A. Rb is underneath K in the alkali metal column (group 1) of the periodic table. There is a general trend for density to increase lower on the table for elements in the same row, so we select choice I. Rb and K experience metallic bonds for intermolecular forces and the strength of metallic bonds decreases for larger atoms further down the periodic table resulting in a lower melting point for Rb, so we do not choose II. Ionization energy decreases for larger atoms further down the periodic table, so we do not choose III. Both Rb and K would be expected to have a charge of +1 and therefore an oxidation number of +1 in a compound with chlorine, so we do not choose IV.

64. At room temperature, $CaBr_2$ is expected to be:

    A. a ductile solid
    B. a brittle solid
    C. a soft solid
    D. a gas

B. Ca is a metal because it is on the left of the periodic table, and Br is a non-metal because it is on the right. The compound they form together will be an ionic salt, and ionic salts are brittle solids (choice B) at room temperature. NaCl is another example.

65. Which name or formula is not represented properly?

    A. Cl_4S
    B. $KClO_3$
    C. Calcium dihydrogen phosphate
    D. Sulfurous acid

A A is the answer because the atoms in the sulfur tetrachloride molecule are placed in order of increasing electronegativity. This formla is properly written as SCl_4. B is a proper formula for potassium chlorate. Calcium dihydrogen phosphate is $Ca(H_2PO_4)_2$. It derives its name from the Ca^{2+} cation in combination with an anion composed of a phosphate anion (PO_4^{3-}) that is doubly protonated to give a $H_2PO_4^-$ ion. Sulfurous acid is $H_2SO_3(aq)$.

66. The curve below resulted from the titration of a _____ _____ with a _____ _____ titrant.

    A. weak acid, strong base
    B. weak base, strong acid
    C. strong acid, strong base
    D. strong base, strong acid

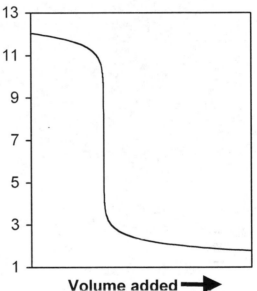

D The pH is above 7 initially and decreases, so an acid titrant is neutralizing a base. This eliminates A and C. The maximum slope (equivalence point) at the neutral pH of 7 indicates a strong base titrated with a strong acid, D.

67. **Which statement about thermochemistry is true?**

    A. Particles in a system move about less freely at high entropy

    B. Water at 100 °C has the same internal energy as water vapor at 100°C

    C. A decrease in the order of a system corresponds to an increase in entropy.

    D. At its sublimation temperature, dry ice has a higher entropy than gaseous CO_2

C At high entropy, particles have a large freedom of molecular motion (A is false). Water and water vapor at 100 °C contain the same translational kinetic energy, but water vapor has additional internal energy in the form of resisting the intermolecular attractions between molecules (B is false). We also know water vapor has a higher internal energy because heat must be added to boil water. Entropy may be thought of as the disorder in a system (C is correct). Sublimation is the phase change from solid to gas, and there is less freedom of motion for particles in solids than in gases. Solid CO_2 (dry ice) has a lower entropy than gaseous CO_2 because entropy decreases during a phase change that prevents molecular motion (D is false).

68. What is the heat change of 36.0 g H₂O at atmospheric pressure when its temperature is reduced from 125 °C to 40. °C? Use the following data:

A. −92.0 kJ
B. −10.8 kJ
C. 10.8 kJ
D. 92.0 kJ

Values for water

Heat capacity of solid	37.6 J/mol•°C
Heat capacity of liquid	75.3 J/mol•°C
Heat capacity of gas	33.1 J/mol•°C
Heat of fusion	6.02 kJ/mol
Heat of vaporization	40.67 kJ/mol

A Heat is evolved from the substance as it cools, so the heat change will be negative, eliminating choices C and D. Data in the table are given using moles, so the first step is to convert the mass of water to moles:

$$36.0 \text{ g H}_2\text{O} \times \frac{1 \text{ mol H}_2\text{O}}{18.02 \text{ g H}_2\text{O}} = 2.00 \text{ mol H}_2\text{O}$$

There are three contributions to the heat evolved. First, the heat evolved when cooling the vapor from 125 °C to 100 °C is found from the heat capacity of the gas:

$$q_1 = n \times C \times \Delta T = 2.00 \text{ mol H}_2\text{O}(g) \times 33.1 \frac{J}{\text{mol °C}} \times (100 \text{ °C} - 125 \text{ °C})$$

$$= -1655 \text{ J to cool vapor}$$

Next, the heat evolved during condensation is found from the heat of vaporization:

$$q_2 = n \times (-\Delta H_{vaporization}) = 2.00 \text{ mol H}_2\text{O} \times (-40.67 \frac{kJ}{\text{mol}})$$

$$= -81.34 \text{ kJ to condense vapor}$$

Incorrect answer B results from using a heat of vaporization of 40.67 J/mol instead of kJ/mol.

Finally, the heat evolved when cooling the liquid from 100 °C to 40 °C is found from the heat capacity of the liquid:

$$q_3 = n \times C \times \Delta T = 2.00 \text{ mol H}_2\text{O}(g) \times 75.3 \frac{J}{\text{mol °C}} \times (40 \text{ °C} - 100 \text{ °C})$$

$$= -9036 \text{ J to cool liquid}$$

The total heat change is the sum of these contributions:

$$q = q_1 + q_2 + q_3 = -1.655 \text{ kJ} + (-81.34 \text{ kJ}) + (-9.036 \text{ kJ}) = -92.03 \text{ kJ}$$

$$= -92.0 \text{ kJ (Choice A)}$$

69. What is the standard heat of combustion of CH₄(g)? Use the following data:

A. −890.3 kJ/mol
B. −604.5 kJ/mol
C. −252.9 kJ/mol
D. −182.5 kJ/mol

Standard heats of formation

$CH_4(g)$	−74.8 kJ/mol
$CO_2(g)$	−393.5 kJ/mol
$H_2O(l)$	−285.8 kJ/mol

A First we must write a balanced equation for the combustion of CH₄. The balanced equation is:

$$CH_4(g) + 2O_2(g) \rightarrow CO_2(g) + 2H_2O(l).$$

The heat of combustion may be found from the sum of the productions minus the sum of the reactants of the heats of formation:

$$\Delta H_{rxn} = H_{product\,1} + H_{product\,2} + \ldots - \left(H_{reactant\,1} + H_{reactant\,2} + \ldots \right)$$

$$= \Delta H_f^\circ(CO_2) + 2\Delta H_f^\circ(H_2O) - \left(\Delta H_f^\circ(CH_4) + 2\Delta H_f^\circ(O_2) \right)$$

The heat of formation of an element in its most stable form is zero by definition, so

$\Delta H_f^\circ(O_2(g)) = 0 \dfrac{kJ}{mol}$, and the remaining values are found from the table:

$$\Delta H_{rxn} = -393.5 \frac{kJ}{mol} + 2(-285.8\frac{kJ}{mol}) - \left(-74.8 \frac{kJ}{mol} + 2(0) \right) = -890.3 \frac{kJ}{mol} \text{ (choice A)}$$

70. Which reaction creates products at a lower total entropy than the reactants?

A. Dissolution of table salt: $NaCl(s) \rightarrow Na^+(aq) + Cl^-(aq)$
B. Oxidation of iron: $4Fe(s) + 3O_2(g) \rightarrow 2Fe_2O_3(s)$
C. Dissociation of ozone: $O_3(g) \rightarrow O_2(g) + O(g)$
D. Vaporization of butane: $C_4H_{10}(l) \rightarrow C_4H_{10}(g)$

B Choice A is incorrect because two particles are at a greater entropy than one and because ions in solution have more freedom of motion than a solid. For B (the correct answer), the products are at a lower entropy than the reactants because there are fewer product molecules and they are all in the solid form but one of the reactants is a gas. Reaction B is still spontaneous because it is highly exothermic. For C, there are more product molecules than reactants, and for D, the gas phase is always at a higher entropy than the liquid.

71. Which statement about reactions is true?

    A. All spontaneous reactions are both exothermic and cause an increase in entropy.
    B. An endothermic reaction that increases the order of the system cannot be spontaneous.
    C. A reaction can be non-spontaneous in one direction and also non-spontaneous in the opposite direction.
    D. Melting snow is an exothermic process

B All reactions that are both exothermic and cause an increase in entropy will be spontaneous, but the converse (choice A) is not true. Some spontaneous reactions are exothermic but decrease entropy and some are endothermic and increase entropy. Choice B is correct. The reverse reaction of a non-spontaneous reaction (choice C) will be spontaneous. Melting snow (choice D) requires heat. Therefore it is an endothermic process

72. 10. kJ of heat are added to one kilogram of Iron at 10. °C. What is its final temperature? The specific heat of iron is 0.45 J/g•°C.

    A. 22 °C
    B. 27 °C
    C. 32 °C
    D. 37 °C

C The expression for heat as a function of temperature change:

$$q - n \times C \times \Delta T$$

may be rearranged to solve for the temperature change:

$$\Delta T = \frac{q}{n \times C}.$$

In this case, n is a mass and C is the specific heat of iron:

$$\Delta T = \frac{10000 \text{ J}}{1000 \text{ g} \times 0.45 \ \frac{\text{J}}{\text{g} \,°C}} = 22 \ °C.$$

This is not the final temperature (choice A is incorrect). It is the temperature difference between the initial and final temperature.

$$\Delta T = T_{final} - T_{initial} = 22 \ °C$$

Solving for the final temperature gives us:

$$T_{final} = \Delta T + T_{initial} = 22 \ °C + 10 \ °C = 32 \ °C \text{ (Choice C)}$$

73. A proper name for this hydrocarbon is:

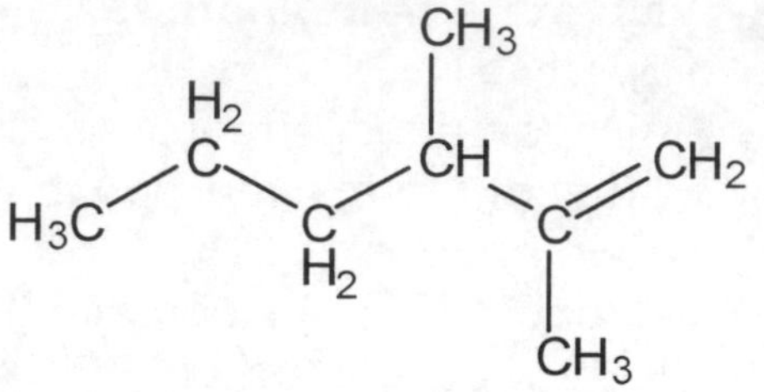

A. 4,5-dimethyl-6-hexene
B. 2,3-dimethyl-1-hexene
C. 4,5-dimethyl-6-hexyne
D. 2-methyl-3-propyl-1-butene

B The hydrocarbon contains a double bond and no triple bonds, so it is an alkene.

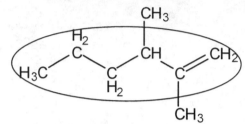

Choice C describes an alkyne. The longest carbon chain is six carbons long, corresponding to a parent molecule of 1-hexene (circled to the left). Choice D is an improper name because it names the molecule as a substituted butane, using a shorter chain as the parent molecule. Finally, the lowest possible set of locant numbers must be used. Choice A is an improper name because the larger possible set of locant numbers is chosen.

74. Given the following heats of reaction:

$\Delta H = -0.3$ kJ / mol for $\quad$ $Fe(s) + CO_2(g) \rightarrow FeO(s) + CO(g)$

$\Delta H = 5.7$ kJ / mol for $\quad$ $2Fe(s) + 3CO_2(g) \rightarrow Fe_2O_3(s) + 3CO(g)$

and $\Delta H = 4.5$ kJ / mol for $\quad$ $3FeO(s) + CO_2(g) \rightarrow Fe_3O_4(s) + CO(g)$

use Hess's Law to determine the heat of reaction for:

$$3Fe_2O_3(s) + CO(g) \rightarrow 2Fe_3O_4(s) + CO_2(g)?$$

A. -10.8 kJ/mol
B. -9.9 kJ/mol
C. -9.0 kJ/mol
D. -8.1 kJ/mol

B $\quad$ We are interested in $3Fe_2O_3$ as a reactant. Only the second reaction contains this molecule, so we will take three times the opposite of the second reaction. We are interested in $2Fe_3O_4$ as a product, so we will take two times the third reaction. An intermediate result is:

$3Fe_2O_3(s) + 9CO(g) \rightarrow 6Fe(s) + 9CO_2(g)$ $\quad$ $\Delta H = -3 \times 5.7$ kJ/mol $= -17.1$ kJ/mol

$6FeO(s) + 2CO_2(g) \rightarrow 2Fe_3O_4(s) + 2CO(g)$ $\quad$ $\Delta H = 2 \times 4.5$ kJ/mol $= 9.0$ kJ/mol

---

$3Fe_2O_3(s) + 6FeO(s) + 7CO(g) \rightarrow$
$\quad 2Fe_3O_4(s) + 6Fe(s) + 7CO_2(g)$ $\quad$ $\Delta H = (-17.1 + 9.0)$ kJ/mol $= -8.1$ kJ/mol

However, D is not the correct answer because it is not ΔH for the reaction of the problem statement. We may use six times the first reaction to eliminate both FeO and Fe from the intermediate result and obtain the reaction of interest:

$3Fe_2O_3(s) + 6FeO(s) + 7CO(g) \rightarrow$
$\quad 2Fe_3O_4(s) + 6Fe(s) + 7CO_2(g)$ $\quad$ $\Delta H = -8.1$ kJ/mol

$6Fe(s) + 6CO_2(g) \rightarrow 6FeO(s) + 6CO(g)$ $\quad$ $\Delta H = 6 \times (-0.3$ kJ/mol$) = -1.8$ kJ/mol

---

$3Fe_2O_3(s) + CO(g) \rightarrow 2Fe_3O_4(s) + CO(g)$ $\quad$ $\Delta H = (-8.1 + -1.8)$ kJ/mol
$\quad = -9.9$ kJ/mol (choice B)

75. Classify these biochemicals.

I.

II.

III.

IV.

A. I-nucleotide, II-sugar, III-peptide, IV-fat
B. I-disaccharide, II-sugar, III-fatty acid, IV-polypeptide
C. I-disaccharide, II-amino acid, III-fatty acid, IV- polysaccharide
D. I-nucleotide, II-sugar, III-triacylglyceride, and IV-DNA

A   I is a phosphate (PO_4) linked to a sugar and an amine: a nucleotide. II has the formula $C_nH_{2n}O_n$, indicative of a sugar. III contains three amino acids linked with peptide bonds. It is a tripeptide. IV is a triacylglyceride, a fat molecule.

76. **Four nearly identical gems from the same mineral are weighed using different balances. Their masses are:**

   3.4533 g, 3.459 g, 3.4656 g, 3.464 g.

   The four gems are then collected and added to a volumetric cylinder containing 10.00 ml of liquid, and a new volume of 14.97 ml is read. What is the average mass of the four stones and what is the density of the mineral?

   A. 3.460 g, and 2.78 g/ml
   B. 3.460 g and 2.79 g/ml
   C. 3.4605 g and 2.78 g/ml
   D. 3.461 g and 2.79 g/ml

B   The average mass is the sum of the four readings divided by four:

$$(3.4533 \text{ g} + 3.459 \text{ g} + 3.4656 \text{ g} + 3.464 \text{ g})/4 = 3.460475 \text{ g (caculator value)}$$

This value must be rounded off to three significant digits <u>after the decimal point</u> because this is the lowest precision of the added values. The four is an exact number. This means rounding downwards to 3.460 g, eliminating choices C and D. The volume of the collected stones is found from the increase in the level read off the cylinder:

$$14.97 \text{ ml} - 10.00 \text{ ml} = 4.97 \text{ ml}$$

The density is found by dividing the sum of the masses by this volume:

$$\frac{3.4533 \text{ g} + 3.459 \text{ g} + 3.4656 \text{ g} + 3.464 \text{ g}}{4.97 \text{ ml}} = \frac{13.8419 \text{ g}}{4.97 \text{ ml}} = 2.7850905 \text{ g/ml (caculator value)}$$

This value must be rounded off to three <u>total</u> significant digits because this is the lower precision of the numerator and the denominator. The first insignificant digit is a 5. In this case there are additional non-zero digits after the 5, so rounding occurs upwards to 2.79 g/ml (answer B).

77. Which of the following pairs are isomers?

I.

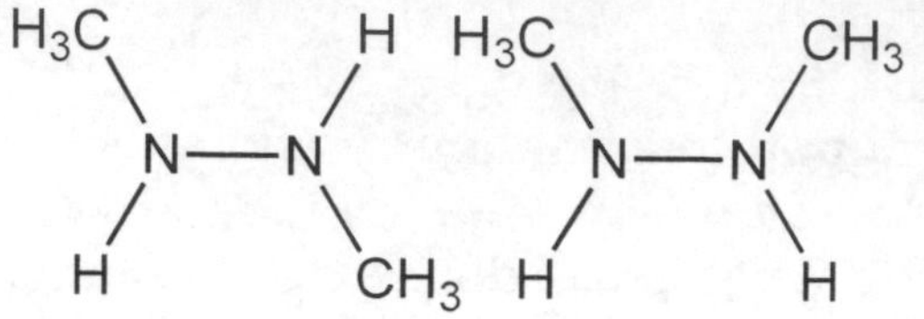

II. Pentanal 2-pentanone

III.

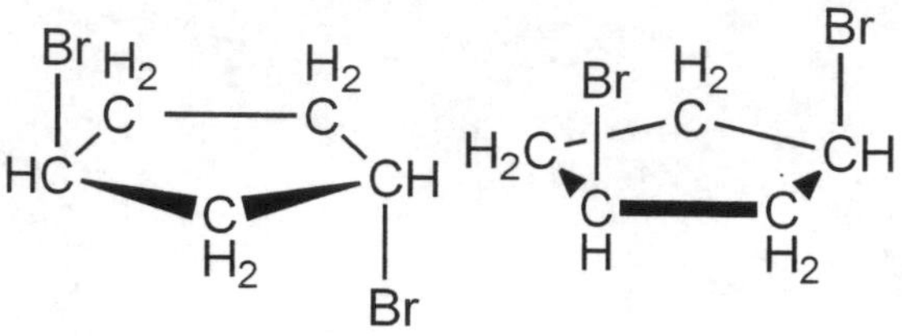

IV.

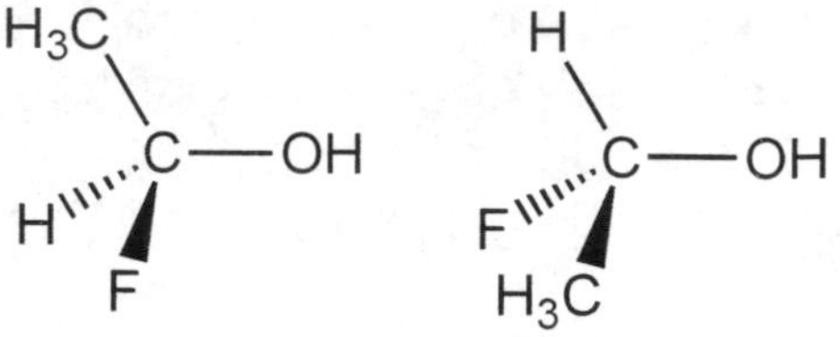

A. I and IV
B. II and III
C. I, II, and III
D. I, II, III, and IV

B In pair I, the N—N bond may freely rotate in the molecule because it is not a double bond. The identical molecule is represented twice.

For pair II, pentanal is

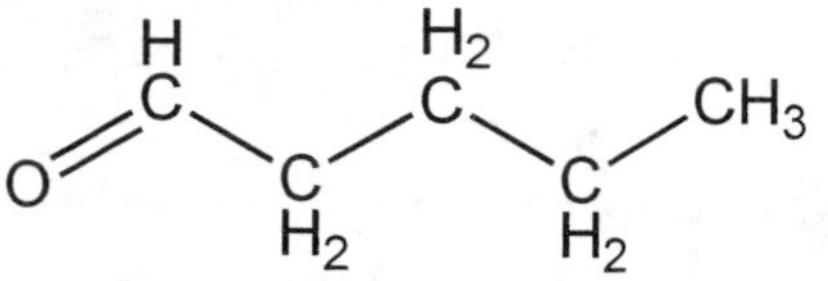

and 2-pentanone is:

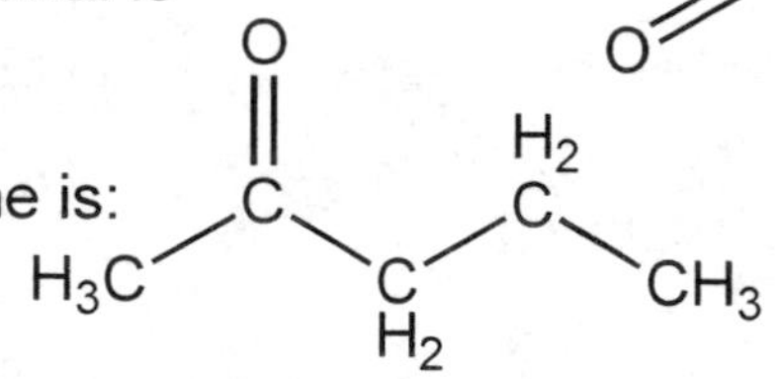

Both molecules are $C_5H_{10}O$, and they are isomers because they have the same formula with a different arrangement of atoms.

In pair III, both molecules are 1,3-dibromocyclopentane, $C_5H_8Br_2$. In the first molecule, the bromines are in a *trans* configuration, and in the second molecule, they are *cis*. The two molecules are also viewed from different perspectives. Unlike pair I, no bond rotation may occur because the intervening atoms are locked into place by the ring, so they are different arrangements and are isomers.

In pair IV (1-fluoroethanol), there is a chiral center, so stereoisomers are possible, but as in pair I, the same molecule is represented twice. Rotating the C-O bond indicates that the two structures are superimposable. This molecule: to the right is a stereoisomer to the molecule represented in IV. The answer is B (pairs II and III).

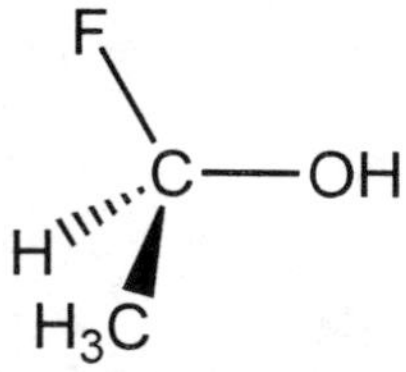

78. The following procedure was developed to find the specific heat capacity of metals:

1. Place pieces of the metals in an ice-water bath so their initial temperature is 0 °C.
2. Weigh a styrofoam cup.
3. Add water at room temperature to the cup and weigh it again
4. Add a cold metal from the bath to the cup and weigh the cup a third time.
5. Monitor the temperature drop of the water until a final temperature at thermal equilibrium is found.

_____ is also required as additional information in order to obtain heat capacities for the metals. The best control would be to follow the same protocol except to use _____ in step 4 instead of a cold metal.

A. The heat capacity of water / a metal at 100 °C
B. The heat of formation of water / ice from the 0 °C bath
C. The heat of capacity of ice / glass at 0 °C
D. The heat capacity of water / water from the 0 °C bath

D The equation:

$$q = n \times C \times \Delta T$$

is used to determine what additional information is needed. The specific heat, C, of the metals may be found from the heat added, the amount of material, and the temperature change. The amount of metal is found from the difference in weight between steps 3 and 4, and the temperature change is found from the difference between the final temperature and 0 °C. The additional value required is the heat added, q. This may be found from the heat removed from the water if the amount of water, the heat capacity of water, and the temperature change of water are known. The amount of water is found from the difference in weight between step 2 and 3, and the temperature change is found from the difference between the final temperature and room temperature. The only additional information required is the heat capacity of water, eliminating choices B and C. Heat of formation (choice B) is only used for chemical reactions.

A good control simplifies only the one aspect under study without adding anything new. Metal at 100 °C (choice A) would alter the temperature of the experiment and glass (choice C) would add an additional material to the study. Ice (choice B) would require consideration of the heat of fusion. Choice D is an ideal control because the impact of water at 0 °C on room temperature water is simpler than the impact of metals at 0 °C on room temperature water, and nothing new is added.

79. **What could cause this change in the energy diagram of a reaction?**

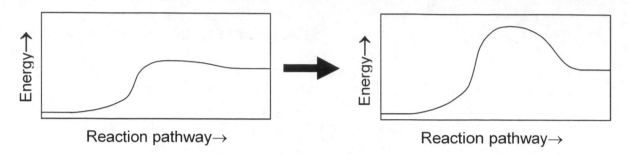

A. Adding catalyst to an endothermic reaction
B. Removing catalyst from an endothermic reaction
C. Adding catalyst to an exothermic reaction
D. Removing catalyst from an exothermic reaction

B The products at the end of the reaction pathway are at a greater energy than the reactants, so the reaction is endothermic (narrowing down the answer to A or B). The maximum height on the diagram corresponds to activation energy. An increase in activation energy could be caused by removing a heterogeneous catalyst.

80. **Some scientists have hypothesized that life on other planets may not be carbon-based, but instead, rely on another element as the primary "building block" for organic compounds. Which of the following is most likely able to fill this role?**

A. Silicon
B. Oxygen
C. Calcium
D. Chromium

A. In the periodic table, silicon is in the same group as carbon. Therefore, it has the same valence electron arrangement and is most likely to have carbon's versatility in forming single, double, and triple bonds and forming compounds with a variety of other elements.

81. An approximately cylindrical piece of wood is found to have a mass of 180 grams. If the diameter of the wood is 5 cm and it is 20 cm long, what is the density of the wood and will it float in water?

    A. 0.11 g/cm^3; will not float
    B. 0.11 g/cm^3; will float
    C. 0.46 g/cm^3; will not float
    D. 0.46 g/cm^3; will float

D. To find the density of the wood, we must first calculate the volume. The volume of a cylinder is $V = \pi r^2 L$. Plugging in our values, we find:

$$V = \pi \times (2.5cm)^2 \times 20cm = 392.5cm^3$$

The density of the wood is simply the mass divided by the volume:

$$\rho = \frac{m}{V} = \frac{180g}{392.5cm^3} = 0.46\frac{g}{cm^3}$$

To determine if the wood will float, we simply compare this density to that of water, 1 g/cm^3. Since the wood is less dense, it is expected to float.

82. Which biomolecule is the primary component in the cellular membrane?

    A. Nucleic acids
    B. Lipids
    C. Carbohydrates
    D. Amino acids

B. A bilayer of lipids, with the hydrophobic regions facing out, forms the cellular membrane.

83. Place the following elements in order from least to most metallic: Carbon, Francium, Chlorine, Manganese

    A. Chlorine< Carbon< Manganese <Francium
    B. Francium<Carbon<Manganese<Chlorine
    C. Chlorine<Manganese<Carbon<Francium
    D. Francium<Manganese<Carbon<Chlorine

A. Metallic properties decrease as position in the periodic table moves from top to bottom and from left to right.

84. Which of the following is the best predictor of an element's chemical reactivity?

    A. Its atomic number
    B. Its group
    C. Its period
    D. The phase at which it exists at STP

B. All the elements in a group have the same valence electron structure, which is the primary determinant of chemical reactivity.

85. Which combination of characteristics would indicate that an unknown substance is an acid?
    I. Feels slippery
    II. Dissolves metals
    III. Turns litmus paper red
    IV. Turns litmus paper blue
    V. Is neutralized by KOH
    VI. Is neutralized by HCl

    A. II, III, and V
    B. I, II, III, and V
    C. I, IV, and VI
    D. II, III, and VI

A. Acids are likely to dissolve metal and turn litmus paper red. Acids will be neutralized by a base, such as KOH. Bases typically have a slippery feel, will turn litmus paper blue, and are neutralized by acids such as HCl.

86. A person holds a paper cup of hot chocolate and her hands are warmed. What type of heat transfer is occurring?

    A. Radiation
    B. Conduction
    C. Convection
    D. Both B and C

D. Most heat is transferred because the cup of hot chocolate is in direct contact with the hands. This movement of thermal energy between two objects in direct contact is conduction. However, within the cup, the hot chocolate nearest the edges will be cooler (as heat is transferred through the cup to the hands) and this will cause warmer liquid in the center of the cup to move towards the edges. This is convection.

87. Which of the following is not a real world example of a phase change?

    A. Dry ice used to produce "fog" during a play
    B. A log in a campfire turning to ash
    C. An abandoned popsicle creating a sticky puddle
    D. The formation of beads of "sweat" on a cold glass

B. Choices A, C, and D are examples of sublimation, melting, and condensation, respectively. Choice B, however, described a chemical reaction, combustion.

88. A test tube containing 5ml of liquid A is placed in a beaker holding 50 ml of liquid B. Some time later, the temperatures of the liquid A and liquid B are both measured to be 45°C. Assuming the two liquids have the same specific heat capacity, which of the following are true?
    I. The liquids A and B are in thermal equilibrium.
    II. The liquids contain the same amount of thermal energy.
    III. The average kinetic energy of a molecule of liquid A is the same as a molecule of liquid B.

    A. All of the above
    B. None of the above
    C. I and III only
    D. I and II only

C. Statement II is not true because thermal energy is a function of the average kinetic energy of the molecules and the number of molecules. Therefore the liquid of larger volume, B, will have a greater amount of thermal energy,

89. In humans, energy stored in adenosine triphosphate (ATP) is released when a phosphate group is removed to create adenosine diphosphate (ADP). The energy is used to cause muscle contractions. What type of energy transformation does this represent?

    A. Chemical to mechanical
    B. Chemical to thermal
    C. Thermal to mechanical
    D. Electrical to mechanical

A. Chemical energy is the type that bonds molecules together, so it is what is released when a bond in ATP is broken to remove a phosphate group. Mechanical energy is the type needed to move objects, such as muscle fibers in a contraction.

90. Alkali metals are most likely to form ionic compounds with which other group of elements?

    A. Any of the transition metals (Groups 3-12)
    B. Halogens (Group 17)
    C. Other alkali metals (Group 1)
    D. Alkaline earth meals (Group 2)

B. Alkali metals, with a single valence electron, are most likely to form ionic bonds with halogens, which have 7 valence electrons.

91. A student designed a science project testing the effects of light and water on plant growth. You would recommend that she

A. manipulate the temperature
    as well.
B. also alter the pH of the water as another variable.
C. omit either water or light as a variable.
D. also alter the light concentration as another variable.

C. In science, experiments should be designed so that only one variable is manipulated at a time.

92. Identify the control in the following experiment. A student had four plants grown under the following conditions and was measuring photosynthetic rate by measuring mass: 2 plants in 50% light and 2 plants in 100% light.

A. plants grown with no added nutrients
B. plants grown in the dark
C   plants in 100% light
D. plants in 50% light

B. The 100% light plants are those that the student will be comparing the 50% plants to. This will be the control.

93.

A scientific theory

    A. proves scientific accuracy.
    B. is never rejected.
    C. results in a medical breakthrough.
    D. may be altered at a later time.

D. Scientific theory is usually accepted and verified information but can always be changed at anytime.

94. **Which is the correct order of methodology? 1) testing revised explanation, 2) setting up a controlled experiment to test explanation, 3) drawing a conclusion, 4) suggesting an explanation for observations, and 5) compare observed results to hypothesized results**

    A. 4, 2, 3, 1, 5
    B. 3, 1, 4, 2, 5
    C. 4, 2, 5, 1, 3
    D. 2, 5, 4, 1, 3

C. The first step in scientific inquiry is posing a question to be answered. Next, a hypothesis is formed to provide a plausible explanation. An experiment is then proposed and performed to test this hypothesis. A comparison between the predicted and observed results is the next step. Conclusions are then formed and it is determined whether the hypothesis is correct or incorrect. If incorrect, the next step is to form a new hypothesis and the process is repeated.

95. **Which of the following is not a legitimate source of unavoidable error?**

    A. Contamination of sample
    B. Randomness of population sampling
    C. Timing of population sampling
    D. Use of measuring devices

A. Population sampling is inherently random because no sample can be guaranteed to be representative of the general population. Similarly, no sample can be guaranteed to act the same over time, and so may not show representative behavior at a given monitoring time. The use of measuring devices is inherently imprecise because it is always possible that important data is not readable by the existing technology. Contamination of a sample is avoidable with the appropriate level of care.

96. Which of the following is <u>not</u> true of the extrapolation of graphical data points?

    A. When exprapolating data of a linear relationship, we extend the line of best fit beyond the known values.

    B. Extrapolation is the process of estimating data points outside a known set of data points.

    C. Extrapolating data will yield appropriate results as long as it is done in a strictly linear fashion.

    D. Extrapolating data is only appropriate if one is relatively certain that the relationship between x and y is linear.

C. Extrapolating data is the estimation of data points outside of the known set, based on a line of best fit through and beyond the known values, and it does depend on a linear relationship between x and y. However, extrapolating certain data in a strictly linear fashion sometimes yields inappropriate results, such as when extrapolating life spans into infinity.

97. Given the choice of lab activities, which would you omit?

    A. a genetics experiment tracking the fur color of mice

    B. dissecting a preserved fetal pig

    C. a lab relating temperature to respiration rate using live goldfish.

    D. pithing a frog to see the action of circulation

C. The use of live vertebrate organisms in a way that may harm the animal is prohibited. The observation of fur color in mice and respiration rate of live goldfish are acceptable because they are not harmful to the animals. The dissection of a fetal pig is acceptable if it comes from a known origin.

98. Who should be notified in the case of a serious chemical spill?

    I. the custodian
    II. The fire department
    III. the chemistry teacher
    IV. the administration

    A. I
    B. II
    C. II and III
    D. II and IV

D. For large spills, the school administration and the local fire department should be notified.

99. In which situation would a science teacher be liable?

    A. a teacher leaves to receive an emergency phone call and a student slips and falls.
    B. a student removes their goggles and gets dissection fluid in their eye.
    C. a faulty gas line results in a fire.
    D. a students cuts themselves with a scalpel.

A. A teacher has an obligation to be present in the lab at all times. If the teacher needs to leave, an appropriate substitute is needed.

100. Which statement best defines negligence?

    A. failure to give oral instructions for those with reading disabilities
    B. failure to exercise ordinary care
    C. inability to supervise a large group of students.
    D. reasonable anticipation that an event may occur

B. Negligence is the failure to exercise ordinary or reasonable care.

SAMPLE CONSTRUCTED-RESPONSE QUESTIONS

Directions: Read the information below and complete the given exercises. Explain your reasoning and show your work.

Part I Content Domains for Science Subtest III:Chemistry (121)

101. Students are learning about equilibrium in a chemistry laboratory exercise. The relevant materials include: an aqueous solution of $CoCl_2$, concentrated HCl, water, a hot water bath, an ice-water bath, and all necessary glassware. $CoCl_2$ dissociates in water into Cl^- ions and Co^{2+} ions which form the hydrated complex $[Co(H_2O)_6]^{2+}$. This ionic complex turns the solution pink. When HCl is added, the additional Cl^- reacts with $[Co(H_2O)_6]^{2+}$ in a mildly endothermic reversible reaction to form $[CoCl_4]^{2-}$. This ion turns the solution blue.

Write an essay describing a qualitative (not quantitative) investigation to explore the effects of both concentration and temperature on equilibrium. In your essay:

a. Describe an appropriate experimental design.

b. Describe the kind of data that will need to be gathered and how the data will be analyzed.

c. Describe the expected results of the study and relate the results to the reactions involved and the relevant concepts of chemical equilibrium.

102. The Haber process was patented in 1908 and is an important reaction used commercially to synthesize ammonia (NH_3). At present, the Haber process is used to produce 500 million tons of ammonia-based fertilizer annually. Gaseous ammonia is formed from nitrogen gas and hydrogen gas using an iron catalyst and high temperatures and pressures. The Haber process is reversible and so production of ammonia depends on controlling the reaction's equilibrium. When this reaction is used industrially, nitrogen gas is taken from the atmosphere and hydrogen gas is obtained from a reaction between natural gas (CH_4) and steam. This reaction between water and natural gas produces hydrogen gas and carbon dioxide.

    a. Write a balanced chemical equation for the Haber process, the conversion of hydrogen and nitrogen gas to ammonia.
    b. Write a balanced chemical equation for the conversion of steam and natural gas to hydrogen gas and carbon dioxide.
    c. If the reaction is conducted at typical conditions of 200 atm and 500°C, how many liters of ammonia gas will be produced if 10 kg of water are used? Assume all the steam present is converted to hydrogen gas via the equation in part b) and that natural gas is present in excess.
    d. If the gaseous ammonia produced under the conditions in part c) is cooled to a liquid for shipping, how many kg will there be?
    e. Write an expression for the equilibrium constant for the Haber process and comment on the likely effect of the lead catalyst on this equilibrium constant.

103. Water is the central ingredient of life: every biochemical reaction that maintains life and has allowed evolution occurs in an aqueous environment. Thus, the presence of water on other planets is considered a prerequisite for existence of life.

    a. Draw the Lewis dot structure of a molecule of water
    b. Predict the molecular geometry of water
    c. Explain the unique intramolecular forces between water molecules, their origin, and the unique properties they confer upon water
    d. Relate the properties detailed in part (c) to the importance of water in allowing life on Earth.

Part I Content Domains for Science Subtest II:General Science (119) and Science Subtest IV:Chemistry (125)

104. A teapot containing 675 g of water at 25.0 °C is placed on a kitchen stove and heated to 100.0 °C until just before it begins to boil. Natural gas is delivered to the stove at a rate of 135 mL per second at 25.0 °C and a constant total pressure of 1.13 atm. Natural gas is supplied with the following composition:

Weight percentage		
Methane	Ethane	Carbon dioxide
94.9%	4.4 %	0.7%

a. How much energy is required to heat the water in the teapot? The specific heat of water is 4.18 J/(g °C).

b. Write balanced equations for the combustion of methane and of ethane.

c. How many moles of gas are supplied to the stove each second? Assume that the gas behaves as an ideal gas. $R = 0.08205$ L atm/(mol K).

d. How many moles of methane and ethane are supplied to the stove each second?

e. How much heat is produced by hydrocarbon combustion each second? Assume complete combustion and use the following values:

Heat of combustion (kJ/mol)	
Methane	Ethane
890	2900

f. What is the mass of carbon dioxide released into the atmosphere each second? Assume complete combustion.

g. Using only the answers from A and E, estimate a length of time for the water to reach 100.0 °C. An experiment was performed and the water was observed to reach 100.0 °C in 258 seconds. Provide a reason why this value differs from the estimated value.

SAMPLE CONSTRUCTED-RESPONSE ANSWERS

Note: Many constructed-response questions on chemistry certification exams consist of quantitative problem solving with the requirement to show your work. Questions 102 and 104 are of this type. For additional practice, I recommend solving quantitative problems from the multiple-choice sample questions with an "constructed-response mindset" and comparing your answers to the solutions shown in the "Sample Constructed-Response Answers" section. Some constructed-response questions require little or no quantitative problem solving, but they ask for an experimental design or analysis of a design. Questions 101 and 103 are of this type. These questions usually have no single correct solution.

101. The dissociation of $CoCl_2$ in water and the formation of the pink-colored complex is described by the reaction:

$$CoCl_2(s) + 6H_2O(l) \rightarrow [Co(H_2O)_6]^{2+}(aq)_{\textbf{PINK}} + 2Cl^-(aq)$$

The dissociation of HCl is described by the reaction:

$$HCl(aq) \rightarrow H^+(aq) + Cl^-(aq).$$

When these two solutions are combined, the pink solution is expected to turn blue due to the formation of $[CoCl_4]^{2-}$. The equilibrium reaction under study is:

$$[Co(H_2O)_6]^{2+}(aq)_{\textbf{PINK}} + 4Cl^-(aq) + heat \rightleftharpoons [CoCl_4]^{2-}(aq)_{\textbf{BLUE}} + 6H_2O(l).$$

The relevant concept under study is Le Chatelier's principle and its application to the impact of concentration and temperature on equilibrium.

The only data that will be gathered in this qualitative study is an observation of color changes. Every color change should be recorded in the students' lab notebooks. A color change from pink to blue indicates the reaction above is occurring from left to right. A color change from blue to pink indicates the reaction is occurring from right to left.

The first step will provide a large volume of uniform experimental material for the students. This step will utilize concentrated HCl, so it should be performed by the instructor while the students watch. The instructor should wear gloves. Concentrated HCl should be slowly added to the cobalt(II) chloride solution until the entire solution changes color. Students should note the color before and after the change takes place. This should be a change from pink to blue because the equilibrium reaction under study has shifted to the right to partially offset the impact of added chloride ion. A sufficient volume should be prepared to provide every student or team of students with an aliquot of 10 mL of this blue solution.

Even though these volumes are small, the students are still handling a corrosive acid at moderate concentration and should wear gloves to minimize their risk of contact. The students should perform the following procedure and answer the following questions:

1. Label six test tubes 1 through 6.
2. Place half of your blue solution in tube 1 and half in tube 2.
3. Add water to tube 2 until a change in color takes place. Which direction does the equilibrium shift when water is added? (Answer: Adding water shifted equilibrium from right to left)
4. Divide the solution in tube 1 in half. Place half in tube 3 and half in tube 4.
5. Divide the solution in tube 2 in half. Place half in tube 5 and half in tube 6.
6. Test tube 3 and 4 should contain blue solution and the solution in tubes 5 and 6 should be pink.
7. Place tubes 3 and 5 in the hot water bath. Which solution changes color? (Answer: solution in tube 5 turns blue) Which direction did the equilibrium shift? (Answer: Adding heat shifted equilibrium from left to right).
8. Place tubes 4 and 6 in the ice-water bath. Which test tube changes color? (Answer: solution in tube 4 turns pink) Which direction did the equilibrium shift? (Answer: Removing heat shifted equilibrium from right to left).

The following table summarizes the experimental study in terms of predictions from Le Chatelier's principle and the expected results in the lab:

$$[Co(H_2O)_6]^{2+}(aq)_{PINK} + 4Cl^-(aq) + heat \rightleftharpoons [CoCl_4]^{2-}(aq)_{BLUE} + 6H_2O(l)$$

Test tube	Treatment	Prediction	Result
1	Instructor added Cl^-	Shift to the right	Pink to blue (moved to 3 and 4)
2	Add H_2O	Shift to the left	Blue to pink (moved to 5 and 6)
3	Add heat	Shift to the right	No change (or deeper blue)
4	Remove heat	Shift to the left	Blue to pink
5	Add heat	Shift to the right	Pink to blue
6	Remove heat	Shift to the left	No change (or deeper pink)

102.

a. Remember first that hydrogen and nitrogen are diatomic gases, so the reaction we must balance is:

$$\_\_N_2(g) + \_\_H_2(g) \rightarrow \_\_NH_3(g)$$

Balancing yields:

$$N_2(g) + 3H_2(g) \rightarrow 2NH_3(g)$$

b. Here the reaction to balance is:

$$\_\_CH_4(g) + \_\_H_2O(g) \rightarrow \_\_CO_2(g) + \_\_H_2(g)$$

Balanced:

$$CH_4(g) + 2H_2O(g) \rightarrow CO_2(g) + 4H_2(g)$$

c. We begin by converting the mass of water to moles:

$$10kgH_2O \times \frac{1000gH_2O}{1kgH_2O} \times \frac{1molH_2O}{18.015gH_2O} = 555.1molH_2O$$

Now we must consider both reactions to determine how many moles of NH_3 are made from each mole of H_2O. In the reaction is B), we see that one mole of H_2O produces 2 moles of H_2. Then in the Haber process, 1 mole of H_2 produces ⅔ of a mole of NH_3. Thus, each mole of H_2O ultimately produced 1⅓ moles of NH_3. Therefore:

$$555.1molH_2O \times \frac{4molNH_3}{3molH_2O} = 740.13molNH_3$$

Finally, calculate volume using the Ideal Gas Law, remembering to convert the temperature to Kelvin:

$$V = \frac{nRT}{P} = \frac{740.13molNH_3 \times 0.0821\frac{L \cdot atm}{mol \cdot K} \times 773K}{200atm} = 234.86litersNH_3$$

d. Condensing the ammonia into a liquid is simply a phase change and the Law of Conservation of Matter dictates that the number of moles present will be unchanged. Thus, we can simply use our findings in part (c) and the molecular mass of ammonia:

$$740.13 \, molNH_3 \times \frac{17.03 \, gNH_3}{1 \, molNH_3} = 12604.4 \, gNJ_3 = 12.6 \, kgNH_3$$

e. The equilibrium constant is simply the concentration of products over reactants, using the stoichiometric coefficients as exponents:

$$K_{eq} = \frac{[NH_3]^2}{[N_2][H_2]^3}$$

The lead catalyst in this reaction, like all catalysts, has no effect on the position of equilibrium. Catalysts serve only to reduce activation energy and, thereby, increase the reaction rate.

103.
a. Oxygen has 6 valence electrons; each hydrogen atom has 1 valence electron, so the Lewis dot structure is:

$$H : \overset{\displaystyle ..}{\underset{\displaystyle ..}{O}} : H$$

b. With two lone pairs and two bonds, water has a tetrahedral geometry and the molecule appears "bent." The predicted angle between the hydrogen bonds would be 109.5°, but in fact, the repulsion of the lone pair electrons is so strong that the hydrogen atoms are forced slightly closer together:

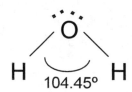

c. Water molecules are able to hydrogen bond. This is a special type of dipole-dipole intermolecular interaction that occurs only in molecules in which hydrogen is bound to a fluorine, oxygen, or nitrogen. The negatively charged oxygen atoms in one molecule of water are attracted to the positively charged hydrogen atoms in the adjacent water molecules. The hydrogen bond between two water molecules is shown as the dashed line below:

The hydrogen bonds confer a number of unique properties. First, hydrogen bonds tend to keep water molecules close together and so water is highly cohesive and has high surface tension. Second, when water freezes relatively large spaces are present between the water molecules. Since these spaces do not exist when the water is in liquid form, ice is less dense and will float on liquid water. Third, extra energy is required to break the hydrogen bonds and so water has a much higher boiling point than other molecules of similar size. It also follows from this that water as a high specific heat capacity.

d. The fact that ice is less dense than liquid water means that water freezes from the top and provides an insulating layer of ice on the surface of bodies of water, thus allowing organisms in the water to continue living. Further, water's high boiling point means that most water is in liquid form, rather than the gaseous state that would otherwise be predicted. The high specific heat of water also means that it resists change in temperature; large bodies of water stay at near-constant temperatures, which is critical for most life forms and acts to moderate the climate, preventing extreme temperature swings. Since multicellular organisms first evolved in water and all higher life forms have evolved from them, the tendency of water to stay liquid and provide a stable environment allowed for all these life forms to exist. Additionally, the water within organisms stays liquid and at a steady temperature, allowing a range of biological processes to take place. Finally, water's high surface tension provides a special habitat for certain aquatic organisms adapted to living on it. Often, these species serve as food for larger life forms.

104.

a. The energy required to heat the water in the teapot may be found from the mass, specific heat, and temperature change of the water by utilizing the expression:

$$q = m \times C \times \Delta T \quad \text{where } q \Rightarrow \text{heat added}$$

$$m \Rightarrow \text{mass of water}$$

$$C \Rightarrow \text{specific heat of water}$$

$$\Delta T \Rightarrow \text{change in temperature } T_{final} - T_{initial}$$

Substituting values yields:

$$q = 675 \text{ g} \times 4.18 \ \frac{J}{g\,°C} \times (100.0 \ °C - 25.0 \ °C) = 211 \times 10^3 \ J$$

$$= 211 \text{ kJ}$$

211 kJ of energy are required.

b. The chemical formula for methane is CH_4 and the formula for ethane is C_2H_6. During combustion reactions, the substance reacts with oxygen, and products consist of compounds with oxygen with each atom at its highest possible oxidation state. For C, this product is CO_2, and for H it is H_2O. The unbalanced equations are:

$$CH_4 + O_2 \rightarrow CO_2 + H_2O \quad \text{for methane and}$$

$$C_2H_6 + O_2 \rightarrow CO_2 + H_2O \quad \text{for ethane}$$

The most complex molecule in both cases is the hydrocarbon, and so a stoichiometric coefficient of one will be assumed for now.

For methane, this results in 1 C atom on both the left and right, so C is balanced. There are 4 H atoms on the left side of the equation and 2 on the right. A stoichiometric coefficient of 2 for H_2O corrects this imbalance:

$$CH_4 + ?O_2 \rightarrow CO_2 + 2H_2O \ .$$

Finally, there are 2 O atoms on the left and 4 on the right. A stoichiometric coefficient of 2 for O_2 balances the equation:

$$CH_4 + 2O_2 \rightarrow CO_2 + 2H_2O \ .$$

For ethane, there are 2 C atoms on the left and one on the right, so a coefficient of 2 will initially be given to CO_2. There are 6 H atoms on the left and 2 on the right, so H_2O will have a coefficient of 3:

$$C_2H_6 + ?O_2 \rightarrow 2CO_2 + 3H_2O \ .$$

There are 2 O atoms on the left and 7 on the right. A fractional stoichiometric coefficient describes the combustion of one mole of ethane:

$$C_2H_6 + \frac{7}{2}O_2 \rightarrow 2CO_2 + 3H_2O$$

Finally, the fractional coefficient could be eliminated by multiplying the entire expression by 2:

$$2C_2H_6 + 7O_2 \rightarrow 4CO_2 + 6H_2O$$

A final check confirms that there are now 4 C atoms, 12 H atoms, and 14 O atoms on both sides of the equation.

c. The problem states that 135 mL of an ideal gas are supplied to the stove each second. The pressure and temperature are also known. The ideal gas equation, $PV = nRT$, may be rearranged to solve for the number of moles of gas flowing in a second:

$$n = \frac{PV}{RT}.$$

135 mL is converted to 0.135 L to correspond to the given units of the ideal gas constant. . 25.0 °C is converted to Kelvin before using the ideal gas law:
273.15 + 25.0 = 298.15 K (the last digit isn't significant)

Plugging these values into the equation for one second of gas flow yields:

$$n = \frac{1.13\ \text{atm} \times 0.135\ \frac{L}{s}}{0.08205\ \frac{L\,\text{atm}}{\text{mol}\,K} \times 298.15\ K} = 6.24 \times 10^{-3}\ \frac{\text{mol}}{s}.$$

0.00624 moles of gas are supplied to the stove each second.

d. Weight percentages of methane and ethane must first be converted to mole fractions using the molecular weights of all three species. These fractions will then be used with the answer to part C to determine the number of moles of each hydrocarbon supplied to the stove every second.

The molecular weights of the three components are:

For methane: $12.011 + 4 \times 1.0079 = 16.043$ g/mole CH_4

For ethane: $2 \times 12.011 + 6 \times 1.0079 = 30.069$ g/mole C_2H_6 .

For carbon dioxide: $12.011 + 2 \times 15.999 = 44.009$ g/mole CO_2

The molecular weights and weight percentages given in the table will be used to find the number of moles of each component using a basis of exactly 1 g of natural gas:

$$\frac{0.949 \text{ g CH}_4}{\text{g gas}} \times \frac{\text{mole CH}_4}{16.043 \text{ g CH}_4} = \frac{0.05915 \text{ mole CH}_4}{\text{g gas}}$$

$$\frac{0.044 \text{ g C}_2\text{H}_6}{\text{g gas}} \times \frac{\text{mole C}_2\text{H}_6}{30.069 \text{ g C}_2\text{H}_6} = \frac{0.00146 \text{ mole C}_2\text{H}_6}{\text{g gas}} .$$

$$\frac{0.007 \text{ g CO}_2}{\text{g gas}} \times \frac{\text{mole CO}_2}{44.009 \text{ g CO}_2} = \frac{0.00016 \text{ mole CO}_2}{\text{g gas}}$$

These intermediate results contain an extra, insignificant digit. The three values above are added together to give the total number of moles in a gram of gas:

$$0.05915 + 0.00146 + 0.00016 = 0.06077 \frac{\text{mole gas}}{\text{g gas}} .$$

The mole fractions of the hydrocarbon components may then be found:

$$\frac{0.05915 \text{ mole CH}_4}{0.06077 \text{ mole gas}} = 0.9733 \frac{\text{mole CH}_4}{\text{mole gas}}$$

$$\frac{0.00146 \text{ mole C}_2\text{H}_6}{0.06077 \text{ mole gas}} = 0.0240 \frac{\text{mole C}_2\text{H}_6}{\text{mole gas}} .$$

Finally, these values are multiplied by the result from part C to give the moles of hydrocarbons supplied each second. The extra insignificant digit for the ethane problem is removed from this final result.

$$0.00624 \frac{\text{mole gas}}{\text{s}} \times 0.9733 \frac{\text{mole CH}_4}{\text{mole gas}} = 0.00607 \frac{\text{mole CH}_4}{\text{s}}$$

$$0.00624 \frac{\text{mole gas}}{\text{s}} \times 0.0240 \frac{\text{mole C}_2\text{H}_6}{\text{mole gas}} = 0.00015 \frac{\text{mole C}_2\text{H}_6}{\text{s}} .$$

e. The heats of combustion are multiplied by the rate of supply for each gas:

$$0.00607 \frac{\text{mole CH}_4}{\text{s}} \times 890 \frac{\text{kJ}}{\text{mole CH}_4} = 5.4 \frac{\text{kJ}}{\text{s}} \text{ from methane combustion}$$

$$0.00015 \frac{\text{mole C}_2\text{H}_6}{\text{s}} \times 2900 \frac{\text{kJ}}{\text{mole C}_2\text{H}_6} = 0.44 \frac{\text{kJ}}{\text{s}} \text{ from ethane combustion}$$

The total heat produced from hydrocarbon combustion is the sum of these two values: 5.8 kJ each second.

f. There are three sources of carbon dioxide in this problem. CO_2 already in the natural gas before combustion is released into the atmosphere. This value is found from its weight percentage and values calculated in parts C and D:

$$\frac{0.007 \text{ g } CO_2}{\text{g gas}} \times \frac{\text{g gas}}{0.06077 \text{ mole gas}} \times \frac{0.00624 \text{ mole gas}}{s} = 0.0007 \frac{\text{g } CO_2}{s}$$

CO_2 from combustion is found from the values calculated in part D and the stoichiometry of the chemical equations from part B.

For methane:
$$0.00607 \frac{\text{mole } CH_4}{s} \times \frac{1 \text{ mole } CO_2}{1 \text{ mole } CH_4} \times \frac{44.009 \text{ g } CO_2}{1 \text{ mole } CO_2} = 0.267 \frac{\text{g } CO_2}{s}.$$

For ethane:
$$0.00015 \frac{\text{mole } C_2H_6}{s} \times \frac{4 \text{ mole } CO_2}{2 \text{ mole } C_2H_6} \times \frac{44.009 \text{ g } CO_2}{1 \text{ mole } CO_2} = 0.013 \frac{\text{g } CO_2}{s}.$$

The mass of CO_2 released is found from the sum of these three contributions:
$$0.0007 + 0.267 + 0.013 = 0.281 \frac{\text{g } CO_2}{s}.$$

g. From A, 211 kJ are required to heat the water. From E, the rate of heat produced by combustion is 5.8 kJ per second. An estimate of the number of seconds to heat the water may be found by dividing the heat required by the rate at which it is supplied:

$$211 \text{ kJ} \times \frac{1 \text{ s}}{5.8 \text{ kJ}} = 36 \text{ seconds}.$$

One reason why this value differs from the observed value of 258 seconds is because the heat supplied by combustion does not transfer perfectly into the heating of water in an insulated, adiabatic process. Heat from combustion will also be used to raise the temperature of the teapot, the stovetop, and nearby air. Heat from the hot water is also lost to the air.

XAMonline, INC. 21 Orient Ave. Melrose, MA 02176

Toll Free number 800-301-4647

TO ORDER Fax 781-662-9268 OR www.XAMonline.com

CALIFORNIA SUBJECT EXAMINATIONS   - CSET - 2007

PO#   Store/School:

Address 1:

Address 2 (Ship to other):

City, State Zip

Credit card number_____-_____-_____-_____   expiration_____

EMAIL _____

PHONE   **FAX**

ISBN #	TITLE	Qty	Retail	Total
978-1-58197-813-1	CSET Art Sample Subtest 140		$15.00	
978-1-58197-800-1	CBEST CA Basic Educational Skills		$19.95	
978-1-58197-809-4	CSET Biology-Life Science 120, 124		$59.95	
978-1-58197-395-2	CSET Chemistry 121, 125		$73.50	
978-1-58197-810-0	CSET Earth and Planetary Science 122, 126		$34.95	
978-1-58197-804-9	CSET English 105, 106, 107		$34.95	
978-1-58197-805-6	CSET Foundational-Level Mathematics 110, 111		$34.95	
978-1-58197-901-5	CSET French Sample Test 149, 150		$15.00	
978-1-58197-808-7	CSET General Science 118, 119		$34.95	
978-1-58197-814-8	CSET Home Economics 181, 182, 183		$34.95	
978-1-58197-806-3	CSET Mathematics 112		$59.95	
978-1-58197-803-2	CSET MSAT MultiSubject 101, 102, 103		$59.95	
978-1-58197-812-4	CSET Physical Education, 129, 130, 131		$34.95	
978-1-58197-811-7	CSET Physics 123, 127		$15.00	
978-1-58197-807-0	CSET Social Science 114, 115		$59.95	
978-1-58197-802-5	CSET Spanish 145, 146, 147		$34.95	
			SUBTOTAL	
			Ship	$8.25
			TOTAL	